THE SPIRIT LIVES IN THE MIND

RUPERT'S LAND RECORD SOCIETY SERIES
Jennifer S.H. Brown, Editor

1 The English River Book
A North West Company Journal and Account Book of 1786
Edited by Harry W. Duckworth

2 A Country So Interesting
The Hudson's Bay Company and Two Centuries of Mapping,
1670–1870
Richard I. Ruggles

3 Arctic Artist
The Journal and Paintings of George Back, Midshipman with
Franklin, 1819–1822
Edited by C. Stuart Houston
Commentary by I.S. MacLaren

4 Ellen Smallboy
Glimpses of a Cree Woman's Life
Regina Flannery

5 Voices from Hudson Bay
Cree Stories from York Factory
Compiled and edited by Flora Beardy and Robert Coutts

6 North of Athabasca
Slave Lake and Mackenzie River Documents of the North West
Company, 1800–1821
Edited with an Introduction by Lloyd Keith

7 From Barrow to Boothia
The Arctic Journal of Chief Factor Peter Warren Dease, 1836–1839
Edited and annotated by William Barr

8 My First Years in the Fur Trade
The Journals of 1802–1804
George Nelson
Edited by Laura Peers and Theresa Schenck

9 The Spirit Lives in the Mind:
Omushkego Stories, Lives, and Dreams
Louis Bird
Compiled and edited by Susan Elaine Gray

© McGill-Queen's University Press 2007

ISBN 978-0-7735-3209-0 (cloth)
ISBN 978-0-7735-3210-6 (paper)

Legal deposit first quarter 2007
Bibliothèque nationale du Québec

Printed in Canada on acid-free paper

McGill-Queen's University Press acknowledges the support of the Canada Council for the Arts for our publishing program. We also acknowledge the financial support of the Government of Canada through the Book Publishing Industry Development Program (BPIDP) for our publishing activities.

Library and Archives Canada Cataloguing in Publication

Bird, Louis
  The spirit lives in the mind : Omushkego stories, lives and dreams / Louis Bird ; compiled and edited by Susan Elaine Gray.

(Rupert's Land Record Society series ; 9)
Includes bibliographical references and index.
ISBN 978-0-7735-3209-0 (bnd)
ISBN 978-0-7735-3210-6 (pbk)

  1. Cree Philosophy—James Bay Region.   2. Cree Indians—James Bay Region—Folklore.   3. Cree Indians—James Bay Region—Religion.   I. Gray, Susan Elaine, 1960–   II. Title. III. Series.

E99.C88B527 2007   398.2'09714111   C2006-905865-2

Typeset in 10½/13 Sabon by True to Type

The Spirit Lives in the Mind

Omushkego Stories, Lives, and Dreams

LOUIS BIRD

Compiled and Edited by
SUSAN ELAINE GRAY

McGill-Queen's University Press
Montreal & Kingston · London · Ithaca

We each wish to pay special tributes:
Louis would like to dedicate this book to his children and grandchildren. Susan would like to dedicate this book to David McCrady, for letting in all the light; to her parents, Al and Elaine Gray, for their support and imagination; and to her aunt, author Barbara Rodman.

Contents

Preface Susan Elaine Gray xi
Acknowledgments xxiii
Illustrations xxv
Map xxxii
Introduction 3

1 WATER, EARTH AND SKIES 6
   The Land and the Spirit 6
   Mooshawow and Wabagamushusagagan 8
   The Shaman and the Narwhal Whisker 10
   Rocks and their Stories 12
   Places in the Skies 15
   Giant Spider and the First People 15
   Astronomy 17
   Moshegiishik (The Universe) 19
   Chakapesh 23
      Chakapesh Gets Swallowed by a Fish 23
      Chakapesh Snares the Sun 29
      Chakapesh in the Moon 36
   Mysteries in the Sky 37

2 INTRUDERS AND DEFENDERS 39
   Encounters on Mooshawow 39

Ostigwan Nowakow (The Place of Skulls) 43
A Mitew Attack with a Lightning Gun 45
Ships, Mysterious and Real 48

3 PAKAASKOKAN, AN ANCIENT LEGEND AND
  MYSTERY 51

4 VALUES FOR LIFE AND SURVIVAL 59
  Dreams and Gifts 59
  Christianity and Our Ways: Fear and Denial 60
  Conversions to Christianity 62
  Life after Death 64
  The Power of the Orphan – a Resurrection Story 64
  Healing and Faith 66
  A Mitew Healer 66
  Omushkego Individualism 68
  Condemnation by Christianity 70

5 RELATIONS WITH ANIMALS 71
  Animal Powers 71
  Caribou Awareness 72
  Caribou Messages 73
  Code of Ethics: Dreams, Gifts, and Knowledge 74
  Sinning Against Animals 76
  Respect and Thanks for Animals 77
  Violations and Consequences: The Hunters and the White Fox 78

6 MITEWIWIN HEROES AND VILLAINS 81
  Mitewiwin: The Power of Dreams and the Mind 82
  Science and Mystery 84
  Dream Helpers 86
  Becoming a Mitew 90
  Dreaming the Elements 92
  Mind Power through Dreams 94
  Seasons and Places to Dream 95
  Mitew Fasting and Self-Discipline 97
  Healing 99
  Animals and Power 102

Mitew Competitions   103
Defence and Warfare: Mitew Powers and Their Limitations   103
Mitew Duels and Insults   104
Protection through Non-Belief   106
Stories of Powerful Mitewak   107
Enduring Practice and Belief   108
Mitew Magical Travel – Not So Long Ago   109
Mitew or Christian, One or the Other?   111

7 WIHTIGOS AND CANNIBAL HEARTS   112
Becoming a Wihtigo   115
Burning Wihtigos   115
Anway and the Cannibals   116
The Mitew and the Cannibal Hearts   122
Ice Hearts   124
Ketastotinewan   125

8 WOMEN AND MEN   127
Women   127
Our Grandmothers' Powers   128
Wilderness Woman   129
Morning Star, a Love Story, and the Spread of the Cree Language   132
Wife of Ketastotinewan   140
A Woman, Her Dream Father, and a Wihtigo Duel   141
Wihtigo, or the Consequences of Not Listening   146
Story of a Woman Helping a Captive Man   148
Story of a Captive Woman Conquering her Guard   151

9 PERSONAGES   153
The Defeat of the Giant Skunk   153
The Legless Man and the Boys Who Disobeyed   161
John Sakeny and Bernard Gull   165
Amoe and Sheweephan   167

10 WISAKAYCHAK   175
Wisakaychak the Rock Mover   175
Wisakaychak and the Woman Who Played Dead   178
Wisakaychak Pursues Women   180

Wisakaychak Tricks the Birds   184
Wisakaychak Cooks His Geese and Loses Them   187
Wisakaychak Tricks a Bear and Loses His Feast   190
Wisakaychak Goes West and Grants Two Wishes   193

Appendix   Recordings by Louis Bird   199
Notes   203
Suggested Readings   207
Index   217

Preface

Susan Elaine Gray

One bitterly cold night in the Winnipeg winter of 1999, I visited some friends who were having a small party at their home. Their living room was filled with people I didn't know – everyone was talking and laughing and I felt shy and out of place. As I got my bearings I spotted someone else who looked as if he didn't know many people there either. Louis Bird was quietly watching everything that was happening around him. We started talking and I noticed how closely he listened to the things I said and how easy it was to make him smile. Then we started talking about music and how important it is to each of us and Louis mentioned that he had brought his violin along. He took up his instrument and I sat down at the piano – and we became friends for life.

Louis Bird is many things – a storyteller, a scholar, a musician, and an artist with words. For over forty years he has gathered the memories and stories of Omushkego (Swampy Cree) elders in communities along western Hudson and James Bays. He has crafted their legends and tales into an oral history of his people and his work conveys, as do great histories, the forces that moved and shaped his ancestors – the saga of the Omushkego Crees.

Louis was born on a trapline in the bush near Winisk, Ontario, in 1934, part of an Omushkego community whose people still hunted and fished, still traded furs – and who had adopted the

Oblate missionaries' Roman Catholic faith for two generations. Myriad changes have deeply affected the community. In 1930, his grandfather and great uncle participated in signing the Winisk adhesion to Treaty Nine. In the mid-1950s, the Canadian government erected a Distant Early Warning radar station – an enormous construction project – directly across the river from his home community of Winisk. This brought a thousand strangers into the area and changed the cultural and linguistic landscape in multi-dimensional ways.

Louis became attracted to the stories of his people early in life. As he recalled a few years ago:

I remember my family in 1938. When we saw Joseph Gull in his camp. It is a famous place, this place. Joseph Gull's father has camped there and many of the people have camped there before them. One family can survive there, or even two families can survive in area....[He] and his wife Helen used to be very kind. And we used to listen to them telling us a story about those legends. I remember them because they tell us the legends that was totally different then I know now. Because they recite the legend for our age group. It was different for the little kids. It was delivered in such a way that the little kids would not hurt them anything but would have curiosity to know more. And that's the first time I remember hearing the legends that we have. And we used to try to work hard in our house and home to help mother and father and try to finish everything before sunset so we can go and visit the elders. So we can sit beside them and listen to their stories. This was the most rewarding memory that I have. And in 1940 I went back for a little while and in 1941 I listened again to our cultural ways and start talking together in the family and spending together as a family in our home and being entertained by our parents by those stories.[1]

Louis spent four years in St. Anne's Residential School at Fort Albany in the late 1930s and early 1940s. He said later:

I lost contact with that kind of life and I miss it, totally miss it. I used to cry so much about it. And when I saw my father and Joseph Gull returned to Winisk it seems to be just a little way to travel but actually they have to travel 300 miles before they get home. They didn't seem to care, as if they were just going a little way. I wanted to go with my father – to go home. But of course I had to stay behind. And the following summer I return home for the whole winter and come back again in the spring of 1944 to residential school and again it disrupted what I had learned when I was young.²

Louis returned home to hunt and trap in the bush – and listen to stories. He remembered, "Finally I return home again for the last time in 1945, and then from 1945 I begin to listen to our stories again. Different stories from all kinds of people. I remember those ladies, and I also remember other elders that I saw when I was in Fort Albany School."³

Louis worked as a manual labourer at the radar station. He moved on to work as a tractor operator, stevedore, line cutter, surveyor's assistant, and section man for Canadian National Railways across Manitoba and northern Ontario.

It was in the 1970s that he began to systematically record Omushkego stories. In discussing this ambition and undertaking he recalled:

I know it is important to try to keep the oral history of our forefathers and try to understand the use and application of the legends that has been passed down to us for ages. One elder told me – by the name of Mr Michael Patrick, one of my best friends, one of my respected elders and also a home that I can be very relaxed with and also have a good laugh at time. And also I have go up to him when I found myself depressed or when I am down of my own making. He never rejected me, he knows why I went to see him. He always welcome me, he never put me down. Yes, of course he laughed at me a little while and I would tell him why. And after I tell him he get a little bit serious a while and talk to me about life. Before the tension get too tight he would make a short quotation that comes from one of the legends and from then on he would break the tension and open up the discussion again. And sometimes I would say, "Let's hear it." And then he would go on and pick up the highest point of the story and then explain. He was very good in using the legends to give a counsel or support for someone who needing some comforting word when they feeling down. So I have done that with this old man many times. He is the only one that I was really able to speak to and to ask a few things and ask him to stand beside me when I am not too sure of myself.

There are other elders that I have spoke to when I wanted their wisdom and also wanted the answer to the question I have in life. I think I have a record here which I have made telling the names of the elders that I have known. All the elders that I have met and all the elders who have contributed the stories that I have know. And some of the stories that I have put into the tape recording, unfortunately as I said before, some elders did not want to be recorded, most of them did not want to be recorded especially when they want to be free. Because when they are recorded they are very careful what they say, they do not mix jokes in their stories, but when there is no recording or no note taking they are free to speak. And they can speak any way they like and they can sidetrack their stories for a little while to create a laughter and to break tension and also they sidetrack the main story to interpret the story where its applicable in our lives. They also sidetrack the story for a time to explain why this happen. These are the ways the legends were applied and used in the past and these legends now are not used. They are not used the way they were used to be.

They were the basic education information for the youngsters. If they could listen to the stories as they watch intensively as they watch the television programs with the characters in there something like puppets. Our elders used to tell us a story just like that. They created the image in our mind that we could mentally see what they are taking about. And their stories were so good. It captivated us and we always know there was something beyond the stories that was hidden from us as a young kid. As we grew up we remember those things and we ask the elder to tell us about these things a little bit at the time but none of the elders that I have listened to ever completed the information that I have seek for so long when I was young.

Finally, as I get older when I begin to be fifty and I was able to speak to the elders that were seventy even older, they understand that I am fifty years old, they understand that I am the chairperson – they understand how to take the mysteries that have existed among our people and what made out of it spiritually and physically. What exactly was their beliefs – how did they get it and how did they develop it. It's fascinating how they developed their mind to understand things without using scientific system. They did not study the things by breaking, or cutting apart, or breaking into pieces, or using magnifying glass to look at the things that cannot be seen by the naked eye. They use their mental power – they develop their mental power that could go into the microscopic world and also that could go into the universe. These are the powerful things that they have developed within themselves. These were the people who were called medicine man – some of them were called general shaman. General mean knowing almost everything – a bit at least. And these are the elders who have explained this to me – putting it together many as fifty elders. Fifty times of knowledge, fifty pieces of new information that I have listened to and I have managed to put it together to make it into understandable story or information for someone at least to picture how it was. And these are the information the teachings that have been given to me by our elders in Hudson Bay and James Bay Lowland.[4]

In this decade he also worked as an interpreter, translator, and economic advisor. Louis served as chief of the Winisk First Nation in 1972–73. After this experience Louis wished to break away from political life and he committed himself to gathering Omushkego stories from elders.

Since the 1980s Louis has devoted his life to making his people's stories known while acting as a translator and advisor on issues that affect Omushkego communities. A gifted performer, Louis has been invited to storytelling gatherings throughout Canada, the United States, and the Netherlands and in 1999 he won second prize at the International Storytelling Festival in Louisville, Kentucky. Sharing his knowledge of Omushkego oral history and legends, survival in the bush, and the spiritual practices and beliefs of his people, he has both moved and delighted the countless students, teachers, and others who have been privileged to hear him.

Louis's work has received support from the Canada Council, the Social Sciences and Humanities Research Council of Canada, and the Ministry of Canadian Heritage. In 2003 a grant from the Canadian Culture On-Line program of Canadian Heritage facilitated the digitization of his large collection of English and Cree-language audiotapes and the creation of a web site, http://www.ourvoices.ca , which presents about eighty of Louis's English-language stories. In 2005 Louis published *Telling Our Stories: Omushkego Legends and Histories from Hudson Bay* – a selection of his stories with commentary, notes, and introductions written by contributors working with him at the University of Winnipeg.[5]

Louis Bird has worked intensively with me to direct and shape this book and has participated actively in its compilation and editing. He is deeply engaged in preserving his people's history, language, and values, and committed to bringing his listeners and readers as far along the road to understanding as he can. His voice is in the foreground of the text and ideas in these pages.

In editing and compiling this volume I was blessed with over a thousand pages of transcriptions of Louis Bird's stories compiled by University of Winnipeg students and others over the last several years, some of which are on the Our Voices website. Working with these documents was like helping to landscape a vast garden. Louis had made hundreds of tapes that were jam-packed with stories, thoughts, teachings, and ideas and they reminded me of a glorious flower garden, bursting at the borders with colour and variety – discussions with others and with himself, thoughts, ponderings and musings, useful digressions, abrupt swings to still other gardens holding other exquisite plants – unbelievable complexity. In working through each transcript I realized that the underlying theme of much of Louis's work has to do with Omushkego spiritual beliefs or, in Louis's words, the Omushkego world view. Once I settled on this as the focus, I worked to piece together important ideas and highlight overarching categories that could showcase the beauty and complexity of Louis Bird's tellings of his rich Omushkego cultural history. I sought to illuminate the main ideas, training my mind to see the patterns and to shape the paths through those gardens, helping to order and link the stories so that the reader could clearly grasp Louis's intended whole.

The stories can be read and analyzed on many levels, just as stories in the Bible have been read by children for centuries but have also yielded rich material for scholars like Northrop Frye, whose analysis brings out additional complexities and great codes. For me, perhaps the most startling beauty of Louis Bird's stories is that, while they resonate with the very young, the very old, people across cultures, and people who have little formal education, they also offer limitless scope for new questions and insights that can illuminate the multitude of layers in the text. I have grappled with the gigantic lion and the tiny mouse in my efforts to lead readers through this book and create a vehicle that brings disparate pieces together in an order that gives form to Louis's vision of the whole as he has experienced it.

This book is meant to be a source book for readers who wish to gain an insider's view of Omushkego Cree culture and its spiritual underpinnings. The book organises key themes, stories, ideas, and teachings into a repertoire that describes the Omushkego world view. The work is a true collaboration between Louis Bird and me. While I have compiled, organized, edited, clarified, and highlighted overarching themes, the stories are told in Louis's voice. It has always been very important to me that my partnership with Louis is *truly* collaborative. To this end I have worked hard to seek Louis's opinions and listen carefully to everything he has said.

There are few footnotes in this book. To stay true to Louis, I have accommodated his wish that my own voice, and the voices of other scholars, be kept to a minimum. Louis was explicit from the beginning that he wants his stories to be presented simply, with no explanatory footnotes from scholarly sources and no additions by me except the introduction and references. The notes point readers to the written transcripts that hold the original stories or sections of stories. A list of suggested readings at the end of each chapter cites useful sources that provide historical and cultural context and guides readers to other publications that deal with similar or related subject matter.

Much material on Aboriginal world views is heavily mediated by outsiders – there is a real dearth of writings that present the heart and historic roots of the Omushkego world view. Louis was an active participant throughout the process of creating this book. He approved my proposed ideas, helped to define structure and continuity, and, when necessary, added new material to fill gaps and enhance the content and unity of the chapters. I tried to keep my editing of the text minimal, recasting words only in cases where the written transcription of the oral narrative was not clear.

Louis has an almost musical rhythm when he speaks, and those who know his voice can hear his cadence as they read his words in print. I have made every effort to preserve this quality. Louis's first language is Cree, and his English speech reflects this background. I have worked hard to strike a balance between clarity and authenticity. While it is true that some readers will have to become used to reading written text based on a distinct oral style, to modify this text further would be to lose its authenticity. My effort met with sincere gratitude from Louis, who says in his Introduction to this book, "This book that you've worked on – you edited my stories that have been written down into English and you have put them into a proper text. But we have understood that we would keep it alive with my voice just as it is when I tell the stories – and that's the great thing you did! I am very happy with that – I appreciate that very much, to keep the story person alive – his voice, and his ways of telling stories – to bring it alive on the page."

THE SPIRIT LIVES IN THE MIND

Chapter 1, "Water, Earth, and Skies," establishes contexts for understanding the Omushkego world view. It presents significant ideas and specific stories about sacred places, parts of landscape that have significance in Omushkego legends, and the importance of celestial bodies and the universe in Omushkego cosmology.

"Intruders and Defenders" follows with accounts of significant human happenings within this landscape: stories of attacks, defence, and remarkable escapes. Louis has often said that the problem with writing stories down is that they lose their emotional impact. Here, however, his tellings recapture their drama through the revelation of dramatic, even epic, themes that readers might never have imagined to exist around Hudson Bay. The stories in this chapter capture aspects of Omushkego history that have never been pulled together before and that convey powerful emotion and a sense of the Omushkego homeland under fear and duress. They also show that, even before Europeans arrived, this land was not so very isolated and remote.

"Pakaaskokan, an Ancient Legend and Mystery" is an Omushkego mystery story involving a flying skeleton. It has counterparts in Ojibwa and Plains peoples' world views.

"Values for Life and Survival" and "Relations with Animals" look at the ideas that comprise the essence of the Omushkego world view. The stories discuss prophecy, power, morality, and consequences of various behaviours. They teach about how Omushkego people saw their land and their world, and how they thought about what they encountered in their environment.

Chapter 6, "Mitewiwin Heroes and Villains," details the training and development of mitewak, or what Louis calls shamans in English, by such means as dream quests, as well as kinds of shamans, shaman powers, shamanism before and after Christianity, challenges between shamans, and guidance for confronting danger through dreaming. This chapter explores concepts that lie at the heart of Omushkego views of life and the universe.

The final four chapters look at personages, both human and other-than-human. These stories present powerful characters – giant animals, Wisakaychak, wihtigos (including stories of the origin of killing wihtigos and famous male and female cannibal exterminators), the Wilderness Woman, and other powerful female figures. The links between the mind, the spirit, and power are vividly expressed in stories about some of the most powerful human and other-than-human persons in Cree cosmology.

Certain powerful ideas underscore the narrative and provide a foundation for Omushkego cosmology. One of these is the power of belief and the importance the Omushkego people have attached to cultivating the power of the mind, for it was through superior mindpower that people could protect themselves and their families from evil and danger. Louis has taught me, in fact, that the spirit lives in the mind and this is why we have chosen this phrase as the title for this book.

Another equally poignant idea is the importance of humility. In Omushkego lore, people who were full of themselves or arrogant, using their position and powers to hurt others, always came to no good. The stories also clearly illustrate the belief that the seemingly weak and mistreated, old people or orphans for example, could have the greatest power for good. The humble could destroy the strong.

The stories also celebrate adaptability and flexibility. The Omushkego people lived in an unforgiving environment and in their efforts to cope with their harsh landscape they moved – physically to where the food was and mentally in their willingness to include new ideas into their cosmology. They sought spiritual help so they, as mere humans, could overcome the challenges of their environment and adapt themselves to the land. Christianity, in contrast, was developed for non-nomadic people living together in large communities. As Louis put it to me, "people living together, one mind, one God." But in older times the Omushkego Cree did not live in settled communities. They had to travel to where the food was, and they had to break into small groups of relatives to subsist by hunting and trapping for most of the year. Their world view suited their lifestyle – there was no predominant unified religion and, consequently, no need for church doctrine or priestly hierarchy. Their cosmology was based on the ideas of continually increasing faith in one's self and in one's spiritual connection with the land, birds, and animals. Within this was an implicit code of ethics that demanded that the people respect elders, animals, the land, and one another. Louis put it best when he explained that the Creator set up a system of control and balance to ensure survival of all species. Some animals prey and some are preyed upon, and the legends show that there has been an order and purpose to everything. These legends, he explains, contain all the lessons that were needed by a tribal people. If life follows the systematic plan set by the Great Spirit, there will be order and balance.

While he sees great contrasts between religious traditions, Louis also draws strong parallels between Christianity and the Omushkego world view. One of these is the great emphasis in both cosmologies on the power of belief. Another is the connection between fasting in isolation (in the wilderness) and suffering in order to gain blessings. The magnitude of mitew (shaman) powers was directly correlated with the amount of time one spent fasting, dreaming, and sacrificing comforts in the wilderness. The Bible documents that Jesus spent time fasting and in isolation in the desert as well as the suffering he went through on earth. Both, Louis explains, were undertaken based on faith, belief, and prayer.

Christianity held real appeal for many Omushkego people, especially women, in that it offered them a kind of safety net. Many lived in fear of bad mitewak (shamans) or of offending some human or other-than-human being and many stories in this book illustrate the Omushkego concept of striking back against your enemy – the opposite of Christ's New Testament teaching that one should turn the other cheek. Belief in Christianity meant for many that they were protected from bad medicine. However, Louis also makes clear the tragic effects of Christian missionaries condemning the positive and beneficial aspects of Omushkego culture through narrow and judgemental intolerance and ignorance. As he has said, "If only they had taken the time to see the good." This resulted in mitewak going underground to practise and, ultimately, in the loss of much of Omushkego culture.

There is some overlap between these stories and some of those included in *Telling Our Stories*. Different versions of Giant Animals, Chakapesh and the Sailors, and Story of a Woman helping a Captive Man exist in the first book. We include them here for the sake of continuity and to paint a fuller landscape.

A tradition common to European writers when viewing the history and cultures of northern Aboriginal groups is to interpret this material in terms of people accruing personal power as a means for survival within their brutal world. It is true that Omushkego peoples have lived for centuries in a harsh environment that they recognized as fraught with challenge and danger. Louis Bird, however, loves the area in which he lives and views it as a beautiful, powerful, capricious landscape full of sacred places and rich in resources. His is an authentic Omushkego view that is central to our book. The view that Cree cosmology was based on survival alone is an outsider's view. In reality Cree people have a more complex view and their spiritual beliefs are not based simply on personal reaction to fear and pain. We have organized the manuscript around this premise and include sections that do not deal directly with power. The Intruders and Defenders chapter, for example, provides essential history and context. From intruders and defenders to Wihtigos and Wisakaychak, these narratives have evolved through encounters over time between Cree peoples and their landscape, their places in the sky, and non-Cree people. Cree perspectives on and concepts of history are critical components of the Omushkego world view.

Acknowledgments

Louis Bird wishes to acknowledge the elders who told him stories that they had heard from their parents and grandparents: David Sutherland, Patrick Sutherland, Jane Sutherland, Charlotte Sutherland, Maggie (Sutherland) Bird, John (Bird) Pennishish, Scholastique (Okimaweeniniew) (Bird) Penneshish, Fanny Augustin, Anna Nakogee, Toby Hunter, and Michael Hunter. He is indebted to these elders for sharing their stories with their children and ancestors. His only regret is that, because so many elders from Omushkego communities have contributed to his knowledge, he cannot name them all here.

Great thanks are due Jennifer S.H. Brown. This book was produced with the support of her Canada Research Chair in Aboriginal Peoples in an Urban and Regional Context, funded by the Social Sciences and Humanities Research Council of Canada. She has provided tremendous guidance and moral support and has been devotedly generous with her time and her resources. David McCrady lent his expertise and imagination to this effort. He sat up late into the night sounding out my ideas, provided a wealth of perspective, helping me to see the forest for the trees when I was discouraged or lost, helped me through myriad computer hang-ups and breakdowns, and helped in so many other ways to birth this book. I thank Maureen Matthews and Charles Feaver for hosting the party where I met Louis – they were the catalysts for a wonderful collaboration and friendship. Finally, I thank Louis Bird himself, and all those who worked to preserve his tapes and transcribe the texts that made this volume possible. I deeply appreciate the support that the Social Sciences and Humanities Research Council, the Ministry of Canadian Heritage, and the Centre for Rupert's Land Studies at the University of Winnipeg have given for work with Louis and his stories over the last seven years. None of this would be possible without their contributions.

Louis Bird, 2002.

Louis Bird and his wife, Thelma, on a Sunday canoe trip on the Winisk River.

Winisk circa 1948–55. "Local lumber produce this small shack. It is a home. The snow geese are hung temporary to keep them from rodents." Louis Bird.

Louis and Thelma Bird with three of their daughters and the community nurse (centre), 1972.

"This is just one of the scenes on Hudson Bay's south-west coast line. Flat and wet, where snow geese love to eat. Cree people look at this land as if it's full with food on the table." Louis Bird.

"Mrs Thelma Bird emerging from her cooking tipi. She is smoking meat and fish. Trying to hang onto the past." Louis Bird.

"A scene away from the community. Setting camp to show children how it's done – setting up tent, stove, and cutting firewood." Louis Bird.

"Louis Bird shows his grandson how to handle a gun on the outside of a goose blind. The boy nearly shot my foot." Louis Bird.

"1993. I went up river with my wife and one of my granddaughters, Roxie Bird. We nearly got caught up on winter. The snow began to drift, and the river began to slush, and it turns cold. We repaired the last year's moss house, which someone had used. We cover it up with thick moss. In two days we completed it and ready for winter. We had moose meat." Louis Bird.

The Winisk River in front of Peawanuck.

"This picture is 65 miles due north-west from the old village of Winisk at a place called Shagami. As a guide, I was taking hunters on afternoon fishing upriver. We run into a moose. My fellow guide shot it. We also saw a polar bear that afternoon on the river. No – we did not kill it!" Louis Bird.

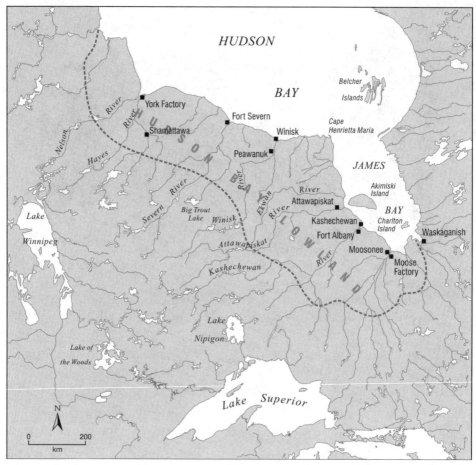

Western Hudson Bay and James Bay Lowlands. Adopted with permission of Broadview Press and Weldon Hiebert. Prepared by Weldon Hiebert.

THE SPIRIT LIVES IN THE MIND

Introduction

Hello, hello. This is Louis Bird. Today is October 16, 2005 and I am at Timmins, Ontario – I came here Friday night and I stayed here last night too. Okay. Susan I want to tell you first of all that it has been a very busy summer and I have travelled a lot – I have been hopping all over the place, going to meetings and workshops and things like that. I am now going to speak plainly, honestly, about this work.

Dear Susan [laughter] – this is not a letter – this is just speaking [on tape] for a time. Dear Susan – it has been good to know you and also to have worked with you and I am very thankful. This book that you've worked on – you edited my stories that have been written down into English and you have put them into a proper text. But we have understood that we would keep it alive with my voice just as it is when I tell the stories – and that's the great thing you did! I am very happy with that – I appreciate that very much, to keep the story person alive – his voice, and his ways of telling stories – to bring it alive on the page.

This book is specifically bringing out the spirituality of our Omushkego people – the Omushkego people that live on the southwest coast of Hudson Bay and the west coast of James Bay. There is a strip of land there which is approximately 200 miles wide and about 700 miles in length, and that's where the Omushkego people live. And that language that's there definitely belongs to that piece of land. The lives that existed there before the European came is what we are trying to record. Anyway, this book is built around the main theme of Omushkego culture history: the spiritual connection of the people to the land and the spirituality of the Omushkego people *before* the European came. Did the Omushkego people actually believe in, or know, the God – the Almighty – the Creator – the most powerful being? Were they actually aware of Him – or It – or Her? And that's what this is all about – it's a spiritual-connected storytelling.

We take the stories that have actually been brought down for generations because they have a value. Even though some of them sound horrible and terrible to different cultures, for the Omushkego culture it is a necessary type of teaching system. It saves lives. It saves the families. It saves the children. It allows people to have a serious understanding about where they live. These stories are about shamanism (in English). As humans, when we listen to the exciting part of a story – whether the story is bad or good – we always listen to parts that are horrible and terrible. We remember them vividly, and we like those kinds of stories.

And that is what happened in the Omushkego land. When we were small and we listened to the stories that were terrible and horrible, they stayed in our minds. They were created for us young people to remember – to help us to avoid going into the kinds of situations that are described in the stories. They do not teach us to become the horrible people that are in the stories – they try to teach us *not* to – they try to show us the negative side of life and they have similarities to any other nationalities' moral teaching. We hear the statements that say: "thou shall not kill; thou shall not steal" – all these ten commandments of the Jewish people tell the things *not* to do. With the First Nation Omushkego, they tell you the stories that actually happened – and in listening to it, we learn to avoid it. It's almost the same thing as saying, "thou shall not do this," but it tells us a story that will imprint on our mind so that we will always remember not to do things that are bad.

So that is why this book has come out – to emphasize that – to teach us the teaching system of the Omushkego people. They are not just horrible stories to entertain you. All these stories have a definition, an explanation – they are there to open the subject, or to melt the ice – whatever you want to call it. So they're here to help us to understand the Omushkego cultural experience, and also to show our Omushkego history.

They were structured in such a way, those stories, that we will remember them. We will not forget if we hear them early enough, as young kids – as I have experienced myself. I listened to them when I was small and I still remember them today as I get older. Writing them down doesn't mean you have to convert into their ways – no you don't – you just have a richer history in Canada when you know the truth about the past and can admit that these people lived here many years before the visitors came – and that they survived. If the Great Spirit had not liked them, they would have died many years before the European came – but these are stories about them surviving. For example, there are stories in this particular book which tell about the powerful giants who wanted to take over the land, and powerful people who sacrificed themselves to kill those monsters. There are other things, like the rattles which they used for singing and for healing – I have described them in the stories – and plants and herbs in the land that people used (even though they didn't try to define them) to make potions for healing. Maybe there should be a project on that now – to find some elders yet that still remember how they make the potions for healing, aside from singing, and drumming, and rattles and things.

I think this book covers the most important parts – and thank you very much, Susan, for the work that you've done. This is a book that has to be printed in a plain, story-telling way. We will not ask any other experts to put anything else in.

Water, Earth, Skies

THE LAND AND THE SPIRIT

Now we concentrate on Hudson and James Bay district. Different part of the Omushkego-speaking First Nation. Now, what was their spiritual value? What was their spiritual practices? And how did they acquire it? How did these people ever put up with the harshness of the country where they live? How did they master the land? How did they become self-sufficient in time before the European came in? The only answer that I can find after going through many times is that our ancestors, before the Europeans came in, have their spiritual practice. They have the spiritual beliefs and practices. Which gives them to be strong. To be powerful enough to withstand any harshness they may come upon in the land. And this spiritual belief and practice stem from the wilderness. You could only get it from the wilderness.[1]

I want to repeat the importance of our legends, in our culture. At least on the southwest coast of Hudson Bay, and the west coast of James Bay. The legends that we have there are applicable only to that area. There are other legends that are similar to ours, that are also applicable within the land. Bearskin, Big Trout Lake, Kasabonika, Webique, Lansdowne House, Marten Falls. All those other communities that are clustered around that lake heads, I mean, the headwaters of those major rivers, which are flowing into the Hudson Bay.

Our legends there are similar to the coast region. And in fact, our legends in this area are similar across the country of Canada. We have the characters that plays the roles in legends, who are very similar to ours. Although they have a very slightly different names. But the ground and the land they involve in is different. It is noticeable. When you listen to these legends from the west coast, the character that plays there is actually involve in mountains, lakes and creeks. And also when you listen to legends that are in a prairie. The character that plays in that legend is also dealing the land that is flat. And the legends that we have, in the Mushkego land, character that plays the leading role in that legend is has to deal with the muskeg area. And the bays of water. So that's the geographical difference of the legends.[2]

What truly is their spiritual belief and practice, that's a part Europeans never understand, and that's the part they didn't want to understand. But they made a mistake. Our ancestors' physical makeup is fifty percent and the next fifty percent is a spiritual belief, that's what gives them strength, that's what gives them to be independent, and that's what makes them to continue to want to be independent. That's why they need an area where they can practice their spiritual practice, alone away from anyone. And they needed that area what they call hunting ground or territory, where they can roam and practice of this spiritual belief around that ground. And the ground is very sacred to them. That is why they say the ground is sacred because there's places, particular places where they go by themselves alone, to fast or to commune with their spiritual belief. There is a place they used to go where is nobody else walk on. They go there and practice their rituals in all the land that is expanded here in the James Bay Lowland. There is no place that our ancestors have not used as their temple, I mean the church, or a place where to pray, a place to commune with God, so this is what the Christian missionary did not understand. And so is today the politics, the major society doesn't understand that, and they don't understand why the Native has to have so much land. They don't understand that.

I am going to expand a little bit more about the meaning of the sacred ground. It means when the Native people go out into the bush, an individual to practice this spiritual part of his culture, he usually have his own place where he go and stay there by himself and commune with whichever spirit he is contacting. And that place is sacred for him. The place has to be isolated, the place has to be clean – the place is a sanctuary for his purpose to connect with spirits or commune with nature. These things are never fully explained why. It is the part of the spiritual belief and practices of our ancestors that they considered that land so sacred that individual person must have his own ground where he can commune his sprit or the creator, or commune with nature.

When a Native person has this belief and practice through his life he begin to respect and almost worship the land where he walks because of his spiritual belief. Such individual thoroughly and holistically practice his spiritual beliefs and practices usually found a place where he can be alone. Sometimes it's within his hunting territory or sometimes it's even far away from his hunting territory, sometimes it's easy for him to go away far to find some land marks, usually a hill or a ridge or a spot on the river system where he could choose for his area or spot to communicate, isolated from anybody of this nature or of his God or his Creator whichever he has established individually to contact the spirit world.[3]

We always associate the spiritual part on the hill, on the mountain, on the high ground. Nobody ever goes to underground. We don't hear of any church where someone goes underground in order to achieve his prayers. Well, our ancestors are the same. When they want to fast and develop something, they would go into the higher ground. Sometimes there are very thick and inaccessible place. Too extreme. Some people go into where no one can go. No animal can go even, so they can be totally isolated. Some people go into the high ground where not so many animals want to live, except for some caribous who want to get rid of the flies. So anyway, so that's the way they were doing.

And they also believe the higher the ground, the easier to access to the spirit world. Because they believe that up there in the atmosphere, that's where the power lies. Because that's where they see this power of thunder and the thunderbird. That's another story.[4]

MOOSHAWOW AND WABAGAMUSHUSAGAGAN (WHITE MILK LAKE)

It was in this area that the people used to see a strange phenomena about the weather, where they have witnessed something like a whip being hung on that area. For that reason is that people have watched the hawks, the eagle and perhaps the turkey vulture. Those people that soars up there, you know gliding, sometimes they used to see those things disappear to the sky, and they can hear them, and they were scared. And then they would never see them again; they just simply sucked up into the air. And that's where they say it was in that place – Mooshawow. And it was there also that the people always talked about this mystery thing, which they called Pakaaskokan – in English, a human skeleton. And it was there that they hear this thing, and it was there, they saw it – a human skeleton – traveling in the atmosphere, or sometimes with the storm, they can hear it.[5]

And it was there also that the people starved sometimes because they get caught too late in the fall, when there is no caribous, when the geese have left already, when everything is gone. I want to mention that, in the centre of that headland between James Bay and Hudson Bay, where there is lakes, is a story. The Omushkegos were attacked and they were killed, and those who were killed were slaughtered, including women with the child breast feeding. And their breasts were cut off by those people and thrown on to the lake, and therefore turns the water into the milk white.[6]

Today that small lake, it's still there, and it is actually white-coloured water, but it is not milk. I assure you that it is something else that causes it to be white. It is in the area of one of those high ridges, the old beaches that are located there. It is very close to where today the radar base has been built because it is the highest point of land. And it was there that the lake is located. And it is it is actually white-coloured water. One day I went to check these waters and what makes it so. It is a shallow water, it's only about a foot or so, maybe two feet deep and it's all sand. And it's a limestone sand, and that's what makes it white. And in it, on that lake, there is millions of bloodsuckers. Tiny, they look like just like a thread, a black thread that is all you see if you go there. If you ever walk into that ankle deep, you would see them in your skin going by or some of them attach themselves. And these are the ones that stir up the bottom. And in that lake you can see about five or ten loons living there, literally just staying there all the time during the summer and arctic loons, red throated loons, arctic loons, and common loons. And that's what they eat. They eat those bloodsuckers, because there is thousands of them. They have plenty of food. So that is why those lakes are white in colour. But the story brings us down because it has happened one time that the women were killed and these enemies literally cut the breast off women and throw it into the lake, whatever the reason. So that's a story that took place in that in that particular place. So that's why Mooshawow story the story of the area is so historic and dramatic and also very exciting. And for our culture it is the area where the story originate and it's a common place for the Omushkego of the area. Both sides of the Bay, not only there, along the shores are also the same. And then this happens before the European came.

THE SHAMAN AND THE NARWHAL WHISKER

Recently, not so long ago, after the European came, after the fur trade begin, our Omushkego people still practiced their own beliefs and practices and shamanism. And some of those were extraordinary people. Some of them were very discreet, or should I say not showing off. But there were those that abused their power and sort of took advantage of their own people. And it was not long ago that there was a shaman that lived in the Cape Henrietta Maria, who knew how to trick people because he wants to get something out of them. So he made up a story saying there is a beast out there in the land – a beast that emerged from the land which is going to be very dangerous and it's going to eat humans. And he says that it was created by a mitew [shaman] – a person from the distance created this for us to be killed. So he says, "If I don't have enough power to resist or to fight against it, I will be killed and then we're all going to be killed!" So he make these people really get worked up. And it was in that area again, in Mooshawow, that this took place.

So everybody was scared and really worried and worked up and they bunched up together in one place because of this. And this old man says, "It's coming! It's coming!" And it was getting cold, it was snowing and it was fall, perhaps in the middle of November, by this time. Literally this guy says, "Yes, this beast is coming." So then he says, "It's either we all die, or I will die myself, so I will go fight this thing, with this power, with this mitew power." So the people says, "Okay, we give you all the luck and everything." So they tried to pay him, they gave him everything what he needs because he has to go away, because he was fighting this thing every so often with his mind. So he did not have to work for himself. Finally one day he says, "Okay I have to go now."

He has to go in the evening. He went out, almost naked, from his home. He didn't want anybody to look at him because he had taken off his clothes and then he has very little on his mid-section – and he left with nothing. And he says, "Just wait – if you hear anything that is terrible towards where I am going, just remember I am fighting, and, towards in the morning, if you hear it stop, you know something has happened. It's either I am dead or I have win. If I win, I will return before sunrise. And if I don't win," he says, "all you are going to hear is me, my voice out in the air, being turned into a wihtigo, because I have been beaten."

So they were so scared, so they just spent all night. They actually hear a rumbling sound and the ground shaking, according to some, all night. Sometimes it stops – and then it came again and the ground actually shook, they say. And then finally towards the morning, no more sound. So they all wondering what happened to our defender. And before dawn, just when the light came out, he arrive all exhausted – he was stark naked. So they go meet him and cover him and put him inside, and he just collapse into his bedside. And he sleep for a little while.

After the sunrise he wake up and he says, "We will be safe. I was able to beat the beast, the thing that is supposed to threaten us, and we will be okay. If any one of you have enough courage to see what is there where I came from, go follow my trail, back track my trail." And there was snow, probably about four inches already. So he says, "I left something over there a little ways – but don't let the children go there, just the adult, because you can see the size of this thing. I just managed to get one whisker out of its whiskers." So everybody, those men and women, just run over there to see what it is.

And a short distance away, there stood something that looked like an ivory, it's sort of flexible but about six feet long and at that bottom there is still flesh attached to it and this is the whisker of the beast. And everybody was awed and scared and thankful and so they all literally worshiped their saviour and from that time on they gave him everything what he want. When this guy didn't hunt, they just gave him whatever he want because he has saved the group. And that was the end of the story.

In my own way of thinking, the whisker of the beast, the way they describe, it sound like it is a tusk of narwhal. We have some narwhal in Hudson Bay and James Bay, the odd one come around. I think he may have killed this narwhal in the fall before the ice break, before the ice pieces arrive on the shore. He may have killed this one and took the tusk and created a story out of it, because he wanted to trick his own people, because he wanted to take something out of them. But how did he ever make the sound like the earth is shaking? There is a thing that he could have beaten on to make that kind of a sound. It is about three feet and flat, and if you whirl it around with a string, it will make a sound like a rumble and you will actually feel the ground totally shaking. Or he could have set up a shaking tent just a little ways away. That would also make the sound. But to actually see the material that came from this mitew's vision – no one can ever see these things, they usually disappear, yes. So to actually see the blood on the snow that has been where the whiskers stem from, whatever it is, that's what makes me doubtful of this guy. I think he may have killed the narwhal in early fall before the slush began to drift (the time of year when the water begins to freeze but isn't quite solid yet) and kept it somewhere and just went to put it there when he comes in the morning, just to get his way, to trick his own people. He could have created the illusion for these people to believe.

So anyway that's what happened in that Cape Henrietta Maria. It is where there have been many kinds of stories that are extraordinary stories, about unbelievable things. And it was there that people used to see the shining objects that fly on the air. They concluded that this must have been from a mitew who was challenging the other mitew amongst them.[7]

ROCKS AND THEIR STORIES

And then they also found another thing. They have found a stone that has fall from the sky. But they have always find strange things about the stars that came. Some of them, they say it's very light, lighter than ordinary stone. And it doesn't look like ordinary stone. And some of them say it's actually different. They say it glows, with a bit of a light emerging from it. Emanating – coming out of it at night. So they say. So it's another mystery for them. They aren't quite able to explain what it does.

And they also talked about some strange behaviour of some stones. In the place where we are, where there's muskeg, they say that you can see these stones if you walk in the bush. There are places sometimes where there's no lakes and no creeks, and if you happen to get stuck there you could get really thirsty. If you ever walk into one of these stones, they say, "Dig under it." If it's about six inches or a foot into the ground, they say, you will always find the water, and the water is always drinkable, it's very nice. All around it there will be no water – but under these stones there will always be water. And that's a way you could find a drink when you get thirsty, or if you get caught in the hot summer in a place where there's no lakes or anything.

They talk about stones that have fallen from the sky and stand on top of the ground. And some elders have been mystified by these stones around the coastal region. Some of the elders that I have listened to say that these stones made a big splash when they landed. If you walk on the shores of the Hudson Bay and James Bay, you could also find that, too. Because, the west coast of James Bay is a marshy place. It's muskeg, it's mud, it's clay – there is no solid rocks. There is no outcropping. It's all sandy, muddy beaches and everything. And the farther away from you go from the shore, there is lichen moss and sand ridges. And in between those sand ridges sometimes you will see a rock, sitting there on top – just grass or even some small type of wood around it. And there's always water and it's always fresh. So people say these rocks have fallen from the sky.

But I studied a little bit of those stones myself. Some of them are limestone. Some of them will be sandstone, some of them granite, black, grey, it depends. But it sits there. So, I ask an elder one time why is it that this stone don't seem to grow over? There are other stones you can just see the top of them, they've been overgrown. And he says, "No," he says, "this is a stone that has fall from the sky. Nothing grows on them."

They could be very right. But I thought about it myself. Maybe, because it's so fat at the bottom, every time when there is a rain, there is water all around it – and the rain goes under it and stays there. In the winter coming this water that is under it will maybe start to freeze. And then when it freezes, it pushes the rock up every winter. Probably just go up and down. We will surely see this rock moving. So it's not because it's been fall from the sky, but because of the nature's way. The water freezes and the water thaws and then it doesn't have a chance to grow over. Because of the way it sit.

Now there was a story. There is an elder, from those people who have came from York Factory. We were talking about these stones – we were sitting on the riverbank and having a tea as the river goes by. And there's beautiful sand there that is so nice – these sandstones – so sparkling and everything. And we were talking about where did those things came from, why is it sparkling and all? And so he begin to tell me about the stones. There are larger stones, and he says, "We call it *inninassini*." In translation would be, "a human rock." We, the Omushkego people, we have named rocks. Like we call those limestones *waapassini* (white stone). And then we have those grey looking rocks, and we call them *waapitewassini*. And then we have those black rocks, solid rocks. We call them *makate-wassini* (black stone). And then we have a mixed colour of rocks. They are sometimes bubbly looking and they come out in the outcropping, and they have many colours. So they say that's where you find the flint, amongst those things. And they call it the flint rock, or a flint stone if you want. And then there's also the rocks that actually look red. We call them red rocks. And then we also have some rocks that are mixed with quartz. They call them quartz. There are such rocks in this area that came out from the muskeg and outcropping, you know, out shoreline. And they are speckled with the quartz. Sometimes mix, sometimes there is a lines of it in there, and they just come out from under the underground. You find those also in the river. You find them many places. Sometimes a huge rock, which has been broken off from someplace. Wherever they come from, we don't know.

And there are many more stories about rocks. Some Native people say that the moon is just a round rock. I guess because the way it looks. And they never go any further than that. They say: *wanihichiapiskohochin piisim. Aapisk. Piiwaapisk*, is a stone, not actually a stone mixed with anything. *Waaweyaapiskakoochi assini. Waaweyaapiskiswassini. Waawiiya michaapiskisiwaassini. Maaktakaapiskisiwaassini.* The *"pisk"* is a name for something which is harder than mud. But it also has a generalization of different kind. *Assini* (stone), I think, is a most general meaning. But *"pisk"* is something harder.

So, there are many other mysteries about the rocks. There's one right over here in where I am staying. The community is called Peawanuck. That's where the flint is found, in this kind of rock. Right across from the village there is outcropping of rocks. And there is an old man who has said, "If you look at that area you could see that the rock melted down and cascaded down into this river a long time ago." Where did he get the idea? He actually saw a picture of a volcano, I think – that's maybe what he thought when he saw this rock. There were elders long time ago who talked about the mountain exploding and cascading fiery stone. There are some elders who have pass on the story like that, but we don't know exactly how the story went.

And we know there is someplace in the earth that stone actually bubbles out of the ground – they know it is hot down there somewhere. Our Native people have passed this story down – it could have come from another tribe. I never believe this when I was young. But then I saw this story in a book and on TV. And this is Yellowstone Park. That's within this continent, right here in North America. So our elders must have hear the story from other tribes.[8]

PLACES IN THE SKIES

Giant Spider and the First People

The first human beings who appeared on earth was these two people, a man and a woman. They were not living in this world, but in some other dimension of life. We don't know for sure exactly where, but they were there. And they noticed that there was a land down below, a land that was so beautiful, and they so wished to go and see it. So there was a giant spider named Ehep who noticed that they were longing to go there. He said to them, "Do you wish to go and see and live in that land?" So the people say, "Yes, I wish we could go there and see that land." So Ehep says, "I will help you if you do what I say. I will lower you down with my string and you will sit in this sort of basket, like a nest." He says, "I will lower you down in this nest, but you must not look at the land – even when you are think you are getting closer, you must not look down until you touch down. If you look before you hit the ground, you will not be happy – you will have to suffer to live in that land, even though it's beautiful."

And so they got in and agreed not to look. Ehep lowered them in his nest – they went down and down – we don't know how far but it took some time to lower them into this land, which was more like the earth, sort of. They were so eager and excited. And when they thought that they were almost there, they wondered what it look like now that they were closer. So they looked – they looked over the side and noticed the land. At that moment the string that held them up sort of let go and they landed on the ground forcefully.

They didn't get hurt really. But Ehep had told them that if they should look down, they would not be happy on that land – that they would be suffer, in order to live there. And that was the end of the story.

The man and his wife wanted to experience another land – they wanted to see it and they even wished to live there. But they just simply couldn't get there. But this Ehep was a giant spider who could help them that way because he had a string. He could bring them anywhere at all, and they were so eager to get on.

This basket that they got into was part of creation. They had to go through this to get to that world – they have to be lowered with the string. And the string they say is represented when a child is born by the cord that gives them their life. If the kids is born with their eyes open, they get hurt – the eyes would be sore and they would get sick. That's why midwives are instructed to clean the eyes first, as soon as the baby is out, so they won't suffer. And this is why the people in the basket were told that if they opened their eyes they would suffer.

The elders lived for so long that they understood life, so they created some stories to interpret life for people. As soon as the humans came into consciousness, they knew that this life is not all there is. They knew that there is some place we originate from and that's what they usually call the Great Spirit. They said we originate from the spirit world and we come here for a short journey in this world – and then we have to go back where we came from. Nobody actually understands where that is. It's not this material world, it's a spiritual one. That's why they created this legend of Ehep.

Ehep is a mystery thing. He is a spider. Whan a spider lowers his self from someplace, you don't know where he is attached – you see him but you can't see his web. It stretches and everything. And no one understands exactly how he makes that line. And it's strong enough to lower him down and to go up. So that is the mystery put into this story to make you think. When the child is born, he's attached from somewhere and has to come out in this world, and only then is he a person. In this story, the two people were being materialized in this world, just like when a child is born with a cord attached to the mother. So when they interpret it, the mother represents the Great Spirit, who is actually giver of life. And when you come to this world you are separated from that world and you go into this material world. The mother is the creator; that mystery.

We still have a question. What would have happened if they didn't look down? They could have just enjoyed the world and there would be no suffering – and then they would go back to the Creator, to the Great Spirit.

The string makes a life very powerful and strong, if you do the right thing. And if not, the string can be very weak also. The same string is used to lift you away from here to go back to where you originally came from. It is the connector which lowered you down and is supposed to pull you up again. So there's that idea. You are here temporarily, but you need something to pull you back. Maybe it's a faith, strongly believing in the Great Spirit, that pulls you back. There's no heaven in our story. There's no heaven for our Omushkego people. What you enjoy in this world will be similar to what you're going to get in the next world.[9]

ASTRONOMY

Our people acquired the knowledge of astronomy. Astronomy is knowing the position of the stars and knowing which moves, which not move. Our ancestors, the shamans, understood their planet. Understood the stars that move. Our ancestors then use the stars to navigate during the night. And also they could study the stars and understand what kind of weather they're going to have in the coming winter or summer.

There are many stories that involved this astronomy, or the bodies of the universe. Our people, our shamans, understood these things. The only thing is that they didn't have the language to describe them. Shamans lived in the bush by themselves, they lived in the wilderness so they never had any gatherings – they didn't have meetings, they didn't have any public speaking. So they know all these things by themself. They have their own education. Just like what the Europeans know today. They know. They know it all.[10]

Many of our elders who watched the stars mentioned about the stars that wander – there are five stars that wander in the sky through a year's time. And almost every elder that I know can easily pick out the North Star. They knew this a long time before the European came. So they know this – they have noticed this – so they are astronomers. They know there's time – just like a clock – a year or even a month. Unfortunately, they never write nothing. The only thing they didn't do was write.

And they saw the meteorites – they have seen some rocks fall from the sky – bits and pieces of those things. And they also study places on the ground where the lightning struck. The only thing that they never actually explain is what happens when there's lightning. It's one of the greatest mysteries for them. Some people believe that the lightning strikes the ground and sticks there on the ground, so that it's like a stone. But we don't know.[11]

Our ancestors didn't have any obstacles to stop them from observing the sky. When they lay on the ground and when they hunted they had no tent, no roof. Whenever they opened their eyes they see the stars at night. They knew that they move. They knew the whole universe is shifting, but they didn't know that the world was moving. They knew that the stars move along with the sun.

They knew the morning star. The morning star sometimes became an evening star, or different seasons. And they knew the North Star, they know that for a long time. They knew that there was one star that did not wander off into the sky – it stayed the same and the rest of the stars went around it.

They didn't know why it was so cold up north, they never could explain that. This was a mystery. So they dream about the north, and they begin to form it as a being, they formed it as a human. They did this with all four directions – as human males, not females.

So they respect all those things, but they did not have any scientific explanation. I mean that they just didn't have enough words, I guess. The only words they used were practical words, practical things which need to be described, need to be named, and it was the only kind of language development they had. But the mind knowledge is not describable in their language. The shamans that I talk about who studied the sky, they dreamed about the stars. And they say every youngster that is aware of the sky at night looks at the stars and he dreams about the stars. Almost every young person dream that he goes to the stars, and travels there in his mind. And that's the beginning.

But why? Why does a man reach out there? The elders have always asked, what is out there? How come those things are there? How did they work so precisely? No chaotic situation. There is nothing colliding out there. Everything they saw, our ancestors understood to be round. The earth seemed to be round. The sun was round, not square, the stars seemed to be round, and the whole universe seemed to be round.

They were aware of many other things. For example, people in James Bay and Hudson Bay, who lived close to salt water, understood that this water is different than fresh water. If they went out with the canoe and they marked the water line, the water into the bay seemed to lift them higher up. So they think that the salty water has something to do in connection with the moon.

MOSHEGIISHIK (THE UNIVERSE)

Okay, these are the little mysteries that are unexplained by our ancestors. They knew that they were there, they never were able to name it. My grandmother tell me this, that if you lay flat on the ground in the month of September and you see that white line that goes from east to southeast, she said that turns in September, and goes directly to the south. And that's when the geese move. They take off from here and go south by guiding and navigating by that line. At first when I was young I didn't see that line, so she says, "Go out there, away from the camp, and go lay down flat on the ground and look, away from the trees and everything."

I went. I think I was about six or seven years old. So I went out there a little ways from the teepee, and went to lay down there. It's dark, really. I see a white line that looks like a white line. She says, "Stay there, stay there. Look at it," she says, "soon, in time you will see all white. There will be no darkness. There will be just white." She says, "All that white stuff is the stars." And this was simply my grandmother. So I didn't see that light at that time. I was too impatient.

And there was another old man that I hear say the same thing, and then three elders say that. Finally when I was 15 years or so I went out to watch the night sky, when it's purely clear when there is no cloud or anything. I think it took me a half hour or so, maybe one hour, looking at the same place, not moving. I begin to see in that line there is just white! But it's all stars – just exactly what an elder had said. So these were astronomers. They studied the sky, they studied the stars.

Because they had no explanations they dreamed about the universe, the stars they called Moshegiishik. So they know there is something further away, far away, very far away, and they think that's where this Great Spirit is – not only there, but here also. And they know that there is a Great Spirit. One of the things that many elders have told me is that there is a good spirit and then there is an evil spirit. Long before the European came they know that there was a good and there was an evil spirit.

One elder says that everything has an opposite. For example, you will be laughing one day, one minute – as a kid you laugh so much. It will change in time – you will cry, you will hurt yourself for some reason and you will cry. There is something that happens opposite. First you laugh and then you are sad, you're in joy and then you're sad, you will be happy and then you will be sad. There is cold and heat, there is dark and light. This was told to me when I was young. So, everything has an opposite. There is positive and negative. Some people are very kind and some people can be very mean, vicious. People can be strong, and some men can be very weak. The variation is always there. So this is also the stuff they dreamed about. In dreams they got this.[12]

So the story goes like this. About a man called Moshegiishik – it means "the universe." Long time ago there was a man who was known as the Moshegiishik. He acquired this name – he studied the stars every time there was a clear night's sky. When he was young, he used to hear his mother say, "This is the morning, get up now, my son. The dawn star is rising."

In First Nation culture, the hunter must be up before sunlight, so that he can be away out from camp by sunrise. First Nation being hunters, they know the animal behaviour – that animals are hunters most of them, even those who are vegetarians, start early in the morning – like moose, caribou, ptarmigans, sharp tailed grouse, and some others. The partridge are always on the move before sunrise. Moose start to eat as soon as the sun rises, so does the caribou.

Nature has it that the noise is sharp early in the morning; thus the animals take advantage of that. Moose can eat broken twigs in winter – trees, or poplar tree seed buds – and he eats them. This makes noise, but other noises are also sharp too. Therefore he can eat but hear almost any sound made by an animal like a wolf sneaking towards him as he eats. So he use this situation for his safety. So do the other animals. Caribou eats lichens, white moss in the winter. He has to dig in snow to find lichen, which he eats. In the morning when it's cold, the snow is brittle and cracks easy. This carries sound. When the caribou is digging, the hoof dig, he puts his head down in the hole. While doing this he can hear the sound of snow noises either made by his own hooves or any other kind. This is the reason why most animals – vegetarians or meat eaters – use this situation.

Caribou can make noise too. Their hooves click as they dig in snow looking for their food. In the early morning the noise carries distance; thus the humans, as meat eaters, have understood this also. If humans are hunters and gathers, they must understand these things. You must start very early age in order to be an expert hunter or to survive as a hunter.

So that is why Moshegiishik took interest on the stars. He was told to get up before morning star rises high, before dawn, so that he can be on his way where he can be hunting.

Moshegiishik did not like to be awakened at the time when his sleep is most enjoyable. Then he begin to study the star, especially the star, morning star. Later then he begin to learn more about the movement of certain stars. He himself counted five moving stars that wanders on the night sky. He studied them very thoroughly. He even begin to name them. *Ochakatak* (the Great Bear), and *Ochakwish* (Little Bear). He also noticed one star that did not seem to move – all through night and seasons. He calls it the stationary star, later known as the North Star.

He was an old man when he acquired his name, Moshegiishik. His main interest was to study the night sky. He would get up at night, if it's a nice clear night, and lay down flat on his back and simply look at the night sky. He studied the sky and saw many things which an ordinary man would not notice. Later, in his old age, he was an expert in teaching of the motion of the stars. People then respected him, Moshegiishik.

He also find out many things than just the stars. He saw raining fires, he called them – exploding objects which appeared larger than the stars. He knew these were not ordinary stars. Many different things made up the moshegiishik, the universe.

He also examined the objects that seem to have explode so brightly that they carry sound. Some of these objects must be very far out in sky. He noticed that some of these exploding objects seems to fall in pieces to the ground as a small sparks. He saw enormous numbers of shooting stars. He said that whenever you saw a star shooting, its direction is where the wind will come by morning.

He saw mystery objects that seemed to have their own will in terms of which direction they wanted to go. And these he believed were created by a mitew, a shaman. Shamans knew Moshegiishik was studying these things. He believed they were jealous of him and thus created illusions to harass him, to bug him. But Moshegiishik knew better. He didn't bother, he just let it go. Anything he could not understand he just put it aside. Therefore Moshegiishik had seen flying objects in the night sky. It has been said about him by the people who grew up with him that he actually get in touch with these objects when he's alone. People say he used them, that he was able to summon them when he needed to get somewhere fast. He would surprise his family to have walked such distance in short time and prove it that he has been there and back.

No, nobody quite understand how he knew mysteries that an ordinary person would not be able to encounter in his lifetime. This man amongst the Omushkegowak, Omushkego men respected this man. They say he taught many things to his people. He tells people, "Man can predict weather from the movement of the stars. Like Ochakatak, for example, when these clusters of stars hung in such a way during the winter, there is an indication of a short winter season or the early spring." Most of the things he said was found to be fairly accurate. He really did study the movement of the stars to predict the weather.

He also studied the Northern Lights. He said that if you see red Northern Lights dancing to the northwestern sky in January it means it will be a mild winter and early spring. When you see the Northern Lights spread all over the night without much movement it means cold spells during the winter. Other ancestors didn't say so much. Some say the Northern Lights are the ghosts of our dead ancestors dancing in a distant world. Therefore our own, our Moshegiishik, was a person who studied the night sky.

Many of his findings were useful to his people. Some for navigation, weather prediction and other prediction which may not be scientific. Moshegiishik said, "When the sky trail has turned from North to South, that is when the migrating birds take off for the sudden migration. Sky trail is the Milky Way."

Moshegiishik used stars' positions in the night sky. He knew when something will happen or will come to pass. Some of his findings seemed to be true. He knew the whole night sky. The stars moved – he said that some were going to west. Some seems to move opposite direction he said. This he did not explain why and where in the night sky that he saw this. He said that when the stars are blinking, that means strong wind next day.

Moshegiishik did not study only the stars, he also studied the sun, the moon and the Northern Lights. Most of what he had stated have been used by the Omushkegowak[13]

CHAKAPESH

Now I'm going back to the time where the legends come from. This is one of those legends that we called Chakapesh. This character, the little guy, plays a great part in one of the famous legends which is called Chakapesh. Chakapesh was a mystical man, he was a powerful shaman. Small as he may be, like a midget, he was a man, nevertheless, who possessed all kinds of powers and spiritual things. And he was a person that usually challenged anything that is not supposed to be done.

He lived with his sister who was the wisest woman that ever lived, who had knowledge about everything. Any question that he has, this little man would just bring it to her and then he would get some answer – and sometimes some very good, sound advice. One of the usual pieces of sound advice from his sister was not to do anything dangerous. And, of course, he crossed his heart that he would listen to her – but then he would go right and do exactly the opposite of what he promised. Because he was a shaman, he could travel far with his mind power and be instantly where he wanted to be. He only used this skill when he needed it – not all the time.[14]

Chakapesh Gets Swallowed by a Fish

Chakapesh plays a variety of characters. He was a very mystical person. He was also like a kid – a very mischievous sort of person. But, at the same time, he is fully grown, fully powerful in his mind – capable of controlling even nature at times. So he's an adventurous kind of a little character. Any question that comes into his mind, he will ask about it. And then, if he was told that such a question should not be fooled around with, if there is any caution of a dangerous item, he would go – investigate! – and give it a try and see for himself – find out for himself. So that is what Chakapesh was all about.

It was said that at one time there were extraordinary people – giants – living on the land, a long, long time ago. I don't know why we had giants in those days – but there were giants! Human giants, living in this time of Chakapesh. And there were giant bears also. Those things are very powerful.

So Chakapesh grew up just the same way as any tribal kid. He had two parents and a sister – and these giant bears and giant beings were close by. Then when he was just maybe five years old, it so happened that one of these giant beings came into their camp and his parents were killed. The sister managed to run away with the little boy while the parents were trying to lure the giant away from the children. In some stories they were giant bears and in some they were giant humans who killed his parents. I am more comfortable with the giant human story.

These giant humans were actually cannibals, and they were very feared by people. And every family that lived around there, they would have to develop an extra power amongst themselves so they could detect the danger of these giant beings – and defend themselves. And that is the reason that every young boy has to be taught to go out and do the fasting, to develop the extra spiritual power for his protection and, if he grows up to be a married person, for the protection of his family.

So Chakapesh's parents were killed at their camp by the giant humans. Chakapesh and his sister managed to live in the bush by themselves and they grew up, they survived. They walked into the camp of other human beings and they were raised by these families. Eventually, when they got a little bit older, they managed to live by themselves, because the sister was getting older and much wiser. They needed to develop their own defence system, so Chakapesh was trained to go out there by himself, same as any other person – any other child.

So he developed his own spiritual stuff, which we call shamanism. He began to be a very good student. He automatically acquired these things because he had lost both his protective parents and he didn't have the comfort of being loved by them. The only thing he could rely on was his sister. And his sister was like a mother to him – an educator, and teacher, and comforter, and everything. Anything that he didn't know his sister knew automatically because she was a gifted person. She had developed her own powers and she was able to help him with whatever he found. She always told him never to venture out into the unknown or never to investigate something if he wasn't sure what it was. He must always try to come home and tell his sister what he had seen, or what he had heard.

He had heard his sister saying that his parents were killed by the giants – but he was not satisfied with that. He knows there is something wrong. He always wanted to know where was this place where it had happened. But his sister would always deny him this knowledge of where and how. So he had that problem that bothered him so much – because he wanted revenge. He wanted to kill those who had killed his parents – he wanted to hunt them. A small being such as him, only the size of a six-year-old boy, doesn't have a frightening appearance – but he was very powerful by now because he was nearly an adult person, even though he was only the size of a child.

His sister never got married, and he didn't get married because of his size – because of his deformity, I guess I would say – and there weren't too many midgets in our tribes (although there were small beings sometimes – I've seen some in the Omushkego country, we still have some today).

So he was trained to report to his sister about everything he had seen or heard during his wandering during the days. Then she could teach him to either avoid these things or learn how to deal with them. So it was always the same way – he would first return home and tell his sister about what he'd seen and the wise older sister always explains because she knows all these things – she had visions, and that's why she knew everything. She also had that powerful women's intuition. And so anytime she wanted, she could have a visualization and find out anything she wanted. If, for example, Chakapesh came home and said he had seen a certain track in a certain terrain, his sister would go lie down and have a little snooze. A few minutes later she would wake up and say, "Ah! Now I know what you saw." And then she would explain what it was. So that's how great she was.

But even though she kept him well informed, sometimes he was very mischievous! He would deceive his sister. She would make him promise not to do something dangerous and he would swear to her that he would be obedient. But then he would go back to the same place and investigate this thing that was dangerous. And that was his problem! Many times in his life he encountered something that would nearly kill him.

One day Chakapesh was using his shaman powers (because he had mastered the power of mind over matter) to project his mind and his body to a lake. Once he got there, he started walking along the shore, carrying his tomahawk and a bow and arrows – of course all fitted for his size. But don't be fooled! This bow and arrows may have been small, but they were mystical – and so was his tomahawk. He could kill anything with his bow and arrows – he could kill anything with his axe. He was an expert axe thrower! He could split a big log by just throwing his axe. He could knock down anything with one of his tiny arrows when he wanted to put the power into it. So that's how powerful he was, and that's the reason he always dared to go out to the dangerous areas – he didn't care because he so had the full confidence of his powers and capabilities.

So he had projected himself to this lake because he had heard that there were big fish there. It was the afternoon of a quiet, calm day. He skipped a piece of flat limestone along the surface of the lake so that it skidded far, far away – because this was a magic throw. He knew that whatever was swimming in the water would jump at this rock. Then he tried the same thing with a clam shell. And it was very calm – no waves and no wind.

And sure enough! As it got far from the shore, there jumped the biggest fish that he ever saw. He had seen a sturgeon that was six feet long – that was the largest fish he ever saw – and he also knew about the white beluga whales. This lake was so big that he couldn't see clear across it and was very deep with very high banks. So now he knew for sure that what he'd heard about big fish being there was true – that was a very, very big fish that he saw jump. Big. Bigger than six feet. And he wasn't even two feet tall. So now he knows for sure.

He went back that evening and told his sister what he'd seen. Sure enough, she was startled and said, "Did you go there?" And he said, "Yes, I went there! It's quite a distance, but I wanted to see that lake because I heard that there were big fish." So she told him, "You should **never** go there again! Don't even walk on the shore because that fish could grab you!" And he says, "Okay! Okay, sister – I swear I will never go there again!" So finally she was satisfied and she went to bed and went to sleep.

Of course he wants to go and try it again tomorrow. To be grabbed by a fish would be very exciting! He wanted to know what it would feel like. Finally he fell asleep also. And he dreamed – he dreamed about the fish and how he would fight it.

Early the next morning before dawn he got up. His sister was already preparing his breakfast. She had dried his little moccasins and smoothed them out for him to put on. Then finally he picked up his hunting bag and grabbed his hunting axe – his tomahawk. Men never kept these bags in the house – they always hung them outside a distance away so they wouldn't get any human smells on them. So he says, "Bye bye, sister – I'll see you tonight." And his sister says, "Be careful!" Off he went – in the opposite direction to where the lake was, because his sister was looking at him.

Just as he crossed the horizon of his camp he made a u-turn towards the direction of that lake. And from there he travelled very quickly and he arrived at the lake by the afternoon. First he had stopped to hunt and whatever he killed he just left it for when he was going home later – that was just habit. So now he was finally here and his curiosity was just so strong! He wanted to taste the power of that big fish because he had dreamed that he had won and he wanted to fulfill that dream.

He walked around the shore and was glad that it was warming up because it was the afternoon. That was another reason he had waited until the afternoon to come to the lake – because if a fish was going to jump out of the water to grab him it would be very cold and it wouldn't be so bad if the day, at least, was warm. So he strolled around and lay around – and then purposely he shot one of his arrows into the lake quite a distance away, just far enough so that he would have an excuse to go out in the water and get it. That way, he could tell his sister, "Well my arrow went over there and I had to find it." Exactly where it landed I cannot say, but he did shoot it out there on purpose.

So now he had to take off his little jacket and just dive into the water. He knew the big fish would be there. So he swam and he swam until he was almost up to where his arrow was drifting. And he says, "*Where* is the *fish??*" He grabbed his arrow and started swimming back and he called, "Come on, Fishy, Fishy, Fishy! Dare to come and grab me!"

And as he was half way to the shore – wham! – a big splash – and that's all he knew. He swept through rushing water and into some kind of a hole – and he knew it was a fish! And so he was swallowed! And down the fish went, and he was inside. He had been all prepared to fight this fish but the worst thing – the thing that really bugged him – was that there is sticky stuff in the stomach of fish, and it stinks! It's really nauseating, and he just was almost throwing up constantly while he was trying to get out from the fish. Finally he was almost passed out and he thought, "Well this is it! I'm not going to survive this thing." He knows because he was dissipated. So he sent this mental telepathy message to his sister, he says, "Sister – I have been swallowed by the fish!" That's all he could send.

And sure enough, his sister was working outside of the tipi and all of a sudden she heard this voice in her head. And that's Chakapesh saying he was swallowed by the fish. She also knew exactly where he was. And so she went there. She took whatever she usually carried during the day – a knife and also a tomahawk – and she travelled towards that place. She had what's called a path-finding mind, so she could pinpoint exactly where her brother was. So she got there in good time because she was travelling with the mystical power – I don't know what kind – nobody has ever explained how she travelled exactly, but she got there.

She took a fishhook that she had brought and she put power into it. Then she got special bait that the fish could not resist and she threw it out over the water. Maybe three times she did that and, at the same time, used her powers to force the fish to come to the bait. The fish was forced to come to that area and then saw the bait that was so delicious to his mind. Chakapesh was still in there, barely conscious now. The fish grabbed the bait and the sister reeled the fish in – pulling so tight on the string – she knew this was the fish. Once it was on the shore, she hit it over the head with her tomahawk. She took her knife and the sun sparkled on its side. She began to cut the stomach open, and as she did this there Chakapesh could hear her. "Careful! Careful!" he says, "You're going to cut me!"

She was so mad that she just wanted to spank him – but her heart was kind and she was careful with him. Finally she got the guts open and out slid the Chakapesh – all slimy and sticky. He was nearly suffocated. She grabbed her brother and washed him right down – actually she almost drowned him because she was so mad. She was too mad to say a thing. Finally he said, "Please, sister – please! You're drowning me!" And she says, "I should! I should! You're stubborn and a disobedient person! Why do I even bother to come and save you?" But anyway she forgave him and all that stuff and she was happy that he survived. So they went home together in a good spirit. I think she took a bit of the fish for a meal. Nobody ever says what kind of fish it was. Was it northern pike? They are big. The northern pike can grab a duck – or even a Canada goose. And they have a very big stomach.

Of course she was still a little mad when she got home and she said, "Why do you have to do that? I have to go out there and rescue you each time you disobey! When are you going to stop doing that?" But he just kept on saying that he was sorry. And she says, "Some day I am not going to come and you will be by yourself!" But when they went to bed they had made peace with each other. And that's the end of the story. Truly Chakapesh had the power, but that time he had to learn a lesson and that's why he was not able to free himself from that fish.

Chakapesh Snares the Sun

Years went by and Chakapesh and his sister were happy. They moved around one place to the other. One day he asked his sister again, "Where is this place where our parents died?" And she was strict actually – she was not going to tell him – but she did say that it was east from where they were living – the east, where the hills are a great height. She told him that giants were living in those big hills. So he asked her, "How far is that place?" She measured the distance by days of travel and told him, I think, that it was about a month's travel from where they were. So to travel on foot for a month – that's a long ways away.

Chakapesh didn't care how far it was. He decided to go check. This was in the springtime. He went there to see, but he didn't do anything – he just travelled around and then he came back to his sister. He told her that, as he travelled east, he went past those hills and went to the edge of the land. He told her, "I was sitting there looking at this great lake that seemed to have no land on the other side. Then I saw a trail that seemed to come from the water – it was wide and nothing seemed to be growing on it. It was all scorched – just bare rocks. And it ended up on top of a hill." He was very mystified about this – what was it and why was it so strange? His sister asked, "Is that exactly to the east? And is it the edge of the land?" And he says, "Yes." "Oh!" she says, "*Why* do you have to travel such far distances when you don't need to?" And he says, "Yes, yes – but what is that? What is that thing?" So his sister says, "I want you to promise me, don't go there! Because I don't want you to bother with that trail again – and I don't want you to snare anything there!" (because that's what he did – he snared most of the animals he killed).

So he had all his snares and he went over there again. He wanted to know what that was. He thought, "No snaring? I'm going to snare here – it can't hurt anything really, whatever this trail is." So, he put the snare there and he went back home. He never told his sister what he had done. He forgot all about it and just went to bed.

Next morning he went to check the snare. The trail was still there – but the snare material had been burned as if there had been a fire! So he began to wonder. He went back to ask his sister again about that trail. She says, "You go *there* again?" "Yes! I was just trying to find out if I had snared anything." And she says, "Don't you ever listen to me?" He said, "I was just curious." So finally the sister says, "Now I'm going to tell you what that is. That thing that you put a snare on is the most powerful thing on earth – it's the sun! The trail is the sun trail – it comes out into the sky from the east at the edge of the earth – it comes from the bay and up the mountain. And if you put your snare there, how would the sun come up if you held onto it? The sun is the one who scorched the land, because it's hot. You don't feel it that much because it's way up there, but in that place – in the east – it's really hot. Nothing is growing where the sun is moving. A stone maybe can withstand it, but there is no material that you could use to snare that sun."

So Chakapesh just wandered about. He went out hunting but he didn't go to that place. He kept thinking, "*Nothing* can snare the sun?" So he went on a dream quest – he went to fast and concentrate on the sun. What could he use to snare this? He wanted to beat anything that was powerful. He wanted to prove himself – prove that he could win at anything. And so he had a dream. He was thinking about the material – the strand – that could not be burned. What could not be burned? What? Everything that he dreamed about using would still burn. His dream quest was to understand this. The roots of the trees have strands in their roots that could be tied together to make a very strong strand. He thought about whales and other things that have strong parts, and in his dream he tried them all. But nothing seemed to work. Then he thought about the about animals and fish – nothing was strong enough to hold the sun. But he wanted to snare the sun so badly because he had been told that there was no way for him to do this.

This dreaming had been going on for about a month when finally he dreamed the answer – he dreamed of the strand that he could use. But the thing is, where would he get the strand? There were hardly any humans around and he didn't want to go and bother any humans. But the thing was, it had to be from a human – and not from himself – from another person. And so the only human he had around was his sister. It bothered him so much, but he simply *had* to try – he just had to! So strong was the urge to try!

So finally one evening he decided, "Well, I have to ask her. She is the only person around and she is the strongest person that I know. And I'm sure she can help me." So as they were going to sleep, his sister noticed that there was something bugging him and she said, "What's wrong with you? How come you're so tense?" So he didn't say anything.

Finally on another evening it was time for them to go to sleep. He was sitting around, working on his equipment – his arrows and all his stuff. His sister had worked hard all day and she went to lie down because she was getting sleepy. And then finally he says, "Sister, can you give me a strand? I need a strand for my snare." So she grabbed her basket and dug in there and found some thin strands of weasel hide. She says, "Here – this is the best I can give you. Weasel is usually good for snaring." But he looks at it for a little while and he says, "No – no, no – I got those kind of things." So she dug in again and found something else and threw it across, but he simply looked at it and threw it back and say, "No, no – that's not going to help me." She was very sleepy, and everything that she tried to give, no, that's not what he wanted. It's never what he wanted. And she started to get very, very annoyed. "Why don't you shut up? I want to sleep! Go find the roots from the trees – that might be good for you to snare what you want to snare. Is it a bear?" And he says, "No, no, no, no." He used his power so that she would not know what he was thinking. Finally she was so sleepy and had exhausted all the materials she had – anything to do with a line – not a thing!

Finally she gave her own hair. She had long wavy hair and she pulled some out and said, "Here – this is the last thing I can give you." So he said, "No, no, no, no. Not that one." She was now really pissed off. But he wouldn't go to sleep. He just kept sitting there – he still wanted to ask her for another kind of strand. He kept saying the same thing: "Come on, sis, just one strand will do!" But she was *very* mad by this time. He just didn't know what else to do. Finally – in desperation and madness and everything – he just spread her legs and pulled one strand of her hair from around her vagina – around there – a hair from there. He pulled it out and he said, "Here is a strand!" She was mad.

Finally she says "Don't you touch that thing! Throw it in the fire," she says. "What do you mean?" he says, "This is it! This is the strand that I should use." She just couldn't say anything to this crazy person – and she also knew that he was a really stubborn person. So anyway she fell asleep.

There! One strand – that's all he needed. In the morning when they got up she asked why he took that strand and he told her that he needed to use it. We Omushkego people, when we had a kinky string that we wanted to make straight, we would put it in our mouths and use our lips and our saliva to make it wet and straight. And so she said, "Don't you put that thing in your mouth!" He told her not to worry and then he left.

He made a beeline to the east, to that mountain where he had seen that track. It was late in the afternoon when he got there – he climbed the mountain and followed that trail. Finally he found the place to put his snare. "I'm going to catch that sun," he says. "No one ever did it, but I will!" So he took out the strand and of course he used a magic touch. Now this strand was only short and all curly and everything. He just put it into his mouth and straightened it out and, by doing this, it got to be about six feet long – powerful – nothing could break it because of his magic touch. He didn't know exactly how large it should be to get the sun, but he looked at it in the distance and made some calculation and set up a snare – to snare the sun.

He left it there and went back home. He did what he always did – he hunted his way home so he would bring fresh-killed food for the evening meal. And once he was inside he forgot about everything that he had done that day. His sister asked him, "How was your day?" and still he didn't remember. They had supper together and went to sleep and he didn't think about anything. During the night he didn't even dream about anything.

By nature's clock, his sister always got up at the same time every day – when the dawn was rising to the east. She got up the next day as usual, and made the fire, and made up some sort of soup. She prepared that and a little bit of breakfast for Chakapesh to eat before he left for the day. So she sat there and the dawn was rising. All of a sudden time seemed to stand still. She looked over to the east and realized that the sun was supposed to be rising by this time. But it didn't seem to come out! There was a red spot where it usually came out from – but she didn't see any sun rising from it.

Now sometimes in our territory, in March or April, because it's very flat country, you can see the sun rise way out to the east, it seems to come up on the horizon and then sometimes it disappears again. And so she decided that it must just be the season that makes it appear like that.

And then finally she began to really worry. The sun was not rising! And then she thought, "Just a minute – just a minute! He wanted to snare – he wanted a special strand for a special reason." And then – yes! – she knew that he could be behind this. She took a roasting stick and jabbed Chakapesh in his foot which he had sticking out towards the warm fire. "Chakapesh, get up *now*!" And he said, "What? What? Why are you hurting me?" And she said, "Get up now before I stab you with this thing! What have you done?" And he just buried his head into his blankets and made himself into a little ball. He remembered what had happened because his sister said, "There's something wrong with the sun, it doesn't want to rise! Did you go put a snare out there?" He didn't want to get up and he didn't want to say anything at all. He was scared by this time and his sister was getting madder and madder. Finally he said, "Yes, yes, I set a snare." So she said, "If you don't get up right now, you're not even going to have breakfast and I'm going to chase you right out of here. You're not just going to lay there. What do you think will happen if the sun doesn't come out?"

Finally he got up and reluctantly she gave him something to eat. Then she sent him out to find the sun. So he went over there. On his way he remembered that nothing can stand that sun – not a thing – except that strand that he had used. And then he wondered what he could use to release the sun if he couldn't reach it. On his way he saw many animals just sitting there, as the animals do when the sun is just about to rise and warm things up so they wouldn't freeze. The animals were looking towards the sun and waiting, and Chakapesh was rushing to release it. By the time he got there to that mountain he saw the sun straining to get out into the atmosphere – but it could not, because it was caught in that strand. Chakapesh looked at it and couldn't say a word. Every time he tried to get close, the sun just scorched and burned and there was nothing he could do. He was really getting desperate. Then he decided, maybe the animals could help him.

He tried many animals but they refused to help because they didn't want to burn. Finally he managed to get the white weasel to help and the two of them ran up the hill. "Okay," he said to the weasel, "there's the sun. I want you to go under there and cut that strand with your teeth so the sun can rise." So the weasel ran over there and it was hot – it was hot! – and the weasel was scorched brown. And that's the reason that the weasel turns brown in summer. The weasel says, "No! I can't help. I tried!" Chakapesh said, "Well thanks anyway." He walked down the hill again, trying to think of which animal could withstand that heat. It took some time.

Then he went to ask the squirrel. The squirrel, of course, is a very proud person, so he said, "No problem – no problem! I'll cut it – I'll let the sun get out." So they ran up there together and the squirrel says, "Okay, what do you want me to do?" So Chakapesh says, "Okay – you see under the sun – you see that line there – that strand that holds the sun? I want you to go under there and cut it with your teeth." And the squirrel says, "No problem – no problem." So he runs towards the sun and by the time he got close he was just simply burned and scorched, and he could hear his hair simply sizzling. He just couldn't stand it and he ran back to Chakapesh screaming. And he says, "What do you think? I could *die* there!" So Chakapesh says, "Okay, okay – I'm sorry, brother, I'm sorry. Thanks for trying." He was holding the squirrel and trying to comfort him. And then they went back down and Chakapesh was really getting to be worried. He wondered what he could use.

Finally there was a mouse running across their path. "Hey!" cried Chakapesh to the mouse, "hey! Wait! I need your help!" And the mouse stood there and he says, "Well – what? What? What is it that you want?" And Chakapesh says, "I need your help." And the mouse says, "What can I do? What can I do?" And Chakapesh says, "I want you to help me. Come with me." The two of them walked up the hill and the mouse kept asking, "What are we supposed to do?" Chakapesh told him that he'd tell the mouse what to do once they got there. Finally they reached the place where the sun was straining to go out. And the mouse says, "What's going on? What happened to the sun?" And Chakapesh says, "It's caught. I snared it, but I can't reach over there to free it." "Well what's the big idea?" asked the mouse. "Well," said Chakapesh, "I was only trying. And this is where you come in. You are small and you can go under the sun and cut the strand with your teeth." The mouse said, "No problem! No problem!" And he ran under the sun – he really got under there but he was suffocated and burned and scorched and his hair was just singed all over – it almost caught fire – so he ran back to Chakapesh and told him he was sorry but he couldn't help. The mouse started back down the hill and Chakapesh said, "Wait – do you know where I could find your cousin who is even smaller than you?" "Oh, him! Oh yeah – he's not far from here."

And so the mouse went to communicate with his cousin – the shrew, who is even smaller than a mouse – he has a very long nose and a very small body. The mouse said to the shrew, "Chakapesh wants you to help!" So they went up the hill. "Here I am," said the shrew. "What's the problem?" Chakapesh said to him, "Well, I have a job for you – I have something I want you to do." So the shrew went with Chakapesh. When they reached the sun, the shrew says, "is that the problem? What do you want me to do?" Chakapesh explained about the snare that he couldn't reach and told the shrew that he was the last person who could help him. The little shrew just ran down there as fast as he could, got under the sun, and grabbed the strand that was so strong – just like steel. It was the hardest thing he ever chewed! He chewed, and chewed, and chewed, and almost suffocated. He was just screaming and Chakapesh kept yelling, "Cut! Chew!" Finally, just as the little shrew was about to pass out, he cut it! Off went the sun!

The shrew could hardly walk – it more or less rolled down the hill. Chakapesh caught up the little animal and he just blew on it and cooled it and finally the shrew came to. Chakapesh said, "Thank you – thank you very much for helping me – it will be forever that I will be grateful to you." And the little shrew said, "No problem!" And this is why the little shrew seems to be scorched right down to the skin on his face – there's almost no hair – and his nose is so long. But this animal can chew anything! He'll go into the bodies of animals and just chew everything in there and just live there. Actually he will destroy everything because he is very dirty – and very stinky too. And that's the only animal who was able to chew the strand. And so the sun rose into the sky and brought the warmth, and everything in the world was happy again – back to normal. And so the story ends. Chakapesh came home and lived happily after that.

So the question is: why does the story say that? Why does it say that this strand didn't burn and why could it hold the sun down?

Because, when people grow up to be adult and are in love – the first night that they are intimate together – when they first go to bed together – they don't want to get up the next day – they don't want to get out of bed. They don't care if the sun ever rises! They just simply cannot move away. They just can't get away from the strand! [laughter] So that's the end of the story.[15]

Chakapesh in the Moon

That Chakapesh was a most powerful person who was very seldom beaten by any situation. He always managed to escape his capturer and save his life. He remained the size of a six-year-old but was as wise as any other wise man there is, and he always got advice from his sister. Therefore Chakapesh had beaten almost anything on earth that was dangerous. Each thing he was told not to do, he went ahead and did, to explore meanings and find answers. And by this time he had found out about almost all the things he never quite understood. But there was something about the moon. But Chakapesh managed to get lost and ended up in the moon because he disobeyed his sister.

While she was able to give the right answers to his questions, they were not always answered quite well enough for his satisfaction and he had to find out if what she'd said was true or not. He did that many times, even if it was true when his sister told him that if he did things against her advice he could actually be captured or lose his life. He was always able to contact his sister by mind contact and she would come and bail him out whenever he got caught. And he learned the truth from the words of his wise sister.

Sometimes when he looked at the moon in the night sky, he wondered about it. And each time he did, the moon seemed to jump right close to him and he became sort of startled – and then it would jump back to its place. So he begin to have a queer feeling and asked his sister why it acted that way. So, of course, she said, "Just don't do that any more because the moon is going to take you away!" And, of course, curiosity ruled so he went to try again. He never returned.

And today we see a shadow in the moon that's shaped like a human. There is a pail on one side – and on the other side there is a shape that looks like a wooden spoon. He had been carrying them to put snow into the bucket. So that's the story about Chakapesh, which gives us an idea about how people are always fascinated by the moon.

The First Nation, especially the people in the Omushkego area and around the shores of Hudson and James Bay, have noticed something always happens at the fullness of the moon. It affects even in the human life. For example, why is it every moon that the woman has to have a menstrual period? Is it the power of the moon, or is it something else?[16]

MYSTERIES IN THE SKY

This is a mystery that happened not too long ago – my own mother experienced such a thing. We hear similar stories today, even amongst other nations – stories about UFOs. While we did not call them UFOs, people have seen these mysterious things in their lifetime. When they saw things that were unexplainable they believed the events were indicators of a tragic event that would involve the death of their relatives. My mother experienced such things three times in her lifetime – she saw a ball of fire moving on the horizon and disappearing into the ground. "A ball of fire," she says, "blue, white in front – and the back, red, like a red tail." So she believed this was an indication that one of her close relatives was dying. And she was usually right.

In my mind, I question this thing, and I tried to relate it to what we call today the UFO sightings. Could it happen? Because my mother saw such an object during the day, when there was clear sky – she saw it move on the horizon, and then it disappeared. And this was a long time ago when she was only a young woman – she was married already, but she didn't have no children yet. In her young days there were no helicopters yet. They could have been hot air balloons. Maybe one of them was lost in the atmosphere and landed somewhere in the Hudson Bay area, and that's what she saw. When I ask her to describe, she says, "Yes, it's just like a balloon. It was transparent like."

She saw it twice in her lifetime. Another time, she said, "I could see the outline of the human being inside." I says, "How? Does it stand, or does it sit?" "Ah," she says, "it sits, and then moves around." So I ask her how long did she see it. She says, "I saw it for long time, and it moved, and next time when I look, it disappeared." And this has happened to her right at the mouth of the

Winisk River. She used to go there to set a net on the tidewater – to hang it on a tree, and pick up the fish when the tide is out, and the water is low. One of her relatives died after that, so she believed that was a sign or prediction that her relative would die. So she passed her way on this earth, believing as she believed. And at that time, I didn't know much about UFOs, and I couldn't relate them at the time when she was talking.[17]

And then there is a kind of thing they call a balloon – we used to create them ourselves by blowing up the stomach of birds, especially ptarmigans or spruce partridge or sharp tail grouse and ruffle grouse and all those have what they call the first stomach. I don't know what you call that in English, but there is a container located just at the base of their neck. And some kind of skin holds the frozen food that they eat in the winter time and defrosts it so it can go on to the main stomach. And this first stomach is what we have, for ages, taken out and blown up. And it becomes a transparent balloon, about six inches in diameter balloon.

And this is the kind of balloon that they describe seeing in the sky when our Omushkego people have been hunting. We don't know exactly how many times a person see it in their lifetime, but it has been said almost every individual has seen it in during his lifetime. Maybe some might have seen it maybe two or three times. It is almost impossible to believe that such a thing actually existed. But some people have said that there was a being inside – this balloon was large enough to contain something – and it is powered by itself. It didn't have no sound, but it glowed – very bright, almost like the sun, which makes it so extraordinary.

Some people have said they have seen someone moving within, but they never say anything about whether the object is moving or rotating. People have said it has different colours. This balloon object has been seen in the night and in the day time. Some have seen it actually landing on the ground, and some seen it only flying in the atmosphere. Some have seen it way up there in the atmosphere, traveling at various speeds. Sometimes it's like lightning, faster than anything that travelled in the air in those days – faster than the geese, faster than the fastest hawk. It was hard to say for sure that how high this thing can fly and how high it can be seen, but people have seen it flying above the tree tops. Some people have extraordinary stories that say sometimes the balloon can be in various forms.[18]

Intruders and Defenders

ENCOUNTERS ON MOOSHAWOW

There were other tribes. There were the people they called Pwaatak (Sioux). My grandmother never explain exactly who Pwaataks are. And there were other plains peoples.

And then the other tribes are Aatawewak and Natowaywak. I think there's two, three different kind of names that applied in those groups. So Natowaywak were the ones who seek the captives. They capture the young people. They also take the women to sew their moccasins. These are the travelers. These are distance travelers. They take humans, especially young people, teenagers, they take them with them, wherever they go. And then those teenagers are like the holy sacred calves in the Jewish scriptures. The prisoners were taken care of, well-fed, and treated so respectfully. And then in an appointed time, they were sacrificed – just like in Christianity when people take the holy sacrament to have life for the spirit. The same idea, but it was the human flesh – and it was not raw, it was cooked very well. These tribes cut the human into pieces and then everyone would come and have a taste of this stuff. Even the soup, they just drink it so holy. So they spiritually refresh themself, or regenerate their life, that's what they believed. That is according to the captives who managed to escape from these Natowaywak. They were seeking something.

There is also another tribe that they call Aatawewak. Aatawewak is a people more like adventurers. Whenever they felt like it, they attacked the small group of Omushkegos, and sometimes took some of them. Mostly, they said, they take the women – they used them for their benefit, not necessarily for sexual things, but for their labour, because the women were labourers in those days – they were the providers of the clothing, workers. Horrible stories really, but these are the facts.

And then there's also sometimes a slightly different meaning of "Aatawewak." It also means "people who come to trade." They didn't necessarily always want to kill. They usually came in groups when they wanted to trade with the Omushkegos. The Omushkegos had some things that the other tribes didn't have, so they came as traders. And it all took place in that Cape Henrietta Maria (Mooshawow) territory. That is where dramatic things took place.

Omushkegos used to camp there during the summer, and that's where all these sudden attacks and skirmishes took place, on the James Bay coast. That's where the Inuit people used to kill the Omushkegos, because they fight for the shores of the James Bay – for the seal hunting, and also the geese and ducks. Because they want it for themself, according to the story. But of course, Omushkegos want it too, so it's the only time that I truthfully find it in my research where two tribes fight for the land. That's where the place, where the two tribes actually fight for the piece of land, and that's for the seals, and the fish, and the waterfowl.

So there also took place a time when those Pwaatak came to kill the men and take the captives. Also other tribes we know for sure did this – they were the Mohawks. These were also Natowaywak. They're the ones who seek the human sacrifice to extended their lives. The immortality idea has always existed, and people have gone to extremes to acquire or to achieve that. We still do it today – we look for the medicine to extend our life.[1]

There is a story about the Inuit attacking the Omushkego people on a lake in the Cape Henrietta Maria. It's called Wabagamushusagagan and it is situated on one of those hills that run parallel to the sea. And this was a long time before the European came onto the scene, there was no guns and other European trade goods. And in this raid on a temporary summer camp, the Inuit warriors attacked the group – mostly women and children and elders – while the men were hunting. The Inuit descended from their hiding place and attacked the camp, killing everyone. And, being so excited by killing, they began to act very strangely and very savagely. This led them to cut off the breasts of the women who were nursing the children. And then they threw away these glands into the lake and turn the water white. And therefore the lake was called Wabagamushusagagan. Even to this day it is it is called the same – not because it is the colour of the milk from the woman breast, but it is because it contain some small leeches which stir the bottom of the lake.

The reason we have the good memory of this story is because one of the young men was able to jump into lake and hide under the hanging moss where he was able to breathe. And while this was happening, he heard and saw something fall into the lake – and these were the breasts of the women who were nursing children. He saw the water turn to white. And the young man was able to survive, and relate the story to his people. This is one of the stories that has been passed on to us by our elders. And this name actually means "Milk White Water Lake." And the story came because of one young man who was left behind because he was not old enough to hunt with the hunters.[2]

So it was there in that area that many things happened. In summer time the caribous live there in the open space – and the herding caribous, they don't necessarily herd, they spread out. And one time every summer they would gather together in a group, the whole lot – they make a big circle around that open space, and then disperse again to their own eating area. Then in that place also all kinds of foxes live there. And land is so rich with many other kinds of animals – there are times when the mice are so many, and that brings the fox and other things. The white owls, the foxes, the white foxes even, arrive if there are many mice. And it doesn't happen all the time. But sometimes it's poor and there is not much.

Our ancestors always went there to Cape Henrietta Maria every summer. One of the reasons was that it's a molting area – the geese and the ducks are molting there. They change their feathers during the summer and for that reason they are easy to hunt. It's just like having chickens outside of your house – the Omushkegos just go a little ways to catch what they want to eat, and it's just right there. It's not really bog muskeg, but it's a real muskeg, and it's easy to walk. And there are berries growing there. Blueberries, and gooseberries, and raspberries (not plenty) and strawberries. And other berries we call moss berries, they are black with clusters of six in a stem. And all these berries are just like a Garden of Eden in summer time. So people can live there so easily.

And besides that, people live there because they want to stay away from the flies – because in the open land, when there is a bit of wind, the mosquitoes, black flies will not to be too many, at least on one side of your body they won't bother you. And in your home, when you live in a tepee, they don't bother you too much. So that is another reason that people used to live there.

One of the important things for the Omushkego people living around the coast in summer was that, because it's open land, it's easy for the look out. You can see the distance far away, if any one comes, if there is any danger. You could see animals.

It has been said that, in the past, there were times when something would go wrong. There were times when some animals overpopulated the land, and they became dangerous. Like there would be too many wolves. When there's too many fox and mice, this brings the wolf. And when there is too many caribous it brings the wolf. And the wolves get hungry and they come close to the camps and steal food or even kill humans. So this was a danger – it wasn't always pleasant but it was the way of life.

There was never any community for the Omushkego people before the European came. They always moved with the seasons. They went to the coast when it was summer time, when it's nice. And a month before it got dark and cold, probably in September, people would move inland to prepare their winter camp – so they never stay in one place. They knew that if they ever stay in one place too long they would deplete the resources around them. Their intelligence tell them that it is better to live with the land, rather than stay in one place.

And, as I said, in that Cape Henrietta Maria, when they were in small temporary camp sites (sometimes five or maybe ten families – at the most there will be maybe seventy five or one hundred in the group) strangers would come; different tribes from the distant areas would arrive and kill them. And, because the Omushkegos were not prepared for this kind of stuff, they were usually slaughtered, the whole lot of them sometimes. But sometimes some would be able to escape the killing.

But there is a story. One time, the Omushkegos were ready for those attackers – they have a previous knowledge. One mitew, a shaman, visualized this going to happen. He saw exactly how far away these enemies were, and he knew that they are ready to kill. So when they came the Omushkego were just ready for them, and they beat them. But they didn't kill them all! They wanted some of them to take a message away with them. They said, "Do not ever come and kill us for nothing." The Omushkego leader asked, "Why do you kill us? Why? What is it that we have?" And they replied, "It is our duty to seek and kill humans – we believe that if we take the life of a man, we extend our life. And we kill for ourself and we kill for our friends at home. "

For them, those who killed, it was good reasoning. But the Omushkegos, who got killed, didn't think it was right. When they released them, they said, "Now, go back and do not do this again, because next time we will wait and kill you all."

For some years nothing happened, not from these groups anyway, but other groups came in – different groups speaking different dialects – and they did the same things to the Omushkego. But at least the Omushkegos now understand why they were attacked.

OSTIGWAN NOWAKOW
(THE PLACE OF SKULLS)

And there is another story about a similar thing. There was a man in that same area. He was a good hunter, the best one, and he has friends. He was probably less than thirty years old. And he has many trainees with him, every time that he goes he has a bunch of young people to go with him. And sometimes he was asked to hunt, when there was a temporary village, so he does that. And one day he went out with all the young men, and left only the elders, and women and children at the camp.

And while he was out there, those attackers arrived from the south somewhere. They have traveled on the southwest coast of James Bay, concealing themselves along the way, and they approached these people living in the tundra, the open area. So while all the hunters were out, including this young man, these attackers arrive in the camp and kill all children, elders, and women. And this great hunter had many admirers and he also had a wife. She was extraordinary beautiful with long hair – he had the best-looking wife there was because he was a great man.

And when he got home, there were a few stragglers that had run away, young people and some women. And they met him there, close to his camp, and they said, "We have been killed – slaughtered!" And he said, "My wife, my wife …" And they said, "They kill her too! They have cut off her head and taken it away."

He was very mad and he just didn't want to live any more. So he and his friends became warriors instead of hunters, and he organized a raiding party, or war party. And he goes after those people. He knows where they were going. So he went past them, he went far ahead and then waited for them on their way back to their homeland. He was at the place that today is called Ostigwan Nowakow, meaning the place of skulls.

That's where he met them. He concealed himself and let them walk right up to him. And then he jumped up and he says, "All those who are captured, please step aside." And then those captives simply just run from the group. And the enemy warriors were not expecting this – they were just carrying their bows and arrows on their shoulders and over their backs, and they just couldn't do anything. And him, this young man, the young hunter, he saw the leader who had a spear and his wife's head, and he get so mad. And they were able to kill all those men because they were so helpless. And the young man grabbed this man holding his wife's head and he tortured him – and he spoke to him as he tortured him because he is so mad. And he kept him alive to let him see all his men be killed – every painful thing, every painful way. And he let only one person live – he cut off this man's ears and nose, and fingers, but he didn't kill him. And he sent him home. He says, "Show this to your home! This is what is going to happen if your tribes ever come!" The leader he killed. And he took his wife's head and buried it. The rest of the dead bodies were just piled into the shores of the Bay and buried roughly, and they were buried with the seaweeds on the shores of James Bay, somewhere around there.

And that place is called Ostigwan Nowakow – skull beach. Literally years later that is all left – just human heads, bleached with the sun and saltwater. That's where this took place. And that is the end of the story. That is why I say the Cape Henrietta Maria, which was known then by the Omushkego as Mooshawow, is where dramatic events took place a long time ago.

So many times this happened, I want to tell a little bit more about those raiders who came from which direction, I don't know. Some of them could have been Inuit people. Or it could have been the other east coast Cree people; it could have been them too, because there was times when the Omushkego were able to speak with them, using a different dialect of the Cree language. This seems to indicate that there was quite a division between the west coast of James Bay and the east coast of James Bay.

Mooshawow has always been a dividing line between the Omushkego people, impassable during the early summers. The ice touches the ground up into the middle of July; you can't go there by canoe. And sometimes people who go there, they have to portage over the land, or wait for the high tides so they can sort of pull their canoe along the shoreline. It's not a very nice thing to do, and it's a long ways out and there is not much to make a tepee of, except driftwood. It was not recommended to go there in that period in time. But in August the ice starts to break off and then you can actually go along the shore. And it is way out there, where there is no trees, but grass and sand beaches. And in that place there was lots of whales, walrus and seals. And in summer time it's where everything happens. The ducks would be molting and laying eggs and everything, and the loons are plentiful there. All three kinds of loons – the common loon, the red throated loon, and the arctic loon. They enjoy that place so much; there are so many stories told to us about many things about that place, some small things, some big things.[3]

A MITEW ATTACK WITH A LIGHTNING GUN

Not far from the Cape Henrietta Maria there is a river called Kinosheowisipi, which means "northern pike." It comes out in the same place as the Sutton River. There is a fork just at the bay, right at the tree line. The Kinosheo River goes to the south and the Sutton River goes to the west. There is a junction there where the people used to live. These people usually live inland in the wintertime, fifty to eighty miles from the Bay. Sometimes they would move their family into the bay, to the east from this junction of the river, that area there is where they always camped. And, when they hunt, when they have temporary village, the men will go hunt either to the Sutton River to get fish, or they will go into the Kinosheo River, or they go to the east to the cape. So the men will go a far distance to bring in food for the family.

And this story happened when a camp was set in there, maybe twenty five miles due east from this junction of the rivers Sutton and Kinosheo. I'm talking about the southwest coast of Hudson Bay.

There was an elder who was related to a present day family called Chookomolin. He was a great shaman, a powerful one – the kind of man that controls thunderbirds, or thunder. He left his home and came up to a place they called Koochichii, which means "the outlet of the lake" because there is desirable fish to eat there. He went there to smoke fish and take them home with him and, besides that, to have a sort of a holiday. He was there by himself.

So when he was there, the raiders arrived all of a sudden at a camp and killed off the families. Only two young men managed to run away, and they were also mitew. They were able to travel very fast directly to this old man to tell him what happened. But the old man already knew, by his magic, by his mental contact – he had already seen what happened there and he knew these two people would be coming, so he was waiting for them.

So when they arrive that evening, the same day, he used his special method of scanning. He put water in a wooden bowl, covered over his head, and looked into the water. "Yep, I see them," he says. "They are planning to come to the junction of the Sutton and the Kinosheo Rivers because there is another camp there." So he says, "I am going to meet them right there, not far from that camp, to stop them." So he tells the two young people, "You may come with me if you want – you can follow me – but I don't need your help." He says, "I'm going to have to deal with those guys by myself." But the young people said, "We would like to come with you! We would like to come and help you, because we are so mad at those people who kill off our families." So he says, "Okay. You can come if you can keep up with me!"

So the next morning, the old man took off. He started off walking with his feet, in an ordinary way. And then he began to just travel in different way so that within a short time he was where he wanted to go – almost instantly, along with these two boys. When he arrived, he prepared stuff on a trail there that had been there for centuries – it is still visible today. He knew the raiders would follow that trail to reach the camp he wanted to protect and so he waited about twenty miles away from that place.

So he prepared the place – whatever he did, we don't know,

nobody explain exactly what he did. The young people remembered that he had a musket – so this could have happened just after the European came. They had this front-end loading gun. The old man set this gun right in front of where those people would come. And he tied it very firmly so that it won't move. Then he had loaded – but they didn't see exactly what he put in it, because he says, "Don't look at me." He set it right there behind the bush, and point it directly at where those people would be coming. Everything was ready, so he sent those two young boys ahead maybe half a mile to the east, he says; "Take a look. See how far they are."

So the boys ran as fast as they can and they saw them coming. We don't know exactly how many they were, but there were more than twenty anyway, plus there were captives.

So this old man was waiting for them in the place where they would walk. When they came to where he was hidden, the enemy in front and the captives behind, he was hiding behind a bush beside the trail, and his gun was over where they were walking (I don't know how far away). When the boys came back, he told them to stay back a little ways because what he's going to use was so dangerous.

This man had dreamt of the thunderbird; he knew how to use the lightning, the thunder – that electric power. He used this substance in his gun. He pointed it right where they were going to walk. As soon as they walked in front of him, he got up and said, "Those of you who are captives, step aside! Run away!"

And these guys were not ready, the enemy was not ready – they didn't expect anything. They had their bow and arrows tied together and they were just walking, expecting to find this camp just a little ahead. Then the shaman took his gun, lit the firing mechanism, and disappeared. He did this very quickly, in the fastest time! And this gun began shooting flames of lightning into the enemy and killed them all – their bodies were burned and hardly recognizable. But the captives managed to run aside and they were safe. Some enemies also managed to jump aside with the captives – they were shot with bow and arrow by this old man.

So he beat them by using the power of his dream – of the thunderbird – actually he used its thunder and lightning, he didn't use it as a bird. He used that flash lightening and had the gun as a medium. And he kills those enemies. And that was it! So that's a story about the power of shamanism, the power of dreams. It is about forming that power to your advantage.

That's the highest level of shaman – one who can control the thunderbird. He doesn't need the shaking tent. And this guy also can do many other things: he can heal, he can restore life if he wishes. Usually this kind of person is very humble, existing very secretly. So that's a story about the mitew, shaman, using power to his advantage. Was he using it properly? Did he have the right to destroy these people who kill his friends? Yes, I think so, because all other nations have done the same. They have had the right to defend themselves, their family, their country. So this shaman has that right to do it.

The thunderbird is very highly regarded as being part of the power of all First Nations people in Canada. No matter where I have gone, the thunderbird is always highly regarded and respected. A person who have acquired the knowledge of the thunderbird in such a way that I have described in the story is truly a powerful shaman.[4]

SHIPS, MYSTERIOUS AND REAL

When the European begin to arrive, those people who used to live on the Bay saw strange things about ships when the first European came. They saw many times something that looked like ice, and it usually don't move – like ice. Usually it goes west or goes to the east amongst the ice in the month of August, the end of August or September. And they used to wonder what that is. For a long period of time they didn't know there was such thing as a big boat with sails on the mast. They know they have their masts, but such a big thing to be out there, way out, it was out of the question, inhuman. So they absorb these things, but sometimes they don't want to even mention because at that time the Omushkegos and the other tribes of people have their own spiritual belief. They believed that mitewiwin, or shamans, had certain powers. They believed that those who had mastered the crafts were able to create illusions to test other shamans. And this is exactly what the mentality was at that time.

Whenever a person saw something strange, he automatically thought that this was a shaman illusion sent to try to test him – to challenge him – to retaliate against him, or to show him. So they usually don't ever talk about it if you are a shaman. You do not tell any person – your friend or even your wife – but you just keep it to yourself. And at that time many people saw those huge sails before they actually saw the humans. And it was there in Cape Henrietta Maria that the Omushkego began to see that these things were actually associated with humans – because they heard the voices. They also heard noise which resembled sound that comes when the ice pieces on the bay collide with each other – the sound was a booming sound like thunder at times. When it's a nice day on some particular evenings the echo can be heard a long ways. When the ice collides on the shores you can hear like a boom sound. You get used to that when you live there, you just think it is ice.

Of course these ancestors when they heard these things it never bothers them – until one day – it was in the evening – they hear this thing. It was not the right conditions to hear an echo and the wind was not strong enough to make the ice pieces collide with each other. And they heard this thing in the evening, and they became to hear it coming over and over so rapidly – and then they looked. They went to the high ground and look at where the sound come from – and it was late in the evening – and they actually saw the lightning on the water. But by this time they couldn't see no sails or anything – just the light on the water, a lightning sort of thing. And that's what scares them. And they now begin to think there is a thing there – there is something.

And years pass again and every summer somebody saw a ship going by far off the bay, lights off and just went by. They just look at it. And it was later years again that they begin to understand that there is actually human being out there with the big ship and a sailing – and that when they would hear that booming sound, it was the cannon – because these sailors probably were attacking each other with their cannons – and that's what we come to understand today.

So that is why that area is so dramatic – the stories that came out of there are so powerful – fearsome stories. When the European came it became worst because our Omushkego people didn't understand those things. But finally they make a contact with those people in a funny way and they know that they were not that dangerous. (Actually they were much more friendlier than what happened down south with the Christopher Columbus and the other people.) These ones were not actually trying to kill; actually they were looking for help. So they blend well the first time. So that's that happens in the Cape Henrietta Maria where they saw these first ships, and then within the James Bay. Eventually on the James Bay, on the Akimiski Island, literally the Cree people found a ship being washed into the shore on high tide – and it got stuck! And the Omushkego went to help them – to release the boat into the deep water. And that's recent, that's not long ago. And then many things happen after that.[5]

Pakaaskokan,
An Ancient Legend and Mystery

I have said there were strange things that have been experienced by the Omushkego people. For example, they have talked about something called Pakaaskokan, which takes two forms. One of them is an object that was seen by many as a human skeleton, and the other is a voice that was heard up in the sky. It sounded like a human voice, and it brought terror to the human listener. That was not the very nice thing. The one that looked like a human skeleton was sometimes able to communicate with humans – sometimes it required a little bit of assistance from humans, and sometimes it gave people worrying predictions for their lives. Now these are the stories that have existed among ourselves. We have stories that are almost like legends, but that do not fit into the legend category. They are mystery stories. It is our nature to try to explain what we see.

In Hudson Bay and James Bay lowland, as we call it today, on the west coast of James Bay and the southwest coast of Hudson Bay, right up to York Factory, and right down to the tip of James Bay to the south, and around two hundred miles inland into the west – that section of land is where the stories have happened. And these people were there before the European came. They had their own culture, they had their own life style, they had their own spiritual belief. The spiritual belief which they practiced was connected to the whole environment – and life is not only the material world, but the spiritual world also. And that spiritual world exists at the same time as the material world exists. In that spiritual world is a much higher form of living than in the material world.

And in that spiritual world there are supernatural beings – our ancestors believed very strongly that the world is connected to the higher world, the spiritual world. And, therefore, they practiced this thing and they believed it. Since they understand there is a spiritual part of things, they believe they, too, have a spirit. And then they have also a Great Spirit, a good spirit, and also a bad spirit, which is not very nice. Their stories have been carried orally, they are actually the history of our people a long time before the European came – unfortunately they didn't have an opportunity to establish their own writing, so everything was done orally. They passed on to the next generation any knowledge they needed to survive. They created the stories that can be remembered very easily.

These stories were called legends and some people say legends were created out of the history of the people. These stories were actually human historical events. They fit well without any dates.

For example, a story that never begins and never ends says that once upon a time there were giant animals that lived on earth, and roamed the surface of the earth, and somehow disappeared. It says they hibernated, and that they will walk again on the surface of the earth at the end of time. So that's one of them. That's the mystical statement which always catches on to a person's mind. What is it? What happened? What happened to those animals, are they still around somewhere? When is the end of time? Why would they come again? Why do they hibernate?

Those mystical stories, mystery stories, have to do with something that is extraordinary big and unbelievably strong, and powerful, and mystical. That is why they will be always remembered. They describe something that people have experienced, and seen, and heard.

We have five senses in our human body. We can use the hearing, which makes us understand things – and vision, we can see, even smell, feel and taste, all these are always functioning in our human body. These mystery stories have to do with the senses – the vision and also the hearing. Our ancestors have stories about our people who have experienced sounds of a human voice which seems to travel from the northwest into the southeast, very fast. It has been heard on clear days, when there was no wind, and it always travelled in the same direction. And each time when it passed overhead, it usually weakened the person's mind, even made people faint. And when it passed they regained consciousness again, and became well – but usually the fear hung around for sometime after that.

And there is another story about vision. People saw the human skeleton they call Pakaaskokan – this has been repeated by different people. Our people, the Omushkego people, have seen it but some people do not mention it because it's hard to believe that there is really such a thing. Is this Pakaaskokan the thing that makes that sound that people hear and that makes them feel afraid and makes them shiver and become a jelly fish?

Are these things real – or are they the work of a shaman? Our people who had strong beliefs could develop their own mystical powers. People who became shamans, or mitew, had certain powers. They could do all kinds of things, according to their will. They could will themselves to become an animal, to become a bird, or to become almost anything they wanted to become. And they could also use their mind to create a beast, or something that they created in their minds to appear and scare other people.

This was considered the spiritual world blending with the material world. So our ancestors have done that. So when people have that belief and practice, they automatically assumed, whenever they saw something strange, that another mitew did that to them. So it was not easy to thoroughly investigate something that they have seen, or to prove that what they have seen is real. These mitew can cause something strange and it's automatically believed that it is a mitew's power. If it's from a mitew, it's not necessary to investigate – you just simply ignore it. But if you yourself are a powerful mitew, you will understand that someone is challenging your power. And then you have to counteract it with your own power, and you defend yourself that way. So this is the reason people have never actually tried to understand what Pakaaskokan means, and what that other stuff was heard in the air, in the atmosphere.[1]

PAKAASKOKAN

Supposing it is late fall, let's say in the Hudson and James Bay coastal region in late October and first week of November. There is a snowstorm, gusts of strong wind, with thick, fluffy clouds. If the wind is very strong, up to sixty or seventy kilometres an hour, and there is heavy snow, the conditions can bring fear to the soul of the human. Animals feel this too. This condition could bring Pakaaskokan, Mr. Skeleton, or Mr. Bones, the Bag of Bones. That's what I call the legend, Bag of Bones. It is not a wihtigo. A wihtigo is usually in the form of a human or animal, but Mr. Skeleton does not have a fully human form, only partial. The wihtigo needs to eat human flesh – he has a stomach. Mr. Bones does not have a stomach to fill. Was he a real skeleton being, or is it just a made-up story?

In this story the skeleton actually speaks! It's a hollow sound, a metallic sound – like a loudspeaker. If any human heard this sound, it sent shivers down to their spine. This kind of fear is not the kind we can hide or run from – so it's been recorded. The sound would come from the ground or up in the sky. Nobody has explained it logically – this has been one of the mysteries of the Omushkego in the Hudson and James Bay area.

Now there is a story about two men who found a skeleton stuck on top of a tree, and amongst the elders it is still a very great mystery. It seems these two men were able to speak in their own language to Mr. Bones and they asked it about their future. And Mr. Skeleton answered in Cree. So it has been said.

This story about Mr. Bones is, as I said, one of the mysteries amongst the elders, but it is one of the fascinating stories for the youngsters. And it has been applied in many ways. It has been used to tell the children not to eat the first snow. Sometimes people happened to get stuck out in the bush by themselves with nothing to make a fire with and they begin to get thirsty. Usually the younger people would start to drink the snow. These people, if they did not make it home, they would freeze. So it has been said that if a person drinks that icy snow water, especially at the first frost, they will become a wihtigo. That is a scary statement – it was really made to stop young people from drinking ice water (which would give them sore bones).

This skeleton that I'm talking about has proven to some people that it is not a dream being, it's not conjured up by anyone. It had nothing to do with shamanism, it had nothing to do with anything. But it can tell the future. But the question is, why the appearance? That's why the Native people have been so mystified. It has no flesh, only bone, lungs, a heart that is pumping, and a voice box. And it travels in the atmosphere. And whenever it travels, it seems to be talking and mourning. But why? This is what people have always wanted to find out.

Sometimes it does get caught in a treetop when it travels too low in the sky, because it's a skeleton. But if it has so much power, if it has so much knowledge, then why doesn't it have the power to release itself? It has no muscle – no power in its arm, or legs. And it has that echo, hollow sound when it speaks. And it has strong effect, that sound – sends chills through the body. Once they see it, it's alright because they know where the sound came from. But if they don't see the bones, it's even worse, they say.

When the European missionaries came to teach, people thought they were the most wise. They categorized them as a mitew, or shaman, because they spoke about the soul, so the people always regarded them as most intelligent. So one day the elders asked a Catholic priest, "What is it that we hear and call Pakaaskokan. How come it is so scary?" They described the thing to the priest – and then, of course, the priest has an opportunity to convince people about Christianity, to convert them and a method he can use to convince them to change. This was a perfect opportunity. So, through his knowledge about the Bible, he connected this story to the Jewish story which says that God created Adam and Eve and they had two sons, Cain and Abel. The first murder on this earth supposedly happened then, because Cain killed his brother out of jealousy, and he was condemned directly by God, the Creator. And he was condemned to live forever, and everybody that sees him will hate him and want to kill him. That's what the priest explained. So he says, "That could be the story that you guys experienced, because he was condemned to live on earth, to suffer all the time." So apparently, Cain didn't die yet – he still remains. That was a first win for the priest. And Christianity.

In our culture there are many things that are not explained – they are in the mystery stories. Since we have left our culture, most of the answers have gone. Some of these questions that we have would have been answered if I had lived, maybe, fifty years before I was born. So these are some of the mysteries of the Omushkego people.[2]

A friend of mine is about sixty-three years old. I have hunted with him many times and I find him to be a very intelligent man, a thoroughly experienced hunter, and a master of his land and his culture.

And he has trapped by himself when it's necessary. He has spent all his life in the bush. He once told me that he heard Pakaaskokan's voice when he a young boy – he was with his two sisters. He described the fear that he experienced at that moment. And when I asked him what kind of day it was when he heard it, he says it was a very clear day, a nice day. It was sometime after midday. And he says he experienced a terrible fear, and he lived through it, with his sisters. He says, "Wind went in the southeast direction." And when I asked if he had seen it, he says, "No, I didn't see anything. I just heard the voice up in the sky."

I also have an uncle who experienced such things, but he never wanted to talk about it – he's ashamed. But he has experienced that as recently as 1950. I was in the vicinity at the time when this happened to him. The fear forced him to come to our camp where we were trapping, because he was my uncle. So this thing has mystified many of our ancestors, and they don't have a unified explanation about it.

Some elders say it's a being that came out of our ancestors' dreams. They said it is a dream being that our ancestors have created in their dream quests, and their visions have brought it into being. And we experience it because we inherit it. That's as far as people explain.[3]

There were two young men, maybe the older one was about twenty years old and the other one was, maybe, eighteen. These two hunters were travelling out there in the Bay, on the coast, near the coast anyway, where they usually hunt. And this was in the fall, just when it begins to freeze up and we usually have those big storms. They saw this cloud formation coming – very low and lots of snow. So they decided to go into the shelter of the trees and sort of hang around there for a while. And this wind came over, very strong. And then they hear this voice all of a sudden – there was somebody screaming, like in pain. And then right away they remember about Pakaaskokan.

So they know it's Pakaaskokan and they really get scared. The storm went by, but the voice was still there somewhere. It should have gone with the wind, but it didn't. The voice remained there amongst the trees, and they said, "Yeah, maybe it's stuck on the tree." They know this happened in the past. So the rule is that if anybody hears the voice they should go and check and release the bones instead of letting them stay stuck there. So they know this story. They said, "Well we should go and check and see if we can help." So they walk around and then, sure enough, there it was on top of a broken tree. And there is the skeleton, stuck there and making a noise. And it says, "Release me! Come and release me!" Sort of moaning and screaming.

So when they get near, it knows that they're down there and says, "Okay, please release me!" So they said, "Before we release you we'd like to ask you something." And then it said, "What is it?" So they said, "We understand that you can tell us something." And it said, "What is it that you want to know?" So the older one said, "I want you to tell me how long I will live in this world." So the skeleton said, "Since you such are such a courageous person that you are willing to come and help me and release me, you shall live to be very old and have white hair." In those days you got white hair when you were around eighty, or somewhere in that range. So he says, "Okay." And the younger man says, "What about me? How long would I live?" And Mr. Bones says, "Since you were reluctant to help and you discouraged your friend from coming and releasing me, you shall not live to see another winter. You will die soon." And the boy says, "Well." He didn't say "thank you" because it's not a very good prediction.

And the two young men went back home and forgot all about their experiences. And it was a few days or a month later that they began to remember this experience. So they asked their grandparents, "What does it mean? Does this thing actually predict the future?" And the grandfather says, "Yes, it's true usually very true."

So life went on. Before the year was up, the younger man died. He didn't see the next season – he died before the snow fell – and the other young man lived to be a very old man, very white-haired.

And there is another story. One time a person was hunting by himself in the fall. He was a strong person, he knew about the bush life and he enjoyed living there. He never had any fear. And it so happened that he walked into this specific area where there's a hillside and thick bushes. And it was snowing, with gusts of wind and big snowflakes – they call it a whiteout. So he went into this thick bush to shelter himself until it passed. And then all of a sudden he felt so scared, and he heard this voice screaming and moaning at the same time. There were words, but he didn't understand the language. Never had he had such fear before in his life.

So as soon as that storm passed, his fear went away and he

started to go home. Nothing happened to him, no bad luck or anything. It's just that he heard that. That's another form of this experience.

And there were three little kids, two girls and one boy. They were out there picking berries for their mother, sometime in August I think, just the time when the berries are ripe. It was a very clear sky, hardly any wind, and they had filled up their containers. They were halfway home, out there in the open tundra – no trees. They could see their tipi and their mum walking around in the distance. And then all of sudden, they get scared. One girl asked, "Are you scared?" And the other girl says, "Yeah, yeah I'm scared all of a sudden!" They look around. There was no polar bear. There's no nothing.

And then all of a sudden they hear the voice, a terrible voice. But they never heard about Pakaaskokan before and this voice that sounded so terrible, coming from the northwest. And it was a warm day with a blue sky. As soon as they hear it they began to get so scared that they just huddled each other, shivering. Then suddenly it was right overhead, and it was trying to speak and moaning. And it sounded hollow – the way your voice echoes back to you when you scream.

The kids just held each other and it went by very fast – in the next few seconds it was towards to the southeast. Very fast. And the children went back to normal. They got up. They didn't see anything, just the blue sky. So, as soon as they got back their composure, they walked home, and they forgot all about it. And it was only later that they came to remember and they said, "Mum, we have heard something up there. Something that sounds so terrible." And they imitate it and the mother says, "Oh yeah, that's Pakaaskokan. That's what you hear. And that's what happens when you hear it – you get scared." So that's the end of the story.[4]

Values for Life and Survival

DREAMS AND GIFTS

Spiritualism in the First Nations, in time past, was acquired individually. It was not a church. Every young person who wished to acquire such spiritual values, which we call shamanism, had to go through rituals. And they must fast – fasting was required as a ritual. But before they can practice ritual, they had to deny themselves luxuries – they could not eat much because food was considered a luxury. And they had to deny their sexual satisfaction, as young people. And they must deny themselves other things which gives the body pleasure, or even the mind. They must have instruction from their elders, and they must be supervised by their grandparents or, at least, elders who knew the practice. They had to go through severe self-inflicted punishment to condition themself to have a dream. Only in a dream, only in mental activity, could they acquire such spiritualism. It's not the material thing they were trying to acquire – it was spirit itself, it was a consciousness. So they conditioned themselves to dream frightening dreams. The dreams were scary and very unpleasant because they had to overcome these fears and horrors during the training. And the mastery was not acquired in short time – it could only be achieved through life practice.

Rituals were suited to their own particular needs or requirements. If a person wanted to be a shaking tent expert, he must maintain the rules which were provided by the elders, who told him what he must do to acquire the mastery of the shaking tent. Not all shamans were able to master the shaking tent. Some acquired a very little, and some acquired maybe fifty percent of the whole practice. Some had the whole, and they were the ones who were very useful.

And there were those who were given the power to be medicine men. They were given this gift which emerged from them while they were trying to acquire shaman power. That was a blessing to the community and to the individual also. In dreams they would have visions which told them how to cure people, both themself and others.

And there were others who were in a different field. They became shamans who were powerful public defenders. They were very important also.

And there were also those who misused these powers. Sometimes they did not acquire powers properly. Sometimes they overlooked morality. Those who turned bad are the ones we hear so much about. They're the ones who misused the power. They're the ones who were very negative people. And, most often, they're the ones who have been put away, at other people's request, by another powerful shaman.

Acquiring spiritual power is something that not everybody can do. This spiritual value system gave people the strength to overcome the harshness of the land where they live. It indicated that the Creator existed. The Creator is the Great Spirit. The honest shamans respected the special powers they had acquired, and used them properly.

CHRISTIANITY AND OUR WAYS: FEAR AND DENIAL

I may compare these sorts of things with the story of the Apostles of Jesus Christ. In the Bible, the New Testament says that Jesus promised the Holy Spirit to the Apostles. They had to suffer a lot with him. They had to be submitted to shame with their master. And they gave up – they were scared. But Jesus encouraged them, saying, "Wait until I send you the Holy Spirit. Because you have suffered with me I will send you the Holy Spirit, and you will overcome all your fears." And Jesus told them they could not fight evil unless they fasted. This is all recorded in the New Testament. Jesus said you have to fast before you can overcome the things that are hard to deal with – spiritually or physically.

And this is exactly the same teaching that our ancestors have taught their children, to help them acquire a full life: spiritual value and spiritual practice. But they would not all acquire powers. There were ordinary people. They were able to master a few things such as survival skills, and they acquired natural survival instincts. But they did not go further than that – they did not acquire the shaman powers.

And there were many of those who did acquire powers. And the best of the shamans that were ever known were the humblest, and the most highly respected, and the kindest people amongst the Omushkego. And those who misused their spiritual power are notorious in our oral history, even in our legends – Omushkego education stemmed from legends and stories. They are the most talked-about people, but they were the most miserable people.

I can't explain in detail how a person got to be a shaman. I only know the basics because I was not born into a shaman's spiritual practice. I was born into Christianity – I was trained to believe in Christ and God. As a young boy I was not allowed to ask about our ancestral spiritual beliefs and practices. Christianity condemned them as heathen or as pagan. The only thing that I regret in this life is that none of our own people will know about these things. Those who imposed their culture on us never had to defend their own culture. Many are ashamed to be an Indian, without knowing why – without ever having information.

I do not intend to resurrect our ancestors' practice of spiritualism. I do not. Because it is not possible. The only way that that can be possible is if our Native people return back to the land and the migratory life of our ancestors. Only then will they ever be able to get back the spiritual systems which they practiced before the European came – before the Christianity came into this land. And that time has passed.

One of the greatest lessons that I have learned from our ancestors is that they never destroyed the land because they were nomads. And therefore no descendant of our people should be ashamed – they can take pride that our ancestors were nomads. Other nations destroy their own land – this is what's happening today. And that is why I wanted to tell the story this way. It's not to condemn the European people, or to condemn their spiritual practice. No. But to record what was, and what is now so that our people will not be ashamed of being of First Nations descent.[1]

CONVERSIONS TO CHRISTIANITY

During the fur-trading period our forefathers behaved badly to one another, just to please the white man, so the white man can give them some prestige. When missionaries were trying to convert the Natives the Christian teachers used this weakness to make them submit to Christianity. And they used another trick – that was, going first to the young ladies, women, wives, to turn their spiritual beliefs away from their ancestors. That was another trick. That's a white man's trick.

Native people did not have a chance to study Christianity, how it affected people, and what its benefits were. No, they just forced our forefathers to convert. Again, a white man's trick, a European trick to dominate people. I am sorry to speak against the religion, but this is true. This is the way it has been told to us by our grandfathers and grandmothers, and all the people who can remember way back how it was done. And no one ever tell this story in front of other people, it's not written down in books. None of our ancestors were allowed to speak this way. But I am speaking. It's not because I want to beat the Christian teacher leaders, it's because I want to make other people understand our people, how they became to be, how they came to have the problems they have. They don't know these things because nobody shows them, nobody tells them. So we carry these burdens along with us – into the fourth generation – up into the seventh generation since its beginning.

And then came Christianity. It caused the Indian people, our forefathers, our grandmothers, to compete with each other to be the best church-goers, to be the best practitioners, and to be praised most highly in the church. And because those Christian leaders did not speak well in Cree, they usually made mistakes, stressing the wrong points, and the Native people got led off in the wrong way. They heard that if you believe in anything related to the mitewiwin, you are pagan, or a heathen. And this is what the Christian leaders were stressing so wrongfully. They did not understand our culture. Very few of my ancestors ever stood up to the priest to question or correct the priest for what he says. And very seldom did any ancestor of ours stand up to express what he saw was wrong about the church, or the church leaders – not the church itself, not the faith, not Christ's teaching – but the way the church is teaching, or the mistakes the leaders make, or their lack of understanding of everything. Because they want to set up their mission as quickly as possible, they didn't care if they did right amongst our people. And for this reason, their instruction was: if you pray wisely, if you pray in front of people, if you do this, God will love you. But they never say that you can also pray without people around you and God will still listen to you. They didn't say that, those priests, those missionaries didn't say that. But the good Lord has said, "Go inside your home and speak to God directly, your Father." Not in front of people. Because Jesus saw these things when the Pharisees were praising God in front of people, just to be seen. And that's why he said it. So he wanted to tell other people that you don't have to be seen to be holy. You can be holy without being seen, as long as your God understands what you are doing. That's what Jesus said, but that is not how it turns out here.

Native spiritual values were there a long time before the white man came. But there was no church. The church means having one belief that is held by a group of people. That doesn't mean a church with a wooden block or stones piled together. That's not the church. The church means, as I was told by the bishop, that when a group of people, or a community, have one faith, one God, this is a church. The church is people put together to act as one, to help each other in their spiritual life. And, to my understanding, that's the explanation of the experts and theologians for the Christianity.

But before the Christianity existed around the Hudson Bay area, there was a spiritual practice and beliefs that were practiced by our grandfathers and our great-grandfathers and on and on. They have this individual gain by living in the wilderness – not by living in a community. All these individual spiritual beliefs and values and practices of each individual came from living in the wilderness. It gave them more knowledge about how to live in harmony with nature. And each person has his own belief, definitely. Maybe if you put all those people who have a strong religious belief together, they will have a common way of believing. This, I believe, is related to God through the wilderness. This is why what our grandfathers used seems to have worked. That was destroyed when the Christianity was preached to them – but for fifty or seventy-five years they held on to it. They went underground – they kept on believing what they believed, they kept practicing it in the wilderness when they went into the bush. Only when they came to the community do they join the Christianity in the church.[2]

LIFE AFTER DEATH

Our First Nation Omuskego had the idea of immortality. And many people sought ways to live for long time, or forever. Many people who became mitews caught themself off guard, sometimes so unexpectedly and tragically, and lost their lives by the mistakes they made. And some died in such disappointment without ever achieving what they want.

There is one story about something that happened not very long ago – it may have been after the European came, because this person seems to have had a firearm, or a gun. We used to call them fire sticks, or thunder sticks.

This is a story about life that does not die, but continues on existing. This person used to tell stories to the children, sitting inside the lean-to while the rest of the people were making tipis for the night. And he was asked to sit by the fireplace with the children because by this time he was an old man. Very old. Perhaps we can say he was a useless old man, but at least he was helpful in keeping the children occupied when everybody else worked. The children used to love to listen to his stories. And he told them that, once upon a time, he was very powerful shaman. And he was very wealthy, and he had many possessions – everything he wants. And, of course, because he was such a powerful shaman, he was able to do anything.

THE POWER OF THE ORPHAN
– A RESURRECTION STORY

And in this story, he told them that he once died, when he was a single person living with his uncle whom he called the blue-haired uncle. His parents had died, but his uncle had adopted him. And he raised him and teach him everything he would teach his own son. And at the same time, the boy became the most powerful shaman, and there was nothing that he cannot do.

But unfortunately he died one day when he was still a young person – a very successful young man. And he died while he was out on his hunting ground with his uncle. He was buried with the customary burial procedures.

They were camping during the winter when he died, so his uncle created a paatakwaaskwahigan. You make it by laying the logs in such a way as to create upside-down box. There's a hole at the bottom, no planking, just four walls and the top – a box without a bottom. It keeps the animals from eating or breaking something within. And the ground they could not dig anyway because it's frozen. This was usually the burial procedure in the winter-time.

So this was his burial place, and they left there after they buried him. And so there he was. He says, "I just went to sleep one evening. I thought I just went to sleep, and it was later that I realized that I have been dead. I thought I just went to sleep, and then all of a sudden, because of my power, I was able to wake myself up. And when I came to, it was like waking up in the night. I was totally covered and my blanket was around me. And on both side of me it seemed like there was people sleeping. And I tried to push myself away."

According to some stories, he had two wives, and he usually he went to bed between them. And this is why he thought there were people sleeping beside him. He tried to push them away but they wouldn't budge. And then, as he was fully awake, he says, "I begin to feel a hard substance on my right and on my left, I gave a heave but nothing budged. And finally I tried to lift my head, and I banged it into the board of logs. And that's when I realized that I have been put into this paatakwaaskwahigan because I was dead. So it was then that I thought, 'this is cannot be.' And so finally, with my full strength, I just lift off the top covering and threw the rest of the stuff away from me, and got up. And by this time there had been lots of snow – the place where I was buried has been covered and the trail of my uncle was barely seen. They had left me behind. And according to the burial procedures, my snowshoes were there and my gun was beside me. My axe was inside there and my snowshoes were standing beside me. My toboggan was there too. And in my coffin, my blanket was there, my rabbit sleeping bag was there, and all my clothing had been buried with me. Everything that I own had been placed beside me – for, according to our custom, a dead person needs those things in the next journey after life. And so, all my stuff was around me. So I got up, picked up my stuff, and went on living."

So, part of that story tells us the way people believed in those days – that they believed there is life after death and there is resurrection – that a body can get up and live again. But unfortunately this man did not get up in the other world, he got up in the same world, by his own power. He resurrected himself because he was a powerful mitew. The important thing about this story is this idea that life continues on – that it is possible to have resurrection. And that is one thing that we understand there.

So therefore our First Nation Omuskego believed in life after death. And also they believed that a person who had shaman power could extend his life for quite some time. But none has ever been found to live forever, no matter how powerful they might be – they all died somehow, some way, same way as the rest of the people.[3]

HEALING AND FAITH

I am going to recall the New Testament. It said that when the good Lord walked on earth amongst the Israelites, the people bring their sick to his feet. Some people ask to be healed. Sometimes he walks to the sick. And he will ask, "Do you have faith to receive the healing?" When a person show his honesty and his faith, he would give the healing. He would do the miracle. And when he granted the wishes of the centurion who asked him for his charitable service to heal, he sent him on his way. He says, "Your faith has the answer." The same thing can be applied to our ancestors who were gifted to act as the healers, or providers of remedies for disease – those who had the gift to help the sick, the crippled, and all people who were disabled because of disease or what they inherited. There were such people. Having said that, I want to tell a small story that is very short.

A Mitew Healer

This happens between 1900 and 1920 – very close there. There was a man who had developed a sore knee. He had been very painfully sick and unable to walk for two years.

And then finally he happened to meet a person who was a gifted healer, a gifted medicine man. This medicine man happened to pass by that area and the man who was crippled approach him – not to ask him for healing, but just to tell him that his incapability hindered him from supporting his family. The medicine man was an older person and he understood the griefs that this old man was expressing to him – he understood the feeling that a disability can bring to an individual and the hardship it can bring to an individual's family. He felt sympathy towards the man. And as he was a medicine man, he considered the situation.

He asked the man who was disabled, "Do you wish to get well?" And the man says, "Yes, I do. It is very discouraging to be like this." And his honesty rang true to the ears of this sympathetic man. So the medicine man went home to think.

Finally this medicine man visited the sick person again. He talked to him for just a short while, and he says, "Where do you usually go when you go outside?" So the disabled man says, "When it's a beautiful day I usually sit out in the open and do my work out there." And the medicine man said, "Where do you live in winter time?" So the disabled man pointed to the direction where he spent his winter. And the medicine man said, "Is there a particular place that you go in the winter time?" So the disabled man says, "Yes, there is a tree that I usually go sit beside. I crawl there on my one good knee and then push myself towards the tree, and then I sit there."

So the medicine man says, "Crawl over there now and sit beside it." So the disabled man pushed himself towards the tree and sat in his usual position. And the medicine man stood beside him and says, "Lift your hand up beside the tree. See how far you can reach." So he measured that distance of the man's arm. He didn't say anything, he just began cut a stick, probably about two feet long. And then he drove the stick right into the tree trunk as firmly as possible, and let it stay there. And he tested it with his weight to make sure it wouldn't move and it stayed in place. So he said to the disabled man, "Come here at your usual time. And every time you come, sit here. And each time when you want to get up, hold on to this stick and pull yourself up with your own power and stand on your leg for a short while – as long as it is comfortable enough for you to stand. And then sit down and take yourself back to your home. Each time that you do this, you must wish to be able to walk. And a year from now, if you do what I say, you will walk."

So the disabled man listened, he believed the medicine man was honest, so he obeyed the instruction, he obeyed his prescription in the hope that he will walk again. Each time there was an opportunity for him to get out he would go to this tree where the stick was driven in and do what he was told. He would get hold of this stick and pull himself up and stand there.

After three seasons passed he found that he was not having pain when he got up, holding himself up by that peg. He noticed changes – his knee did not hurt as much as it used to. Towards the end of the year he was able to stand comfortably by holding the stick. Within one year he could walk away from the tree without pain. Through his belief he was healed. And he believed it was the faith in the man who had made a simple gesture that had helped him to walk again. That's the end of the story.

This story shows us the medicine man himself did not perform miracles all the time, but made a person have faith within himself. All he did was to instruct. He did have medical knowledge, but he also understood that faith does many things. In this story this is what he applied, because he knew the disabled person's disease was not inherited, it developed gradually from over-activity. He therefore understood that this disability would take a long time to cure. One has to have a wish and hope and continuous faith to receive the benefit. And through their spiritual belief this could have been considered a miracle. That is the part of our ancestors' spiritual belief and practices. We have a right to question it. Each one of us can ask, "Was that a miracle? Was that an evil deed? Was is evil to do that?" So it's up to us to decide. We can say that when our First Nations lived independently they had gifts which allowed them to survive on the land.[4]

OMUSHKEGO INDIVIDUALISM

The Jewish people have their God, which they associated with thunder on a volcanic mountain and with many things. Our ancestors were not much different. They have one Great Spirit; God and the Great Spirit are the same. But they didn't have one faith only for the whole people.

There is an elder who has said that God created us, the Great Spirit has created us. The Great Spirit created us to use the land, to use it all in season and not to destroy it by staying in one place. That was a very wise saying I think. The Omushkegos actually lived like that until the European came – until the last fifty years when they begin to emerge from the bush and begin to exercise living together. Unfortunately, in doing so, they were denied their cultural beliefs and totally alienated themselves from their own First Nation culture, from their dignity.

I have said before that this is the reason our culture existed in the wilderness and why they never developed what they call "living together" or civilization. When you live in the wilderness, you don't need a bunch of words to express your feeling. No, you don't need high language for that. What you need is a higher level of understanding, faith in yourself, and spiritual connection. That's all you need. You don't need no verbal skills. That's what our ancestors had – did.[5]

They understood that there was a supernatural Person who controlled everything. Each individual developed their own beliefs about everything having a spirit: wind, the storm, the weather, nice weather, and the things that are on the land, or the seasons, or the water, or each animal. They say that each thing, each being, is a spirit, and has a spirit.

But the belief is not universal – they never built a church – they never created a church that was universal, as we know the Christianity. Christianity is a teaching that can be used for the group of people – for thousands of people, even for millions of people. The theology of the Christianity is made for universal use, for any kind of people – not necessarily only one nation, but many nations. And that is why it's called a church.

But our Cree ancestors did not develop such things, not in northern Canada where I'm originally from. They didn't have a church, they did not have a universal theory for them to practice. Each individual guided his own belief and practiced it through his lifetime. But it started in the very early age. I am not condemning the westernization of our people. The European style of living is very good. The standard of living is much more comfortable, and much more useful for the community living. And it's geared for the socialization, and the common good. And it also has its bad points, too.

But in the past, before the Europeans came into our continent, our people have had their ways. They have developed the most useful ways. I'm not saying that our ancestors have mastered the best way of existing in this world – I'm not saying that. I say the majority of them have lived in this world very usefully, and they have managed to survive the conditions in which they established their culture. They established traditions. There must have been some good in them.⁶

CONDEMNATION BY CHRISTIANITY

And their spiritual value system was not far off from European spiritual beliefs. I'm not trying to resurrect our forefathers' spiritual beliefs and practices. But I do question: what is truly evil in what they did?

It is important for our next generations to understand our history, the background of their ancestry. Whenever they face some criticism because of their nationality, they will have this knowledge of their history which they can rely on to retain their dignity. And that is my hope. That is one reason I want to record these stories.

The use and application of their spiritual beliefs and practices is termed shamanism today – it has also been classified as paganism. Christianity has believed it was an evil – that it belongs to the devil's world. Our present Christian leaders understand the mistake that has been done towards the First Nation. I have personally accepted their apology. I am sure our First Nation have also accepted their apology and that there won't be too much hostility towards the religious leaders and those who were leaders in the time when the mistreatment was applied to our Natives.⁷

Relations with Animals

ANIMAL POWERS

There is something else that people knew a long time ago. Elders have said that animals have powers. They don't have to condition themselves to have these powers – they don't have to condition themselves to dream or to practice the dream quest. They are born with it. They live in the forest without any comfort provided to them and so they are conditioned automatically to live in the wilderness – they automatically acquired these gifts for their protection. That means they have know-how. They have gifts for their own survival. They know the dangers. They can feel dangers ahead of time, as if their minds can see ahead. Their minds are awakened when danger is near.

   Black bears have this for sure. They can hide – they can actually almost make themselves invisible. If they suddenly come into a close encounter with a human person they just freeze, they just don't move – they're immobile and, at the same time, they make themself almost invisible. They can hide very easy. The wolves have it, all the big game animals have it – moose – and even some smaller animals like otters, beavers, mink, and others. The birds have it – ravens have it, the owls, the eagles – most animals have it for their survival.

The human develops these things by conditioning themselves to dream. But the animals don't have to condition themselves, it's just automatically in them. I am going to tell a small story about this.

CARIBOU AWARENESS

A man who still lives today once told me he had a strange experience one time. The Native people believe that you must never mishandle an animal carcass or misuse any animal which you use for your food. "For some reason," he says, "I could not kill a caribou." And he is a master hunter, he has mastered the technique, so there should be no question that he will kill a caribou if he looks for one. So he know this.

And then one day, he says, he simply couldn't kill a caribou no matter how many days he hunt. So he says, "I don't remember ever abusing this animal. But whatever I have done," he says, "I have offended the caribou." So he says, "Whenever I hunted that winter, never, never did I have a chance to kill it. It was as if my rifle had no bullets at all." So he tried three times when other people could simply kill a caribou – and he could not hit. He was so frustrated, he says, that one time he just took his gun and threw it in the snow. He had given his gun to his partner to see if it was shooting straight, and the guy had taken it and shot the caribou down. And he says, "Nothing wrong with it." So he tried again and still couldn't hit anything – that's when he got frustrated and threw his gun down. He was actually going to leave it there, but his friend said, "No! Don't do that. Maybe it's just something temporary." So he took his gun back and just simply didn't try to hunt caribou anymore. So for that winter he never did hunt, he went out with the hunters but he never tried to shoot.

And then he told me: One time he had been by himself and he had followed the caribou, using his best technique to make sure they don't know him. He says, "I was here in this location. I was very sure there was no way the caribou would know me – I was behind the wind and I hid in the thick bush. I watched the caribous move closely by. And then, all of a sudden, the leader of the herd seemed to stand up in the high ground as if to try to see something – and he looked my way. His tail was up. As soon as he does that, other caribous begin to shuffle around and lift their tails up, which is the indication that they are now aware there is a danger. And as soon as they do that," he says, "this leader just simply make a move to run." And he says, "I didn't even want to shoot because I know they know me. The leader knows me even though he didn't see me. Then he just took off away from me, not towards me, even though I'm down wind." Usually the caribou, when they sense some danger, they just run down wind a certain distance to try to smell what they are feeling. "But this particular caribou who was the leader," he says, "simply run away from my direction without any investigating. Certainly he knows exactly who I am."

This is why people know caribous have an instinct to tell them when there is danger. Humans possess a similar thing – shamans can use their power to scan with their mind and sense if danger is around. So this is a story which is true. Omushkego people have said that animals do have similar powers to shamanism. So the herds of caribou have a leader, a look-out who keeps them alive. Many expert hunters have said the same thing – not all suspect that the caribou leader has shaman power, but they know he has a scanning system which tells him there is danger. So the animals are gifted. There is such thing as an animal knowing something – he actually has knowledge. He has a mitewin.

CARIBOU MESSAGES

I personally have experienced that too. Myself, I can kill a caribou almost as easy as I can kill a ptarmigan or a sharp-tailed grouse. I am lucky. I am not the best hunter, but I am lucky. Sometimes I think that the caribous just simply want to die – and so they come my way. Sometimes I find them – walk up on them – and they just simply stand around as if waiting for me to shoot them. So my father told me I am going to be the luckiest hunter – I will always be able to get the caribou. And it was the truth. So many hunters that I have been with have noticed that. They always want to take me with them because they know they will get the caribou. I have noticed that myself too.

But one particular year, this was 1985, in February, me and my friend were hunting caribou. We were so sure of ourselves because we never failed. So we went to a place that he knows well and we found a herd of caribous. And the first day we thought it was just bad luck, we just simply couldn't shoot any. We didn't hit anything. They seem to know we were there. He says, "Well, it's a bad spot." That's what we were saying.

So we caught up to the same herd the next day. The same thing happened – early in the morning we caught up with them, and they just simply know we were there. We chased them for maybe three hours, and we caught up to them again – and they know exactly where we are! They go into the thick bush and they just hide from us – they know exactly how to get away. And that's when he says, "Louis, forget it, we cannot kill them." He says, "Three times we tried it." He says, "If we were lucky we would have killed them." So he says, "I think there is something wrong." He says, "The caribou are afraid, they are telling us something." I didn't listen, I was sort of mad at myself, but we gave up anyway and came home. We never even bothered to look for any other caribou trails, we just went home. And I was very angry that we came home anyway. So he says, that evening, "I know they are trying to tell us something."

And then in 1986, on May sixteenth, the whole village was wiped out and destroyed and one elder died and one young person died. In June sometime I happened to run into my friend who happened to have been in the village during that time. So I asked him, "Was it very dangerous?" And he says, "Yes, it was dangerous. It is amazing that we are a lasting people, lots of us could have died, even myself," he says. "So," he says, "that is the reason the caribous tell us that there is something wrong." So that's what the caribous were doing, animals do that. Are they shamans who were they trying to tell us something, or was it just instinct, or was is just simply a smart herd of caribous that knows exactly what the human hunters do? Was it a coincidence? No. I do believe it was such a thing because it happened to me.

Our ancestors experienced the same thing and they considered that animals do have a shamanistic powers. Just like the shaman who has the scanning ability to see things around him through his mind, so they think caribous have it, moose have it. And the rest of the animals have it, they say, for their survival. So that's the end of the story.[1]

CODE OF ETHICS:
DREAMS, GIFTS, AND KNOWLEDGE

To survive, our ancestors acquired special powers, which we call mitewin. They did this through dreaming. It is in dreams that they find an answer to a question. Once they began to seek a deeper knowledge, they could find answers in their dreams. So they would begin a dream quest to allow them to seeking answers in dreams. And those who managed to do that became mitew and passed on their knowledge to the next generation. The first step in the procedure of acquiring knowledge was to find a dream, or to create a dream. This is how you found something that was supposed to be understood in life.

People established the spiritual nature of their beings by doing this. They already knew there was a Great Spirit who knows everything and has created everything. And they wanted to understand the nature of where they lived. To do that they established the procedure known as mitewin. And it started with the dream quest and the practice of dreaming. Some people were gifted specially to create the shaking tent – shaking tent experts. Or some dreamed of a drum, how to use a drum, a hand drum that is, in our area. Some dreamed of how to be an expert hunter, how to use their mitewin for good hunting, for survival – and how to understand nature, meaning all the things that are in the land. And there were those who were gifted in their dream quest to study the universe, the stars, the moon, the sun – to readily understand what are these things were for and how they were useful. A mitew was a person who had created or obtained things in dreams and applied this in his lifetime, he is a mitew.

In time past legends were created as the medium to pass on knowledge to the next generation. And these things happened before other nations ever appeared on the land.

According our ancestors, everything works in order, systematically. Nothing was overused, there was nothing that overextended its usefulness or its benefit to humans. We found a systematic way to survive in the area where we live, the Omushkego country. All these things were extended to us by the Great Spirit and were applied by us in our lifetime through the teaching system that was passed on to us by our elders. Everything worked well, from the beginning of time – until the time of the other nations' appearance.

When other nations appeared everything began to change. The way it was then, before the appearance of the European, the teachings were about how to respect animals and all nature. There were rules about respecting nature and the environment – the animals and the birds. If one of these were broken by a member of the family, a kid maybe, the punishment was a retraction of the benefits from the nature.

If a person disobeyed these teachings, or dishonoured them – he was punished. For example, if a hunter killed more animals than he could use, when he needed that kind of animal again, he could not kill it. When this happened, there was that knowledge. When this denying of food occurred in a family, the leader of the family, or the family members, began to suffer the need for the food which could no longer be obtained. And then they would begin to question, to find out why this was happening.

Before the European came, before the Christianity came, when this happened, a family would seek out a person who could use the shaking tent to find an answer. The rule at that time was whoever did something wrong in the family must confess, or admit, that he misused the animal. Sometimes it was an elder who would be asked to find out why, if he could. And then he would seek in his mind whether there was anything he had to know – and he would be the one to suggest what should be done.

SINNING AGAINST ANIMALS

In our code of ethics, or the principles in life, there was a thing called *maahchihew*. It means that, when you do something wrong or out of the ordinary to an animal, it will be stop being available to you. And that is maahchihew. Usually, at that time, a lady or a young girl would have stepped over some food, and that would break the law, because she has not done or followed or respected the teaching. Because before the Christianity, there was a rule that said no woman should step over an animal that was being used for food, whether or not she is having her monthly period. That was a taboo, to say the least. And that would stop the provision of that animal if that happened. That's what they believe in those days. "Taboo" is, I think, a translation of maahchihew. *Maahchihew* means, therefore, that the animal, or fish, or bird will stop being killed easily.

When that happened a confession had to be made – there had to be a declaration of such an action before the punishment would stop. In further explanation, if large game animals, like caribou, were abused or over-killed by a hunter; or a woman stepped over the animal meat, intentionally or unintentionally, severe punishment results – food provision is not possible. And when the elders could not find an answer, they usually requested a person who was an expert in using the shaking tent to directly question the animal.

This person usually set up the shaking tent and ask it to bring in the caribou to explain why does he not allow himself to be killed and provide food and life. And then the caribou would say, "Because I have been abused by this or by that person and I will not give up my life for you." And then the wrongdoer will have to declare what he has done. And then the leader will ask the caribou for forgiveness and to please return his benefit. And then the caribou would say, "Okay, yes, you have now shown that you will respect me and so I will give my life for you." And that is the answer to the matter. And that was the use of the shaking tent and the procedures that were used long ago to respect the animals in spiritual relationship. And all of the living things were respected the same way – the animals, all the fish, or any other kind of animal.

So therefore the teaching of girls has always been very careful. She would be taught never to step over any food items or anything that is used for food, when she begin to be a lady and begins to have her monthly period. There was a warning to the young man also. When he was taught to hunt he was instructed never to kill an animal for nothing, never to kill an animal and leave it there to rot and waste. If he does that, he has committed a sin against nature, or *paastaho*, and he will not be able to kill the animal until he has declared that he has done so and why he did it. Only then can he regain his hunting skills.

And all these things changed when the European religion arrived amongst the Omushkegowak, because all this activity was considered a superstition and, therefore, was not practiced any more. But we still practise the conservation a little bit and we still believe in conservation ideas from our ancestors. And we still teach the young women not to step over any animal that is to become a food for a family.

RESPECT AND THANKS FOR ANIMALS

They used to believe that the Creator, or the Great Spirit who created everything gave those animals for their survival. So they did not *worship* the animal, but they *respect* it because it gives its life to them. And therefore they would make a sign in the place where they killed it. And when they have the first meal of the animal they would thank the Great Spirit for his provision for their survival. And whenever the hunter brought the food into the camp where his family were, the elder would give thanks to the Creator and bless the food in the name of the Great Spirit. And at the same time they would thank the animal who gave its life for their survival, for their life. And that is how the old spiritual belief and practices were carried out by the Omushkego people.

And wherever they were provided with food in the wilderness, our people have always made a sign of respect by hanging a part of the animal bone – most of the time it was the skull of the animal. They would hang it there where they have been given this food. And they thank the provider of the food and the animal.

This was their practice, and that is how the hunter had a spiritual relationship with the animals he hunted. These were very important principles and the elders taught them to their children. Hunters were trained to think this way, to know that the animals they hunted are free. The animals were not theirs, no. Animals were provided for them by the Creator. Their practice stemmed from watching the animals.

For example, the wolf is a predator but he doesn't kill randomly, he doesn't kill the animals for no purpose. He kills the animals to eat. And by observing the way animals act – killing only the animals they want to eat and eating every part of the animals they kill – humans knew how to respect the animal.

This is how they practised, our Omushkego. They respect the total environment, for the sake of the Creator. It's the highest form of belief and worship for them, the most highly regarded – the code of ethics. I have heard these stories and wisdom from our elders, those who have lived in my time. I give all the credit to their knowledge and their wisdom. I pass on them to you.[2]

VIOLATIONS AND CONSEQUENCES: THE HUNTERS AND THE WHITE FOX

Another thing that fascinates me is the way the Indian people enforced morality. There were rules amongst the Indian people – moral laws. These rules covered everything for the protection of individuals. One said that the hunter or trapper must never over-kill or be cruel to the animal, even though they want to kill it for their own survival.

Take, for example, the story about the three men. They were very, very good hunters – one of them was especially good. This happens when the fur trade was already taking hold of the people. And they were after the white foxes one winter, somewhere in the Hudson Bay area, and they were having bad luck. They just couldn't seem to catch them, and this made them so mad.

One time in the following summer when they were travelling with friends in the area where the white foxes have their dens, they remembered that they hadn't been able to kill them in the winter before. So they said, "Let's catch them! Let's take them out and skin them alive!" So sure enough, with this enthusiasm they tackled the dens. And they smoked out a white fox and grabbed it because they were waiting for him – and they skin it alive. They take the skin off the body and leave only its paws and feet and head. Then they let him go alive. And the fox ran away without skin – without fur.

And it went again into its den and the men started digging up the other dens. Suddenly that fox popped out from another hole – and it appeared to be holding a human skeleton hand, just the bones.

It shocked them to see that vision. They instantly realized they had committed blasphemy. They were terrified – and they couldn't catch any more foxes. They went home and didn't say anything because they knew they had broken the law. Cruelty to an animal was forbidden amongst the Indian people.

The next winter they were trapping again – and they froze to death. They got lost in a big whiteout and the three of them just bundled together and sat there until they died. The next summer someone happened to come upon these same foxholes – and then he came upon the white foxes among three human skeletons. The hands had been eaten off by the fox. They brought home the remaining bones of the three human beings who had committed a blasphemy, an act of blasphemy punishable by death by nature. That's one of the rules of the Indian people.

My grandmother happened to see one of our own relatives born deformed and she used to describe to us what he looked like. He was a man and his name was George. The shape of his head was just like a seal and his hands were at the elbow, just smooth like a seal's fin. And they say this may have come about from bestiality. That is something else that is forbidden. We don't know who did this, whether it was the mother or the father or the ancestors in the past.

Sometimes blasphemy happened amongst the Indian tribes in actions and also in words. A person that uses very severe words against somebody would live to regret it – they would live to pay. That is why rules of morality were so strongly taught to the young children. And today the old traditional culture is dying off and these things are not expressed to our young people.[3]

Mitewiwin Heroes and Villains

I am going to try to explain the medicine man. The Europeans have attempted to write about this. There are some movies made by Hollywood that touch on the medicine man. There are also anthropologists who have tried to explain what this medicine man is. But none of those have covered the whole subject.

Medicine is another field of shaman development, the spiritual belief and practice of our Omuishkego. The medicine man does not necessarily have to have plants and herbs and things like that. He has acquired shaman character, a standard, or shall we say a degree, and he has been gifted to help others in the field of medicine.

The true medicine man does not have to have any object, or plans, or methods. In the white man's world they call them medicine men but we call them Healers. They would receive a small gift from the person who requested their assistance – after Europeans arrived, when the tobacco was one of the famous items to trade, they usually accepted tobacco, not as a payment but as a good gesture. So that wasn't a payment.

No matter how powerful a shaman he may be, if the sick person didn't believe the shaman, he wouldn't receive no benefit from him because, as it is in all religious practices around the world, one must have faith. When the medicine man had the power to heal or to help a sick person, the first thing he would want to find out was: is this guy genuine? Does he believe that this can be done? At first he could be very reluctant because he first needed to know whether this guy was very honest or not. When he was satisfied that this person genuinely needed some help, that he truly had faith, he accepted the tobacco as a gift, a symbol of faith. So it was only when a patient have faith in medicine man that he will receive the cure, or the remedy for his sickness.[1]

MITEWIWIN:
THE POWER OF DREAMS AND THE MIND

Shamanism is one of the major parts of our Omushkego culture. Without it, we would have been dead a long time ago, killed off by other tribes – but because they had this defence mechanism they survived. Shamans were once feared but they have dwindled down, maybe because they have submit themselves to be controlled.

Shaman power is developed individually and shamanism is not a church. The only time it ever involved communal spiritual stuff is when people used the shaking tent for offensive reasons, or for entertainment. There were times in the past where the shamans came together on friendly terms and showed off their power – what they could do. But they never used it aggressively in these friendly gatherings. There was a rule that said: you do not intimidate your fellow man, you just entertain.

It was just like today, with competitive games – the world champions meet to show who is the best – but they have no intention of starting a war with it. All nations come to a certain area and show their skills – they exhibit their capabilities and they are honoured that way. Similarities existed among the Omushkego people. They came together in the spring for thanksgiving gatherings – to feast, and play games, and exchange marriage vows, and exchange trade goods, and to rekindle friendships. Aside from these gatherings, shamans were out in the wilderness by themselves.

If a person was planning to harass a shaman, he or she may be asking for trouble – there is no pity, there is no mercy. If a shaman intends to get rid of this nuisance, he has the right to kill and that was the law – an eye for an eye – kill or be killed. The survival of the fittest. Many of these things were useful in those days but today they are not – and for that reason the Omushkego culture has come to an end. It began to deteriorate when the spiritual part changed over. I'm not saying that the Christianity is bad. I am saying that the cultural beliefs and practices were eliminated and then therefore is not part of the cultural activity today.

The Christianity has taken over the Omushkego. The old culture was cruel and harsh, but the Christianity is smooth and non-violent and it is very good to be in the wilderness with it. You don't have to fear a man. If you know he is Christianized he is not supposed to kill you, he's not supposed to challenge you – at least that's what we believe. But mostly today we see Christian people kill each other just the same

Now let's go back to the Omushkego culture. The Omushkego, because they live in the wilderness, followed the wilderness rules – nature's law. You see it amongst the animals – they follow these rules – they follow the seasons and the seasons are the law enforcement. The season makes animals move, migrate, and people follow these animals because that's their food, that's their food supply. So nature itself was the law and no uniformed law enforcement humans were required. All the laws in the land of the Omushkego people were right there in the wilderness. And that's their culture, that's their lifestyle, that's their land. [2]

Our Omushkego history is, at least, fifty percent mitewiwin, shamanism. It was obtained through retreat to the wilderness for isolation and fasting. And when one was satisfied that he had as much as he wanted, he was not done. He had to keep rekindling the spirit in the body, reconditioning himself. That meant he had to go into the wilderness again, to get in touch with the spiritual part of his being. It depended on how much he wanted to obtain or what level he wanted to achieve. If you wanted more power, or to have a more successful life, you had to condition and prepare yourself more. You also had to start very early age.

So our culture was based on knowledge of the wilderness. Our ancestors understood each species and knew that they are all gifted. They also knew that a human is more highly gifted than animals. But not all people are equally gifted. Some were gifted just enough to survive.

There were levels, or degrees, of shamanism – just like in the white man's education. One person could have a minimum – just enough to be aware of danger and to understand those other things that are necessary to understand. And there are those who could go higher up and have more power over things. And there were those who went to the second level, who could understand the mysteries – things that are not quite explainable. And the third level was the highest. When the shaman got to the third level he didn't require any material stuff. He had the power to control with his mind – mind over matter. He could do that.[3]

SCIENCE AND MYSTERY

Our ancestors did not deal with matter scientifically – they did not break things apart to understand. But they did understand the animals they ate. They understand fish because that's what they ate – they knew all the inside of the fish's body. They understand that. And they also understand that fish swim under water because it has gills and it needs water to have the oxygen. And then they understand the animals they cut in pieces to eat – they understand about tendons, muscles, blood, the arteries, and veins. But the nerves they didn't know, they have not mentioned that, they didn't explain that. So that's a lack of knowledge because there's no scientific experimentation. Maybe the shaman knew but, if he did, he could not have explained because shaman was not a teacher. He was just a survivor, a gifted survivor – but he could guide others.

Our ancestors feared what they did not understand, just like anybody else. One mystery they never understood very well was the weather. They didn't understand why the wind behaves so furiously and viciously. The most highly feared stuff in nature was thunder. Thunder and lightning is powerful stuff and they never quite understood how it's created. They didn't understand it scientifically.

But because they could not understand it scientifically, could not explain it, they tried to understand it in their own way. What I mean to say is, they dreamed about it. When a kid was dreaming, he dreamed about the thunder because he was afraid of it. When the thunder was scary to a young person, he dreamed of it until he began to understand that it was not actually trying to kill him – it was just a part of nature. But people who developed shaman power wilfully dreamed about thunder.

Before the white man, most of our ancestors believed thunder is a being. It could be a bird, or it could be something else, but they never actually saw. They couldn't see. They could not understand why it was so loud that it makes the earth shake when it sounded, and where the lightning started from.

They have to make up their mind to satisfy that curiosity. So, in a dream, what they do is they try to dream this thunder and lightning and to make it into a being, a person. They called this person a thunderbird – it had to fly, it had to be a bird because it would not be up there if he has no wings. So what would be the most logical bird in their land? The eagle! It's a predator – dangerous, and feared by the lesser birds because he catches them from the air. He is the most feared.

So they made this thunder into a being that took the form of an eagle and called it a thunderbird. Then they could begin to be familiar with it and to use it as a friend or a partner – through their dream they were able to control this thunderbird and use it when they wanted to. The highest level a shaman could reach – the highest level of the mitewiwin – was when he could control the thunder, when he could form it into a thunderbird so he could use that power from thunder and lightning. He wanted to form this energy into a being, a bird – something that he can handle here on Earth. They didn't use any substance to harness this power – instead, they formed it in their minds.

Our Omushkego have also always talked about the north. The north is powerful stuff. It brings the extreme cold weather and the heavy storms which can hold you up for a long time – maybe for three days you cannot move or do anything because of the strong wind. It can create a thunderstorm because of the wind. It can tame the thunderstorm also. When there are thunder clouds in the south and to the west, and the cold north wind come gusting into the land, it dissipates the thunderstorm. So there is power in the north.

They lived in the open country all the time and so they saw the stars at night. They pinpointed the North Star a long time before the white man came. So they have called this *Keewatin* ("Mister North") – as a person in their dream! They have dreamed this stuff. And if you could dream Kewatin, he could become a person and you could be friends with it. You had to be able to associate with it – to talk to it – to control it. Some powerful shamans could control this sort of thing.

The same with the other four wind directions. They turned all these four corners in the world into persons so they could control them in their minds if they wanted a favourable wind. A powerful shaman could do that.[4]

DREAM HELPERS

You can dream about many sorts of characters in different ways: animals and birds, any moving thing – even the weather, even thunder. Even the sun, and the moon, and the salt water, and the fresh water. And you can even dream about under the water – the fish. You dreamed those things to try to use them. You could dream about the fox, because he's cunning. And you could dream about the eagle, because he's the most powerful predator who flies – he's very respected because he's dangerous, even to humans. You had to dream about the eagle for him to become your helper. You could dream about anything that is dangerous to you. If you weren't a good swimmer you could dream about the water and turn yourself into a fish. Therefore you could survive if you fell in – and then you could turn yourself into a human again. That's why the dream quest was there. In some dreamers' dream quests they could turn themself into a bird, any kind that they wish. And it goes on and on. Almost anything.

From dreams you could also be friends with an animal for your own use. Let's say you have dreamed about the muskrat as your helper. What could you do? Well, with your power, because you dreamed about the muskrat, you could use the muskrat as your spy – to spy on beavers – because if you want to hunt a beaver you need to know how many doorways he has. So you dream of using the muskrat to tell you, because he always lives very close to the beaver. And then you could summon him in your mind and say, "Okay, Mr. Rat, tell me exactly where the holes into the beaver house are. How many beavers are there?" So the muskrat will just inform you and even tell you where the holes are. And then when you go out to hunt you just dig right there where the muskrat told you that you would find the holes. That's one way of using the animals.

It's the same thing with the weasel. Some mitewak used the weasel because he's tiny and could go into places the mitew could not go. Same with the mouse – even the shrew, the smallest mouse. You can use him where you want to see. And then also you could also use the birds in the same way.

Like the hawk. You could use a hawk as your helper and whenever you wanted to see something, or to find something, you could ask the hawk in your dream find it for you. And the hawk will do that. And that's for you. That is your helper. And so it went on in the same way – it didn't stop.

The mitew could make a human person do what they wanted, just by using their mind power. They could make a person walk in their sleep and do things without realizing they were doing them – a mitew could just force a person's mind to do this.

A mitew could train himself to leave his body and see where he wanted to hunt, to see whether there were any signs of animals. That was usually very simple for the mitew. And they used many other things. Some mitew could use any kind of thing – a fox, or beetles (there are stories about this), or the wind (if they have controlled the wind in their dream quest). In their dream vision they could use the wind to aggravate another person – a man who had insulted them, or a woman, or another mitew who was bothering them – they could create a small tornado to go and attack that person. A mitew could also project himself into the distance, without moving, and see with his mind's eyes. And it usually actually happened. These are the things that we know.

Some people, during their dream quest, created some kind of a beast who could fight for them if another shaman was sending his beast to kill them or terrify them. They could create their own beast and then fight. Only the beasts fight – the two men just sit there with their minds fighting – and whoever is stronger is the winner. And if one of the beasts is killed, the mitew dies right instantly.

The mitew could actually go inside of a man's dream and fight him there. And whoever was killed in that dream didn't wake up again. So these are the things. This is the real stuff I'm talking about. This is not what we see today when we see Indian powwows and mitewiwin and people running around a fire and dancing around. This is all just ritualization of stuff that was done a long time ago. The real mitew didn't show all these things. It was highly secret because if you started telling things you would lose your will and your power.

It's so totally different from the Christian teaching and our elders have said that it is not possible to practice both of them at the same time. If one wanted to be a Christian, they were supposed to totally deny the old ways – or, at least, put them aside. One had to be totally eliminated, or at least put aside, to practise the other. And they say that if a person tried to use both there were usually consequences – a person lost his mind because he didn't have no guidance to begin with. And a person was advised against trying it after he's already grown up. A youngster had to grow up with this thing to survive it. He had to develop a strong body and a strong spirit. It was just like having a great physical test and a great mental test at the same time. The weak body would succumb to the power of the mind and could not survive it.[5]

Anyway, let's get back to developing this stuff. Not only a man could have it – a woman could be trained that way too. That's why some women were so powerful in those days, because they developed that extra power.

One person could have only one particular kind of dream. Let's say, for example, a young person dreamed only about using a shaking tent. He would be very well off. He could go as far as he wanted – he could go to the highest degree with it, or he could just use it simply for his own benefit – to hunt and benefit his family, and to defend his life. If that's as far as he wanted to go, he didn't have to go any higher. But others, they go to the highest level possible using only the shaking tent. They can do that. There are three degrees – there's this first part, and then, if you wanted, with a bit of instruction you could go to the second level. And then you can go to the highest you can get.

You could understand the animals if you could dream about them – the wolf, the caribou, the moose – if you can dream about these you could begin to understand. You watched them as you grew up and you saw their behaviour – and then you learned *why* they did those things if you dreamed about them. And then you learn to respect them. There are rules that have existed for a long time about how to respect animals and why you should respect them.

There are some shamans who used their dream, or power, to be very good hunters. For example, if a man dreamed about the beaver, he would be able to survive by knowing how to hunt him – and he respected the beaver because the beaver had instructed him as if he were his friend, and gave his life for the man's survival. In return, the beaver asked only, "Respect me." The beaver would say, "To respect me you must always hang my skull wherever you have eaten my flesh." So if this person was using his knowledge very wisely, whenever he ate a beaver for the first time in the season, he would hang its skull, putting a string through the eye and hanging it in a tree. Other people knew what this means and they didn't touch it.

They did not worship the beaver. The beaver also depended upon the higher power, the same as the human. Our people thought that animals know the Creator, the Great Spirit – especially the beaver.

They really respect the beaver because he seems to have a mind – he seems to prepare himself for survival during the winter. He creates a den, he makes his house, he knows exactly how to do it. Where did he get his knowledge? So the First Nations people say he is maybe the most intelligent animal. And, for that reason, sometimes he abuses himself. When he stays in one place too long he begins to deteriorate the land, the tree, the willows, the grass – he blocks the fish and pollutes the water. This is how our people learned that you cannot stay in one place. So, to their understanding, the Great Spirit gave humans the power to use over the beaver – to kill them when they are too many. And, when the beaver lodge has begun to become permanent, they have to destroy the dam so that the fish will go through, if the river is long and it has lakes. These little things were just simple instructions from the elders, but there was a knowledge beyond that.

There is a story about one person who dreamed about whales. In his dream he heard them talking under the ice, and he thought to himself, "How can these whales live under the water without breathing?" So he went out into the Bay and checked the ice condition. Then he saw this buckling ice, and that's where he actually heard the whales breathing – it was a whale breathing hole. So he dreamed this first, and then he saw it. They have to dream these things first, if they want to understand them.[6]

We have talked about the nightmares during shaman development, when a person was young. A young person's mind is free and full of imagination and fantasy worlds. We can create any fantasies in our minds – we can picture something that is impossible, and we can do anything in our fantasies. And that is how our dreams work. Your mind doesn't rest, it just keeps on working all the time – your body relaxes but your mind never stops. I think it's called the subconscious. When you could use the power of your mind to control your dream, this was what the elders called a dream quest. Only when you achieved that could you move on to the next stage, which they called a dream vision.

After developing a dream quest, and passing into a certain state, you were then able to have a dream vision in your waking hours. You could just close your eyes and see things with your mind. And that's what the mitew was – the real shaman. And when you had developed the highest level of shamanism, you could actually travel far distances with your mind – leave your body behind and travel with your mind. I have tried to find this idea in English. I could not find it but I have found a phrase that may almost cover what I mean. It is called astral projection.[7]

There's another branch of this mitewiwin, this shamanism, and this is the medicine man. He was a healer. He dreamed about plants, herbs, and animals – whatever stuff he used to heal someone. But he had to dream about those things first. In his dream quest, he was gifted as a healer and he dreamed about many things that he could use to heal people with different diseases. So he was a benefactor. But the medicine man could sometimes turn to evil. He could kill just as he could heal – he could use his medicine as a power to kill. Very dangerous too when they go bad.

So there is one opposite to another, one good and one bad, it's all there. The medicine man had to dream about each item that exists on the land before he could use it. Also he sang – he used a rattle and sang to heal a sick person, or give him support. But he could not bring a dead body alive again – that was the only problem – he could not win back the dead. A shaman who was at the highest level could use the shaking tent to bring life back to the dead, but the medicine man could not do this.[8]

So that's a small section about dreaming and shamanism. But the word "shaman" doesn't fit, in my opinion. I like to use the word *mitew* to describe one person, and *mitewiwin* to describe his activities. Our elders did not have a church – each elder was a leader, a wise man, and an independent person – he was a protector – he was everything. He was almost next to the Great Spirit and he guided the young people, the next generation. He passed on this knowledge on how to develop, and how to be careful.[9]

BECOMING A MITEW

It has been said that parents would first recognize that their child, especially their son, was gifted, by listening to him talk about his dreams. And then they would recommend this child to his grandfather or grandmother, who became his personal guardian and teacher in this development. Usually the young person would start at a very early age, preferably at the age of five and not later than fifteen. Our ancestors believed that the sooner you got introduced to this practice the better, because your body had to develop along with it. When you develop your mind, your body also has to be strong and in good health, and when your body in good health, your mind also functions btter. That's their teaching.

And then the child was set to receive some instruction and guidance, preferably from his his own grandfather – if not, it would be his uncle, and if not the next best of kin, then an older man. The grandmothers could do that also, they could be perfect guardians for this, as long as they knew the subject. Most of the time, in the past, all the elders used to know about this thing. When the youngster was appointed a teacher, he had to listen to him and follow whatever he recommended.

Now, in the first level of this development you had to obtain dreams. And in order to obtain the dreams that may be useful to you, you first had to get over your fears. The first fear any child can have is the fear of being alone, especially in the darkness, and that was the first thing to try to overcome. Once a youngster got over this first fear, he was ready to further develop himself. Usually he was about six years by this time – it takes about one year for a child of five to get over his fears of being alone at night inside the home and sleep alone.

The following year, if possible, he had to learn to sleep outside, away from home. At that time he and his grandfather or teacher went to spend the night together. The instructor, the guide, would watch over the young person and if, for any reason, this young person had difficulty enduring his dreams, his grandfather, or guide, was right close by and could calm him.

Once that was overcome the child could be on his own and, with the help of his instructor, try to condition himself to sleep and to think about the things he needed to find out about. If he was to get over all his fears, he had to contact them in his sleep. He had to condition himself to go into a half-sleep – he must not have full comfort when he was sleeping. He must have a minimum of covering, a minimum of comfort, so he could condition himself to be half asleep and half awake at the same time. In that state of mind the dream is actually almost real – and sometimes it can be very terrifying. He had to understand that this was not real, this is a dream.

Once he could control that, he could call or command any kind of dream that he wanted. If it had to do with an animal that he feared, he must summon a dream, a vision of this feared thing. He must have enough power to speak to this animal in his dream – to win the friendship of this animal and win its trust so that it could become one of the boy's helpers. The word we use in our language is *pawaachikan*.

Once he got into this state and could communicate with things like animals, he was on his way. All he had to do was develop and maintain this during this stage of his development. Every animal that he was afraid of he had to summon during these dream quests. It would take about five years to encounter all the things on the earth that he feared or was mystified by. By the end of five years he would be comfortable with them all.

In the Omushkego land there are many dangerous animals – one of the most feared is the polar bear. And then there is the black bear and the wolf. Even moose can be dangerous in the special season. And there are also smaller animals that can be dangerous for your health. And then there are other animals in the salt water Bay – not necessarily dangerous, but mystical, because no human can live under the water, and nobody understands readily what the whale is like, what the walrus can be. And there are many other mammals in the water. And even in the rivers – the fish. There are some fish that we don't understand – and we know that fish can even be cannibalistic – they eat each other. And that is not a very nice thing to know. Some of the fish are not eatable, they can make you sick. And the birds that fly – there are certain birds that can be dangerous in certain seasons. For example, the hawks can be dangerous during their nesting season – they can kill. And all these things a child must understand and summon in his dreams – he must tame them in his dream quest.

DREAMING THE ELEMENTS

The elements – the atmosphere, the air, and the water – can be dangerous. One must understand how to deal with them. In his dream quest, one had to develop the ability to solidify elements that are not solid. For example, there are times when the wind is very destructive – it can kill you. And so some people dreamed of the north wind and the north direction as a very powerful being. A dreamer on his dream quest had to visualize the north as a being, a human form, so he can speak to it and come into its favour, so he could use it during his lifetime if possible. It could help him and be kind to him during his lifetime. And in his dream quests he had to turn all four directions of wind into a human form that he could summon or contact.

After being able to do that, he had to go into further destructiveness. When the wind began to be strong, he had to dream about this wind in different form. It was the same thing with thunder. In a changing atmosphere the wind can create a thunderstorm – lightning and thunder close together. People tried to form it in their mind as a being – and this form was called a thunderbird. It is from people who formed this element, this power, into a kind of bird.

But it depended on the individual how much and in what way could use this as one of his helpers, how much he could do to win these powerful forces through his dream quest, or how much he would be able to avoid its dangers. We know today, thunder and lightning is not a bird, but in those days it was through their mind power that they visualized this thing as a bird, a most powerful predator.

Each direction of the wind had meaning and was of potential benefit to man – and it also had potential dangers. They had to dream about all these, to win their favour. And that's what the dream quest, the quest for dreams, was all about. You were trying to create the dream, to contact things by your mind, so you could understand.

The person who methodically developed this in his dream quests could not be overcome by anything – the elements, the animals, the birds, the fish. Fire was also something a person could form into a human form to understand it, and communicate with it, and have a command over it. This is why people we call mitew could overcome these things – even if the odds were against them. The reason that people developed to be a mitew was so they could survive. And it has been said that, in our area, every head of the family had to have a certain amount of these things – not everything, but at least some level.

And now we are going to talk a little more about the dream quest. Some people dreamed about humans themselves to understand their potential benefits and dangers to each other. In time past, men were mystified by women because they had menstruation every month. And if a man tried to understand this, he tried to make it into the form of a woman. And that was a very dangerous thing to do. Many men who were about to be fully grown dreamed this stuff because their bodies felt desire and they wanted to know what that was about. So they dreamed about that menstrual blood, and they dreamed it in the form of a woman – the most beautiful woman. And if they won that woman's love, they thought they had acquired something. But this dream could be very negative and destructive for such individuals. I personally have seen a person who has made this mistake.[10]

If a person was healthy, he would be a fully grown man of about thirty by the time he could acquire the dream quest of all things. By that time his body had stopped growing, he could withstand all these pressures of mind and knowledge. When he stopped his quest for dreams and had acquired, in his mind, the power to command any one of those things that he had dreamed about, they were an accumulation of benefits for his life. He could summon any one of those things and face it without fear because he could understand it, and so did not fear it.

Some men acquired a minimum of dreams during their quests and sometimes that was all they needed. Women did not have to do dream quests because they were already gifted. They could acquire all those things very easily – they were treated very harshly and, because of that conditioning, they didn't have to induce themselves into that state.

People, during their dream quests, also sharpened their senses. We all have five senses, and they say that when a person had acquired dreams, he was able to develop extra senses.

MIND POWER THROUGH DREAMS

Actually, what the man did was exercised his mind. There is an elder who tried to explain these things to me because he had seen it himself when he was young, he had listened to an elder who was explaining those things. He said that when you were at least halfway to the highest level of development you could summon dreams when you needed them and accomplish impossible things.

You conditioned yourself to use your mind power by using the mind's three levels. One level is the one that you used as a primary source of dreaming – the mind that never stops, that goes anywhere, that can do anything. The second level is the one that you use when you are fully awake – this was the creative mind. These levels can be reached by a person using only five senses.

But the extra senses that you sharpened and developed were used at the level that is now called extra-sensory perception – in our language it is called *pimootahgosiwin*. And it means to be able to project yourself where you want to be instantly. At this level you could also summon other beings to assist you. That was your most powerful mind – the third mind. And that was what you were using when you went on the quest for dreams.

It is the third level of your mind that you awakened when you slept, when you wanted to dream something, when you wanted to know something. This mind, along with the ones you used when you were actually awake, could help you dream about something that you wanted – to actually see it in your mind. And that third level of mind was the one you used to accomplish almost anything you wanted. Another way of saying it is that you could perform a miracle. You could command the elements, you could walk on water, you could even walk on air, or travel on air. You could travel instantly in your mind without going there physically. And, with your mind only, you could move things and make other people do things without knowing they were doing them. This is what our ancestors called the *mitewiwin*.

There are certain things that a human mind cannot do, there is a certain level that cannot be reached – and that is where the Great Spirit is located. There is a Great Spirit who can overcome every power on earth and in the atmosphere. The Great Spirit created everything that we see, everything that is here on earth. This is a great spirit, who has the mind power to create anything.

And this is what my ancestors have told me – these are the things I understand. But, unfortunately, I was not allowed to do this. I was allowed to listen, but discouraged from trying to do it.

SEASONS AND PLACES TO DREAM

Sometimes a youth would have enough dreams by the age of fifteen, and he could begin to live his life with these dreams in his knowledge. That doesn't mean he stopped the dream quest there – he continued, not all the time, but at certain given seasons. In the Omushkego land we have four main seasons: fall, winter, spring, and summer. But we have other seasons that overlap: a season between spring and summer, and one between summer and fall, and one between fall and winter.

The time when the Omushkego used to practise dream quests was in the early fall, as soon as it started to freeze, because that's when the proper temperatures existed. It wasn't totally freezing weather – warm enough for someone to be able to sleep out in the wilderness without many blankets and be able to survive. During winter – December, January, February, they didn't do the dream quests because the winter is too severe.

After that, from the middle of March to the middle of April, they could do it again – they called it the spring dream quest. And they could also do it between summer and spring, that season they could do that. So these are the periods that the Omushkego would have the opportunity to practice the quest for dreams.

And now, where did the Omushkegos do this? There was no one place. In our part of the country there are no mountains and no high waterfalls – but we do have small hills that are about 800 feet high from the sea level, and we do have fast waters that you can actually hear from a distance. And we had special places where people did not usually stay in the winter or summer.

Those secret places are where these people would go – usually onto higher ground. Some people looked for a place where there was fast water. Some people made a nest in a tree and went up there to dream, if their instruction called for it. Some people made a nest over the fast water so they would always have that sound in their ears – this helped them to have a special kind of dream.

In the fall, when the water is open and there is no ice in Hudson Bay, they would go at least three miles from the shore of the sea water. On the southwest side of the Bay, when there has been a strong wind for a day or two, you can hear the waves crashing into the shores – you can hear them from a distance. So the people used to sleep where they could hear them at night, which helped them to create a dream. So that's one way.

And other people, when it was allowable, went out into the Bay, if they had a canoe. They would anchor out there in the open water and sleep inside the canoe – and they tried to dream there.

And then also in the early months of June and July, when there's broken ice on the open Bay, it makes a terrible noise every time the tide goes. It sounds like a gun or cannon because the pieces of ice are crashing into each other. It sounds like a thunder. And sometimes that's where they went – close to the Bay – to sleep there during the night, and condition themselves to dream.

In the spring, from March to the middle of May thereabout, walking in the bush is very easy because the frost makes the ground firm. In that kind of condition, they would go onto the higher ground, someplace where they were isolated, to spend the night –

or whatever: a week, three nights – to begin to try to find a dream, or have a question answered in a dream.

And it is during that time too that the water begins to rush out into the creeks – you can hear the water all night making such a noise. People used to make a scaffold over a small creek that was making such a terrible noise, and that's where they slept. The sound made them dream of anything associated with water. And they do that.

And sometimes during the summer some people went a distance from their homes, especially when there was a thunderstorm. They slept wherever – on the surface of the land, or in a tree, or on a scaffold they made as a bed – just to get a dream during the thunderstorm. But the young person who did this always had to report to his own assigned guide.

And then some people would just sleep, on a tiny island, with water close by on all sides. And there they would be – in a half-sleep state. That would bring the dreams into them.

So all these dreams they accumulated were the dreams they summoned when they needed help. That is why they did that. It has been said by some elders that some people, in their quests for dreams, would only require twelve important dreams – that was all they needed in their lifetime. During their dream quests it would be revealed to them whether they were going to need more dreams or not, because their life was predetermined already by the Great Spirit. And those who were predetermined not to live a long life didn't need many kinds of dreams.[11]

MITEW FASTING AND SELF-DISCIPLINE

To become a shaman, one had to practice fasting. This meant they could not stuff themselves with good food. One had to control his gluttony and deny himself a comfortable sleep so he could lay, at night time, in a state of half-sleep.

In that state you developed many dream visions. And these dream visions were the most important things – it was as if somebody was teaching you things, talking to you, and writing on a blackboard. You were supposed to listen and try to stuff it all in your mind for your future use. So the dream vision is like that. And that is the training.

And the person who wanted to develop this shamanism had to

take it very seriously – had to wish for it, and hope for it, and have faith that he would acquire those vision dreams that would be so useful to him. The ones who became master shamans had do frequent fasting, to frequently go into a state of self-discipline, with the advice of the elders. And it was very dangerous. One person could overdo it in a short time if he did not do things in a very well-organized manner or pushed his body to the point where he could not withstand the severity. That is why many, many people fell short – because they wanted to rush it and, thus, put themselves into a state of confusion – and some even, to be very honest, became retarded by their own making.[12]

Another thing to deny was sexual satisfaction. He had to keep himself nice and clean without any tarnishing from another body. He denied himself and lived in isolation and prayer – whatever the kind of praying they used. And whenever a person wanted to develop more skills, or a certain power, he had to go back into the wilderness to fast. If he could not succeed at the first time, he had to go back again. If he failed a second time, he had to approach the elders for their advice. And then he had to follow that instruction which would finally give him the power to achieve what he was seeking.[13]

Mostly people developed these things for their survival – their defence. But if he wants to develop himself to become a more powerful shaman, he had to acquire the vision dreams that would allow him to practise his offensive development – in his mind and in his body. That was the dangerous part, and that's where the old people were very useful.

Not everyone was encouraged by the elders. Some people were naturally gifted to be developed as shamans. They were the best people to have around, because they had developed many things – they had mastered the training and were able to use it properly. They had acquired powers. The longer you lived, the more you developed, and the more you understood the mystery. That is why the elders were so useful and respected amongst our people in time past, before the European came in. That is why they were able to survive on this land. That is why they were able to withstand the severity of the harsh land where they lived.

Those who were most respected and useful were the medicine men because they specialized in healing or helping the sick people, and they were very kind. But not all! Some used it for the good purpose, and some used it for their own satisfaction.[14]

One way that a youngster could develop shaman power without going through much conditioning was if he lost his parents when he was small and was taken in by his grandparents, or aunts, or another guardian. These orphans were usually not well cared for. They knew they were not cared for the way their parents would have cared for them – that people taking care of them did not love them as much as their parents would have loved them – that they were just doing their duty. This kind of a child understood these things and he felt there was no total love from anyone. This was the kind of a child that could easily be trained to dream. Sometimes you didn't even have to instruct them, it came to them so readily. That is why our ancestors passed on the knowledge that no person should ever mistreat an orphan. This is the kind of child that it was very dangerous to make fun of, or irritate – because this will cause them to further develop their conditioning to receive a dream. This is one of the warnings that I have heard amongst our people. That's where the idea came from to respect your fellow man – that's where it came from – and we understand that.[15]

Some people genetically inherited goodness, and they put their gift to a very good use – they could be very holy, and very gentle, and very generous. But it was all individually developed and it was up individuals to practise it and believe it. They believed. They believed – that's it. They had faith in their dreams.[16]

HEALING

What does a medicine man do? Here is an example: There is sickness that is caused by sudden overexposure to extreme cold. This causes a person to have a condition similar to an epileptic seizure – it looks exactly like epilepsy but it's not as severe – these people do not have foam coming out of their mouths. They twitch up and down and they remain partially conscious – they have very excruciating pain and are very frightened. This usually happens during the winter – in a season where there is a very limited number of plants that can be used as medicine, because everything is covered. So the wintertime used to be the worst time for somebody to get sick like this.

In time past, the only emergency remedy was to apply heat – to quickly put a heating device in the patient's bed. Usually this was a stone – a stone can carry heat close to the body. It was placed near the feet because the elders knew that the blood seems to rush into the upper body when somebody gets cold. And usually it was the head that was hurt and that's why the person had such severe symptoms. So they understood this.

If they couldn't find a stone, they used the sand if the camp was located on the sand ridges – they dug up the top moss and made a fire on the sand to heat it. Then they put it under the patient, especially at his feet, and they held the patient under a heavy cover. They then put cold water at the top of the skull or around the head – not ice water, but cold water. And if the twitching continued, they would just gradually apply more heat by giving a medicinal drink called Labrador Tea, which was made of ground spruce. They boiled this plant into a very strong liquid and make a patient drink it – as hot as he could swallow without burning him. A person would test it first in his own mouth before giving it to the sick person. This liquid acted as an internal heater. It went all through the body and relaxed the muscles, I suppose, so the blood could flow easier. And usually that's when the patient stopped twitching and passed out, as if in total exhaustion. But the people who were attending would have to stay close by, to make sure the person didn't kick away the blankets and get another sudden chill. Sometimes it took only twelve hours to heal a person who has such an accident.

Sometimes, when this extreme emergency measure failed, the patient would be in a coma, laying just there he was dead, but with his heart still pulsing – still breathing, but unable to become conscious. The Native people knew that he could remain that way for a long time. If he came out from the coma, sometimes he could not walk or speak – or he would be numb on one side because this was, apparently, a stroke. The people understood that something happened in the head. And sometimes a person recovered very easily.

So, to the point, when all these emergency applications failed and the patient was still in critical condition, a medicine man would be called in. I like to call him a shaman because he specialized in helping sick people after finding out themselves that they have the gift to help somebody. He can help where everything else failed. So the shaman brought his medicine bag.

He sat beside the sick person after he got all the information and understood what had already been done. The only thing he brought was his own medicine. Some medicine man carried symbolic things like plants, and herbs, or even objects. Sometimes it was a piece of bone, or something else to symbolize their actions.

An example of this is a rattle – this used to be a favourite for medicine men and was usually used by the really powerful shamans. They made these rattles from a human bone in time past, before the European came. Later on, they used the skull of a beaver, or an otter – sometimes it was a mink, a martin, even a weasel. A small skull did not indicate that the medicine man had less power – the level of this skill was not measured by the size of any object. Anyway, some people used a rattle and sang – that's all they did. They had a song which, unfortunately, our people have forgotten. Most often they could help the sick person when everything else failed. Sometimes the sick person totally recovered – and that was very extraordinary. Sometimes the sick person only partially recovered, which was better than giving up.

Now, getting back to this rattle – some people used the shoulder blade of an animal. The medicine man would use this bone rattle as he sang – be it for healing purposes, or for simply requesting the help of the Great Spirit in time of need.[17]

Our Cree people used the sweatlodge but, to my understanding, they didn't see it as a spiritual thing – they use it purely for medical purposes. When somebody was exposed to extreme cold and was having a seizure, or fits, they created a little sweatlodge to heat the guy until his muscles relaxed – because they had twitched into a ball of muscle.

Another emergency could happen when a lady was exposed to extreme cold weather. If she had her menstrual period at that time, the flow stopped because of the cold – that's what they believed. So they established again this little sweatlodge and put her in there to get extreme heat in her body and to start the flow again.

If the flow did not start, she would not have a menstrual period again. Every month it would just accumulate inside the womb, become a hardened substance, and make her sick. And when this solid mass of menstrual material got really big, it had to come out – and that's when people had to really try to do something. So the medicine man or lady would know there's no baby in there. They liquidated this stuff somehow by using a douche made with warm water and pressing hard on the lady's stomach so the clotted blood could come out. This saved the life of the person because once they were cleaned, or at least partially cleaned, they could live. But they could never have baby because it destroyed the womb, I guess. So that's why this people used this sweatlodge stuff.[18]

ANIMALS AND POWER

In the land of the Omushkegowak, there is constant danger. There are dangerous animals, like polar bears, black bears, and wolves. They are especially dangerous when they are scared, because then they are always on the alert and can automatically kill anything that startles them. So it's very dangerous and, for this reason, everybody needed some spiritual connection for defence. Living in the wilderness required this.

Every animal has his own gifted defence mechanism. The skunk doesn't have speed, or muscle, or sharp teeth to tear an enemy. But he has a stink! That's his defence and he can save himself with that. The porcupine is slow and very small – very vulnerable to the animals. But he has a defence system – he has sharp quills. That's part of the gifted defence for him to survive. Each animal has his own. Our ancestors believed that all animals developed shamanism, they believed they had a spiritual connection that was partially similar to humans. They don't pray like humans, but they have a mind. If a person spends thirty-five years studying animals, they begin to understand these animals are intelligent.

Polar bears and black bears are the very closest to the Native way of behaviour. They follow the seasons – they have their routine. There is a time when they are dangerous and there are times where they are not so powerful. But they always have that keen sense of detecting danger. A polar bear sometimes can know, will understand, will feel the enemy which is a human. They will feel it before they see it, before they hear it, before they smell it. That is a gift in them. Most have that. Caribous and wolves have a high sense of that. The wolf socializes in a pack – the caribous move in herds. They usually have a leader. In a way, they have shaman power. The caribou herd will be safe because of the leader. He knows when there is danger – when to move, when to run away – he is a sentry. Sometimes there are two or three leaders if there is a big herd of forty. If there is ten, there will be one. Native people used to try to detect the leader first and try to outsmart him. Once they kill the leader, the rest will be in chaos and that gives the hunter a chance to take another shot with the bow and arrow.[19]

MITEW COMPETITIONS

There is a particular place which still exists at the mouth of James Bay called Ekwan River. And that's where most of the Omushkegos used to congregate in the spring after the ice breakup. They would create a temporary village where there were so many tipis that, if you stood in the middle of the camp, you would not be able to see the end. Lovers got married then – or they would wait until the fall gathering. And there they also played competitive games – different kinds of physical competition, like short runs, or carrying a heavy load, or jumping, or skipping – anything at all. There was also a tug-of-war amongst the men.

And then there were the mitew who competed against each other to see who was going to be most fantastic. They did impossible things and showed off amongst each other. They could make a stone rise, and hang in the air until they decided to let it drop. And they could break a stick just by looking at it. And also they had a game they called racing across the creek. There was a creek there, about twenty-five feet wide, and it was pretty shallow. People could walk, or run across, but they didn't do that. They had a long stick, like a pool stick. And one young guy who was really strong might say, "What you do is nothing! I'll show you!" So he might take this long stick, put it in water; step on it, and just skim across the creek and back. So he might be the winner. This was what they called a mitew competition. They used their minds to do what they wanted to do.[20]

DEFENCE AND WARFARE:
MITEW POWERS AND THEIR LIMITATIONS

There are many stories which involve tribes sneaking up to attack the nice, peacefully-camping Omushkegos on the coastal region of the James Bay and Hudson Bay – especially when the men were out hunting. They would slaughter those people. For some reason, these were people who just wanted to kill.

Now, what did the Omushkego do for any measure of defence? They used this spiritual stuff they called mitewiwin. A mitew was a gifted defender, a seer, a radar system, a defense system, a leader. The mitew could be depended upon to watch for enemies because he could scan the area, if he was functioning right.

And if another mitew was coming to attack, this intruder sometimes had power to shield his presence and overpower the defending mitew. But sometimes the Omushkego people got caught unexpectedly. Let's take, for example, the American military defence. In World War II, the defence system was radar. Later, there was an airplane, created by the United States, that could shield itself from radar detection. The same situation existed between the First Nations long ago, a long time before they created airplanes, never mind the radar system.

A woman once asked me, "How come the mitew didn't use the power to fight the white man?" I told her that when a mitew and a non-mitew mind met, there was no connection, they didn't communicate. The mitew's power was useless. The white man didn't know about the mitewiwin, so he had no fear of the mitew – unless he began to get scared by the mitew's exhibition of mitewiwin. Some explorers witnessed this and were mystified by the revelation of the mitew power. Our stories talk about this. An old man could be very powerful – he could move the earth – but a young person who was not trained to be, or to fear, a mitew, could simply hit the mitew without any resistance.

This mitewiwin could not be used in wars. It has been tried many, many times, even between the First Nations and the Europeans. Many tribal warriors have said, "I am invisible in this war, I will not be hurt by the bullet." Somehow, it didn't work. Many mitewak who became leaders in armies of warriors died by the bullet and arrow.[21]

MITEW DUELS AND INSULTS

The Europeans had aristocrats, men with power, men with money, men with intelligence and education. They had their honour. You see in the movies that if a guy dishonoured another guy, the other guy would slap his face and challenge him to a duel to defend his honour. So they fought each other for their dignity – with guns, and rules – and whoever died, lost.

It was the same way with shamans. You could insult them very easily! One look into their eye could be an insult and a challenge. But in their duels they did not take a gun and walk ten paces before shooting. No. They walk away – they could be 500 miles apart. They used the power of their minds that they established from their dreams and they fought with their minds.

They could create a beast, a physical beast, that would fight for them, and if one beast died, that mitew who created it would be dead, even though he was 500 miles away. That's how this powerful stuff was – but that was not the way it was supposed to be.

People who get mad and want to strike right away are not good people to deal with. Usually they are not that powerful, but they like to challenge the other guy. A good shaman, a powerful shaman – a great shaman (*kitchi mitew*) – knew he had power. He didn't have to duel with a guy who challenged him – he would just walk away. But if the man kept bugging him when he's out there somewhere, he could get tired and frustrated. Sometimes he would actually get rid of this person by using his power. So that is the negative side of this stuff. It always did exist among the First Nations.[22]

The shaking tent could be used to fight another shaman. A shaman could summon another shaman, who was out there trying to challenge him, by setting up the tent and using his mental power to bring the guy in there. And they competed in the tent. They would tell each other everything they knew, and whoever ran out of items or subjects was the one that was beaten. Then he died out there, died where he was.

Other shamans, who did not use the shaking tent, used only their mind power. They could cause animals to kill someone, or they could make someone go nuts, by using their mind. They could create a beast that was a combination of many dangerous animals, or they could create another world's beast. These shamans could walk on water, or jump into the water and become water themselves – or become a fish, to escape or to do something they wanted. I said earlier that some shamans could project themselves to a place where they wanted to be – that was one way. The other way was to use animals, birds, fish, or underwater creatures. They could use the animals that walk on the ground, the bugs that fly, the bugs that walk, the bugs that are in water. They could use these in many ways.

Let me tell an awful story about a shaman who used a bug to kill his enemy. This is supposed to be a true story and it happened after the European came in. There was a young man who bothered strangers, always provoking them so they would get mad and go after him – then he could exercise his power. This kind of person existed. One time, in early spring, he made fun of an elder. He threw a small bug into the elder's cup as he was drinking, and then he laughed and startled him, and he says, "Look at the bug in your tea!"

The old man looked at it, and he knew who had thrown it in. He just picked out the little bug. This young person went home and forgot all about it. In the fall, he went down to trap. One day he began to feel that he was being watched. By now, the stranger he had made fun of was far away, probably in his own home ground.

So when he went home he knew he was being bothered by someone, and he was going to prepare a defence for himself. He was very hungry, and he asked whoever looked after him there to make a soup for him from some kind of animal. He began to eat, but he wasn't watching what he was doing. All of a sudden a youngster saw a bug running around on his spoon. It was a bug that usually runs around in the water – and the kid says, "Look, in the spoon – there is a water bug!"

And the man didn't even know – he just spooned it into his mouth, watching the kid who was speaking to him. In went the bug. In a few minutes, he just leaned over and vomited blood until he died. People wanted to know what happened and, since he had just come home from trapping, they concluded that he must have strained his lungs walking too far in the cold. As they were preparing to take the body out and put it away, the bug was still there on the ground, in a bit of blood. And the same youngster came in and says, "Look at the bug! That's the bug that went into his mouth!" The bug walked around in the blood, went into the ground, and disappeared. So there is that small item. A few moons ago, the young man had made fun of the elder – he had thrown the bug into his cup and tried to get him scared, and startled him. The old man gently just put away the little bug, but he was insulted. The young man didn't know that and he died from his mistake. This old man hadn't seemed to be a powerful shaman at all – just a gentle going old man. It was believed that he killed the young man in revenge.[23]

PROTECTION THROUGH NON-BELIEF

Not everybody needed to acquire shaman powers. Sometimes they were better off not having them. People would be in no danger if there was no connection. If a powerful shaman was threatening and being very mean to people, he wouldn't be able to bother you if you didn't believe in him. He couldn't do anything to you. That was a good thing about not having any shaman knowledge. The white man didn't know anything – not the ones who came to explore or the people in the Hudson Bay Company – they were just simply doing their business. They were business people, not spiritual leaders. The Christian belief is totally alien from what the Native people had, so the minds didn't connect. The Omushkego tried to use their powers but they didn't work – they didn't work on the priests, and they didn't work on the Hudson Bay managers. So they sort of thought that maybe the Great Spirit was allowing this to happen, that maybe those white people had truly come to stay. But they could use their powers against each other because they had the same connection of mind. This is missing in the European history books and there are very few people still alive who actually remember the stories they have heard.

I think the original establisher of the Christianity, Jesus himself, said, "Turn the other cheek." That wasn't like the old way of saying an eye for an eye. We had that – our ancestors had that eye for an eye way of thinking. If somebody came to harass you and hurt you, you should hurt him back, even kill him in self-defence. But there was also instruction that said you must not use your powers just for the sake of killing a person.

So these are the Omushkego beliefs and practices which were submerged after the Christianity. Many went underground to practice their spiritual belief and practices – they are the ones who remember it. Their neighbours who watched them do it also remember. The last shaman practice in James Bay that we know of was in 1930. That was the last group of people to hold onto the old ways. We just barely heard things in whispers, but we encouraged those who understood to tell us, so that we would know. That is the reason why I am having these stories written down.[24]

STORIES OF POWERFUL MITEWAK

Many shamans searched for immortality, but none of them ever found it. Many of the ones who tried to dream about it turned very bad because they were misled by this stuff. They were led, in this shamanism development, to kill people. The Omushkego people believed that when they killed an animal for food, if they respected this animal properly, it would give its life up to them every day. These shamans who got misled dreamed that if they took a person's life, this would extend theirs. That's what they thought: my life will be longer if I take this man's life. Many people were misguided by that wrong interpretation of the dream – it was evil that influenced this.

Some mitews believed they had to kill a person every certain number of years to extend their life. There are stories about this. There's a story about a man who killed his wives. By the time he was old enough to marry for the first time, he was being bothered by this dream that if he didn't kill a man immediately, he would die. So, to extend his life, he killed his wife. Then he married another lady after that. They say he killed five wives. When he got older he stole a young girl, about six years old. His mother took pity on the child. When she became a teenager, the man wanted to marry her. His mother knew that he had killed five of his wives and, because she loved the girl so much, she made her son promise her he wouldn't kill this one. So he made the promise and, therefore, didn't kill the girl. He did kill other people – usually women, although he could have killed a man. They say this happened after the European came because this man had a gun, a muzzle loader, and a steel axe – they are mentioned in the story. So that's the story of a terrible part of this shamanism development.[25]

ENDURING PRACTICE AND BELIEF

Even today some elders are afraid that someone may use shaman powers for offensive reasons. For at least fifty years after Christianity came about, most elders and middle aged men practised their own spirituality secretly. Those were people who had, through dream quests, developed gifts for their survival, or for good hunting – to master the animals.

By the 1930s the last of them died – the best ones. Since then we have not heard that any person around the coastal region is openly practising his ancestral spiritual beliefs. We have not heard anyone using drums for those reasons. We have not heard of any person using the shaking tent since the last one died somewhere around 1935. But we can say very easily today that some elders still believe in and fear shamanism because it still exists somewhere – just not in the open. Some people brag about it openly and pretend to have it, just to scare people. But they are lying. A true shaman could never brag or openly talk about it – it's a secret thing, very private.

They had to keep everything to themselves unless they had to use it to benefit other people – they could share that.

MITEW MAGICAL TRAVEL – NOT SO LONG AGO

Now I am going to talk about another person. He received Christianity when he was old, but, before that, it is rumoured that he had acquired the mystical powers which we call shaman powers. Then he managed to set it aside and embraced the Christianity. In this story, he was camping about a hundred miles away from the closest community, and about two hundred miles away from a second community which had a trading post. He had a wife and children and he was getting to be aged – he was somewhere around fifty but, in those days, men were durable and some of them kept their youth longer because of their activity and good health. This man was extraordinarily healthy.

According to his children, he told his wife that he wanted to go to get tobacco. His family wanted to have the ordinary tea that came from the trading post – it was a luxury item for the Native people in those days. So he decided to take a trip to get those items. They were very light so he didn't have to take a toboggan or any other carrying equipment.

Seems the man could travel a long distance in one day, just by walking and carrying his gun and axe. Anybody could travel sixty miles a day with good snowshoes, as long as there is not deep snow. And every man in those days knew every muskeg region, and every creek, and every open space. Those people understood the land so well that they could just pick out the nice places when they wanted to go somewhere. But he was intending to cover four hundred miles, round trip! It was a bit odd to his family, but his wife never questioned him – she just said farewell to him and advised him to take care – and the children said good-bye. She wasn't worried because she knew that he was capable of anything. So he left early in the morning, walking in the direction of the trading post. He didn't say when he's going to be back. The children knew which direction he went. And the night fell and they just forgot about him. But only two nights later the old man arrived home from his trip, bringing the tea and tobacco! Nobody asked where he went – they waited for him to tell the story.

So finally, as he was having tea with his wife, he talked about friends they knew who lived in the nearest community – a hundred miles away. He said he had stopped and talked with them on the first day of his trip. Right away his wife understood the distance but she didn't question anything. All she says is, "How were they?" And he said they seemed to be doing well – they were all healthy and it was nice to see them. And he says, "Then I went on. I stopped along the way – before I reached the trading post – to set up my camp and then I turned back to the settlement where I wanted to go." For whatever reason, he had flown past the site. The place where he camped was quite a distance for the ordinary person. So he said, "I went to the settlement to buy my items and, close to the noon hour, I returned after visiting a few friends. I returned to my camp and spent a second night. And then I left my camp and got here." This was what he said to his wife, and she just say, "Great – that's nice."

A few days later the next door neighbours, who also had children, found out that the old man had done this and they were wondering how an old man could cover such a distance so fast. And the neighbours' older children were very curious too. They were old enough to travel and the boys were training to hunt, so they knew what travelling in the wintertime entailed. So listening to the old man talk about his trip, they were doubtful – no one could cover such distance in so short a time. So they went to investigate his trail.

They followed his trail up to a lake which was quite large, probably about a mile and a half long and, maybe, half a mile wide – that shape. Usually that sort of lake has very hard snowdrifts – and sometimes just bare ice. It was that lake that he walked across, they said. And along the pathway to that lake, his trail just seemed to disappear – as if he didn't walk there any more. They went all the way around the lake and couldn't find no trail – they re-checked the snowshoe marks and re-checked them again. They also found his returning tracks on that same spot. They could not understand and could only conclude that his tracks must have drifted over.

But as soon as they told their parents – those next-door neighbours – that they couldn't find no tracks of him, they said, "Stop looking. The old man has mystical powers which carry him where he wants to go." So that's the story about this man. He lived to be a very respected elderly person. So that's the end of this person.

He was the last man known to have utilized mystical powers. Some of the elders that I knew a few years back talked about him

– most of them are gone now. They said they never saw him but they knew about him because he was famous. He performed a deed that nobody could understand. Some people didn't want to believe it and said he must have stashed away the tea and tobacco somewhere nearby. But the thing is, later on in the summer, when the families got together again, the very people he said he met – the ones he said he saw along the way – they talked about him without being questioned. They said, "We were so surprised to see him there in our camp last winter when he was on his way to buy tea and tobacco!" And there were a few other people who had seen him in the trading post, in the trade store. All he had said was, "We're short of tea and tobacco." And this was the only thing that people could remember – they couldn't remember the date.

MITEW OR CHRISTIAN, ONE OR THE OTHER?

So there we have it. There are many, many kinds of stories like this that pop up. The reality is that a person has to accept either the Christianity or the other faith. If one denies his faith, denies the first spiritual belief, and takes the other, he cannot just practise the same way as he did before. This was impossible according to the beliefs and teaching of the First Nations. You must leave it behind if you join the other faith – and you cannot use it unless you are really are a master deceiver, showing yourself to be a Christian but really retaining your old spiritual practices.[26]

Wihtigos and Cannibal Hearts

Wihtigo. It was something that happened among humans. It means an other-than-human was created from an ordinary human – and sometimes maybe not. There is a question there. There were many kinds.

There is a wihtigo that was created by starvation – humans starved, went crazy, and ate human flesh when it was decayed. Some of us have experienced how awful the human body smells when it's decayed. If you eat human flesh in that condition, of course, you poison your system – but you survive it, it doesn't kill you because your stomach is empty and it can digest anything – and you condition yourself to eat that. And you become a wihtigo – and that wihtigo is very evil.

Another wihtigo was created when a person was driven extremely insane. People lost their human consciousness and were driven to become a wihtigo by another human's abuse – if, for example, a man had a wife who he abused, and beat, and starved. There is a certain point when the mind can not tolerate any more and when that limit is reached it turns chaotic, and then it turns really crazy. A person turns crazy. Sometimes the person actually became an other-than-human and he was not normal anymore. Automatically such a person would want to retaliate and hurt or kill someone. A person who got that way was very dangerous.

Other wihtigos are not understood – it is not known where they came from. One of those is our famous friend the Sasquatch – Big Foot, you name it. These are also in the wihtigo category – they are other-than-human but they were never humans.

There are many kinds of wihtigo that people have experienced. Some Omushkego people actually found a dead wihtigo – it was a terrible thing to find. People who tried to describe how awful it is were not able to do very well, even though the sight stayed in their mind for a long time, because they were always afraid to see it again.

And then another kind came if someone mistreated an orphan – they could create a wihtigo – this child could just take off, become inhuman, and come back to haunt them or even kill them. Sometimes they had the opportunity to kill your whole family. That's why wihtigos were very terrible. The wihtigo which was once human was way worse than the others – especially the ones who were driven to it.

This was many years before the European came. People over-populated the land and over-hunted. They sort of drove themself into starvation. And then some of them became wihtigo – they started to eat each other – many became cannibalistic.

Some of those who became wihtigo were mitews who were capable and powerful, and they became the worst kind of wihtigos – they were cannibals and mitews at the same time. They were not easily killed.

And there were others who became half wihtigo and half human – they were not as bad because they only ate humans once in a while. They became physically cold – their hearts became ice and they didn't care about the cold weather. They could exist. These were what they called the ice-hearted wihtigo, and they were very, very hard to kill. Only a powerful shaman could contact them, and fight them, and kill them. And whenever they killed this kind of wihtigo, they had to cut it in small pieces, take the heart out, really burn every piece, and then burn the heart, if they could. But many times, when only that heart was left, their fire could not keep on going – it wanted to snuff out. The heart was tough, and only when it had finally burned had they completed their destruction of the ice-hearted wihtigo.

Other wihtigo, who did not have the ice-heart, were just as powerful, and evil, and scary – but powerful mitews who had enough dream quests in their development managed to fight them off. The more powerful the mitew who turned into a wihtigo, the more dangerous and feared that wihtigo would be.

Some people, in the distant past, became only half wihtigo and then it was possible for them to live among humans. They were half normal and half cannibalistic. But once they tasted human flesh, they always craved it. Those kind of people were not very nice to have around. At certain times there would get to be too many of these half-wihtigo people and it was not safe. That was when the people would get together to organize some kind of extermination process – they would hire a person who could kill them.

And this is a legend. Those kind of wihtigo lived an ordinary life with humans, ate ordinary food – but they always needed human flesh. They would kill, and then separate from the ordinary people. They were very a nasty people to be around and it was not safe to live amongst them. A mitew who was powerful – who had enough dream power – could overcome them and kill them so the people could live peacefully again.

And there were other monstrous wihtigos who were able to live without their hearts being in their bodies – people who live with their hearts apart from their self. They left their hearts on a scaffold or in some other safe place, and then they wandered off to live like ordinary people. But actually, they ate people. This kind was very hard to kill, but it did happen once in a while – someone was able to get rid of them. There are some stories that are so extraordinary it was impossible to believe them. But they came to be looked at as legends.[1]

At other times disease covered the land of animals, mostly among the wolves and small four-legged animals – not necessarily the big game animals. Sometimes the wolves were known to be sick – today we know this is rabies, but a long time ago the disease could be within the animals for a long time and it would begin to affect their growth – their genetic makeup went haywire. Sometimes a giant wolf, who was full of disease and really evil, would clean out the land and kill people. Maybe it was one of the Great Spirit's ways of maintaining the population of the area. People have said that. But after the European arrived, this dwindled because the Europeans introduced their food products, which helped a lot.[2]

BECOMING A WIIHTIKO

When we have asked the elders why people became wihtigos, they said it was a controlling system – they said that maybe the Great Spirit saw things that had to be cleaned up. When there were too many people, they over-hunted and then starved. And then the starving people sometimes became cannibals – and then it was time to clean. It comes from a strong teaching of conservation – that you didn't kill any animal just for the sake of killing, you kill the animal for use, and you use it all. It was a very strong teaching.

We have talked about cannibal wihtigos and people who became wihtigo from over-abuse. Some people used to abuse their own family member, or sometimes a family would pick out one member that they really took advantage of and mistreated – maybe one of the children or an elder, like a grandmother. Those people committed what we called a sin against nature – our word is *pastahowin*.

Sometimes this grandmother, for example, turned into a wihtigo. She just walked away and she was no longer a human – she was more spirit than human, and very bad. She could be terrifying, she could kill, she could exist without any food, and she could do almost anything she wanted. And sometimes, for revenge, she would punish the people who mistreated her – and that's a certain kind of wihtigo, a very terrible one too. She didn't actually have to eat people, but she was terrifying. And then eventually she would somehow just simply disintegrate – just disappear somewhere. And where did she go?

People have been trying to find that out for a long time. They followed the track but it just went in a circle that got smaller and smaller until there was nothing. That's a mystery our people have never been able to explain.

BURNING WIHTIKOS

The belief was that, if a person experienced a shortage of food for some time, he lost his mind and that led him to have a delusion where he saw humans as animals to eat. To fill his stomach, he ate human flesh – he was already crazy – and he never regained his right mind. His mind was destroyed and he would always crave human flesh, even after the famine was over. He could survive with the beaver and fish, and behave like an ordinary person, but the need to eat human flesh would be so strong. It was just like being an alcoholic who thinks he'll be okay as soon as he can get a little alcohol in his system. And that's the way things were at that time.

And when a person got into that state, he was numb – he didn't have no more feeling. And his heart became like ice – he had no sympathy, no sense of right, no human richness. Eating human flesh was all that counted and he had the evil in him. The evil was so powerful that people would feel it right down to bottom of their spine, if the person was near. And their voice was so terrible that it made you pass out. They usually knocked their victims out that way – they just yelled at them loudly or shrilly and they just went down – passed out. That was the moment when they killed you, usually by hitting you with a stick – that's how they attacked people, those cannibals. So that is why a person who had to fight them needed more power of good than their power of evil.

They burned them because they were such extraordinarily bad things that their hearts were made of ice rather than flesh. That's why, when they told a story, they would say at the end, "All that remained was a heart of ice." That heart was hard to burn – some people used to cut it out with an axe. And any blood had to be cleaned – everything – any clothing, everything had to be burned right down to the ash. And then the people would avoid that area for a long time, some years, until it had healed over and everything.

ANWAY AND THE CANNIBALS

Indian stories always contain shamanism – that is the most interesting part of the story, especially when a young person is listening, because shamanism was not obvious amongst the people. You did not see the shaman – you could not recognize him at first glance. Shamanism was necessary for people to survive on the land. The only problem was that, just like today, if you considered yourself better than the next person you tended to be overconfident and threaten people with your acquired powers. It depended on a person's character. If he was aggressive, he used his shaman power aggressively and he was a very bad person to associate with because he abused his powers to subdue his fellow man. These people were feared, and even despised amongst their own people.

But those who acquired and mastered total shaman power were the best people. They were the kindest and most respected and admired people because they did not take advantage of their powers. Rather, they put them to good use. Again, it depended on character. If a person had a good character and a kind disposition, he used his power for good purposes – for healing, if he was a medicine man, or to be a good hunter, provider, and defender for his family and his group. It didn't necessarily have to be a man – at times women acquired such shaman power and put it into a good use. And these people became leaders and were looked up to. People usually asked for their help whenever it was necessary.

Once upon a time, when the cannibals were too many, there was a cry for a solution from the area people. So the elders and the wise men got together to discuss the situation and seek solutions. Most of them had acquired some shamanism, so they decided use the shaking tent to seek outside help from somebody with the shaman power capable of solving their problem. Because those cannibals were once ordinary people with the shaman power, they were terribly feared – and they were not easy to get rid of, because they had the power also.

And so the guy they contacted through the shaking tent was named Anway – he was a Plains Cree. The elders begged him to come to the area and get rid of the cannibals. He was an expert exterminator of cannibals – that was his profession amongst the Indian tribes – and he agreed to come for, I guess, some price.

When he arrived he talked with the elders and asked them how many groups of cannibals there were and where they were located. And this information was made readily available to him, and he began to decide his strategies for eliminating these cannibals.

So the story goes that he did his job and eliminated all the cannibals in the district, and the Crees lived normally after that. That's the end of one story about cannibalism.

One time, in a different area, the same situation happened – there were too many cannibalistic people in the land. To eliminate them, they asked Anway, the expert killer to help. So he arrived and says, "I am here to do the job."

They briefly told him about the situation – how many cannibals there were, and where they lived – and he went on his way to study the matter. What he did was, methodically, as a killer, he went to study each cannibal family. Where did they go? What did they do in their everyday lives? How often did they travel a distance, and where did they go? How many were in each group?

He was told about one large clan in particular: an old man, his wife, and his seven sons. All the men were powerful – they lived like ordinary people, hunting animals and eating their meat – but they were cannibals who just didn't happen to eat people all the time. When they got the urge to eat human flesh they could not resist – they just had to have it. So they would go out to the people and snatch one and take it home. Anway went to study this family thoroughly.

Five of the seven sons were married and had kids, and the old man, who was the leader, also had his wife with him – so the clan had about seven tipis. Every day he went to watch, always at a distance. After many days he began to plan his actions. He decided to approach the weakest one first.

He went to the old man who was hunting close by the camp – he usually didn't go far. There was an old beaver house with no beavers in it – they had all been killed because there was a shortage of beavers in the area. Still, sometimes an old house will still have one old beaver living there still, and the old man was hoping to find something like that because they needed to eat something besides human flesh. Anway saw him walking towards that house and quickly ran ahead so that he'd already be there when the old man arrived. He knew the sons would be far away, hunting, so he went to meet this old guy in the old sagging beaver dam. As Anway stood there, the old man finally appeared from the bush. Anway says, "Niistaw," which means: hi there, my brother-in-law (it's an informal greeting that was used by men when they met but didn't know each other).

Now this Anway was a big, strong, healthy young man – but his power was very deceiving. He had made himself look like a near frozen, starving old man. The old cannibal didn't know where this stranger came from, but he said, "Hi visitor!" He was startled, and that's exactly what Anway wanted. Actually, in that instant, Anway had beat him already – his mind had tricked the old man and he was confused.

Anway says, "Well we better get prepared – you know how curious beavers are!" The old cannibal knew there was nothing in there – maybe one beaver, if anything. But he played along with

Anway and thought, "We can get rid of him very easily." He saw Anway as a meal. So they checked the dam and found water leaking. The old man, the cannibal, was wearing a poncho made of caribou hide, so Anway says, "Could I borrow your poncho so I can block this water?" And the old man says, "Yeah, yeah – why not?" So Anway just stuck it in the hole and said, "There, that should do it – that should hold the water for tonight, and by morning there should be enough water."

The old wihtigo was just stumped, and he thought, "Crazy man! There is no beaver in here! Well, let him think that way." By now it was getting dark, so Anway says, "Be here tomorrow just at sunrise. I'll be here and we will just block the house and spear the beavers." So the old man said okay and they said good bye and good night, and away the old man went.

When the old man got home he forgot all about what had happened. He saw his wife and she began to cook, because all the men in the family had a habit of eating together. So they all had a good meal and as they sat and talked to their father, they asked him, "How was your day?" And he says, "Well nothing – what did you expect? We just made a camp and we been here." And it was just before they were going to go back home to sleep that he remembered and he says, "I met a man just down the creek – you know, where the dam is – that's where I met this old guy." And the boys says, "Who is he? Do you know him?" And he says, "No, I never seen the man, but he called me brother-in-law."

And right away the oldest brother says, "You know, you may have been tricked. Anway is supposed to be around here somewhere – to kill us off. Could have been him." They all get excited but the old guy said, "No, you haven't seen the man! The guy was so old and poor – he was almost froze to death and starving. He's probably died by now! Nothing to fear – just a little poor old guy." But the more he described this person, the more they believed it was him. They knew Anway was very tricky and could make himself look like that. But the old man said, "No! No! I would have known if he was Anway, you know – I have my ways of knowing about these things."

So, anyways, the morning came. The old man's sons hadn't been able to sleep – they just didn't have a right feeling. And so he called them and says, "Well, let's go before sunrise – if he's there, we'll just hit him over the head and have a good meal out of him."

So they followed their father and had a feeling something was not right. And, sure enough, when they got close to the beaver house, there ahead waited a big powerful looking man, well dressed, and chiselling away the ice. And his chisel had both ends sharp. And they started, "You see! I told you he's Anway!" "Let's go back!" "Let's spread out and attack him from both sides!" And then Anway turned around and pretended he hadn't heard them. "Come on, come on," he says, "you're right on time!"

They could not show any fear, so they just had to walk right up to him. He was such a strong looking man that they know for sure he was Anway. What his next move would be was what they didn't know! So Anway says, "Tell your sons to go get us sticks while we chisel this ice out from around this house." And the old wihtigo says, "Come on, sons – do what he says!"

Reluctantly they went, whispering to each other, "We'll go and get his sticks – and then we'll kill him!" They went as quickly as they could – Anway had made it so they would have to go a long way to find sticks. While they were away, Anway chiselled a big hole in the ice. He was getting sweaty, and the old guy too.

"Well, it's kind of warm!" says Anway. He pulled his shirt open and got down one one knee to drink the cold water. And as he opened his shirt, there was hair on his chest. The wihtigo was startled because a hairy chest was a powerful sign. He knew then that this really was Anway and that he was there to kill them. By this time there was no point in backing down. The only hope was that they could overpower him.

Right at that moment there was a chance for him to stab Anway, but he knew Anway could see him reflected in the water. After he was finished drinking, Anway said, "Well, that was great! Okay, your turn." The old man was reluctant, but he pulled his shirt open – the ribs stuck out on his chest because he was so old – and he kneeled down to drink the water. Anway just struck him right behind the neck and shoved him under the ice – but just before he pushed him in, the old man whispered, "The man is killing me!" That's all he said, and he just spoke in a whisper – but in that instant his sons heard him – telepathy.

So they all turned around, grabbed a stick, and ran back to save their father. The oldest arrived first, but his father was gone – and Anway was ready with his chisel. He just stabbed him with it and killed him instantly. Another two arrived and he did the same thing

– and he took his bow and arrow to a fourth. And when he finished these three, he tackled two more who were coming towards him – he met them and just shot them, one at a time. And the last son that came was the most vicious one – he had the most power. He threw the stick he was carrying as if it was an arrow. It nearly hit Anway, so he just grabbed his bow and shot him. And then Anway saw one of the old man's grandsons who used to tease people and be really mean. He had climbed up a tree to try and get away, but Anway shot him in the leg, and he says, "This is for the people that you used to be so mean to – this is what they felt!" And the boy was screaming and almost falling out of the tree – and Anway shot him again – in the bum. He finally fell to the ground, where Anway shot him in the heart. And then, finally, the youngest grandson came and kneeled down and begged for mercy. So Anway says. "How many times in your life did you let people live when they begged you to spare their lives?" And the boy says, "Never." So Anway killed him, and that's the end of the men.

As Anway ran back to the to the beaver house, he knew the old lady would be coming behind – that was the usual thing, because she would have to cook whatever the men killed. He knew, though, that it would be some time before she appeared. So he sat down at the beaver house and pretended to be watching for beaver. When the old lady appeared with her daughters, and daughters in law, and servants, he looked up and said, "Come on! Come on! You're right on time!" She noticed that there was nobody else around so she asked, "Where is my husband?" Anway pretend not to hear. "Where is my husband? What have you done to my husband?" And she knew already. Anway said, "Your husband's bum is right there – sticking out of the ice!" She looked and – yes – sure enough, her husband's bum was sticking out from the hole.

She turned to her little toboggan and pulled out a stone that was used to pound meat into powder, and she says, "I'm going to kill you!" She let fly the stone, so expertly and so powerfully that it was fast as a bullet – so fast that Anway didn't have much time to duck. She grazed him on his head.

He says in a curse, "The old lady almost killed me!" So he grabbed that stone and did exactly the same thing, but she ducked. He threw it again and again, but every time the old lady ducked and ducked. Finally he walked up to her and hit her over the head with a stone – and down she went. Then Anway grabbed this bow and arrows and says to the group, "Those who are captives, step aside!" Many women stepped aside, and he began to shoot the cannibal women.

So he killed all the cannibals in that group. There would have been maybe fourteen or fifteen, plus their captives. That was the first batch that he killed. And then he said to the captive women, "Now you're free. We will have to cut up all these bodies. I will drag them over to this big pile of wood and we will have to burn them. We will cut the bodies in pieces, in the usual custom, to make sure they don't come alive again." So they cut up the bodies and put them into the fire. They all began to burn, and finally the old man's body was pulled out of the water and they cut his and his wife's body up also. And while they were stirring the ashes to make sure everything had burned, they noticed the hearts were still there, whole – because they were full of ice. So they kept the fire going for a long time and finally they finished the job and everything was burned away.

So that was the customary way to execute wihtigos. That's how they made sure that they didn't come back to life again. So that was the end of that.[3]

THE MITEW AND THE CANNIBAL HEARTS

This story probably happened before the Anway story. The particular cannibals in this story were very fantastic and more fearsome than the ordinary cannibals we talked about in the Anway story. These cannibals, it's said, were hard to get rid of. Many an exterminator simply couldn't kill them. They were somehow able to take their hearts out of their body and preserve those organs – so the hearts pulsed separately from the bodies. They say that if you hit and kill one with an arrow or an axe, you would inflict damage in its body all right, but later on it would get up and walk away alive, because you did not actually kill it. Its heart was still alive and its body mended itself.

It is said that they made a special scaffold where they camped. They kept their hearts in a special basket that was made of down feathers and was very warm and well insulated. They kept the basket on this scaffold, and they lived just like ordinary people, eating animal food – only they also ate human beings. They would kill their own next door neighbour, if the neighbour didn't realize what they were – the ordinary person without shaman power would not know readily; he would think that these were just ordinary people. And so this went on for some years.

Finally the people restricted their movements and avoided the areas where those people were. Once again the situation was so tragic and fearsome, and once again the elders and wise men of the tribes had to discuss the situation. And, therefore, they decided to eliminate these extraordinary cannibals. The exterminator they chose was not Anway – he was a young man who was an orphan who had acquired powerful shaman skills. And he agreed to kill them.

It was said that he went right up to the cannibal camp and turned himself into a small baby that crawled on the ground. He had studied their habits and knew that the young men were away hunting and only the women and old people were at the camp. So he went directly to the heart of the problem by visiting the elders.

In the camp he found an old man, who was the leader, and his wife. Those two elders were just sitting quietly in their home – when in rolled the baby! The old man was so startled that he just grabbed him.[4]

The exterminator, through his power, had contacted the old man through his mind and had already beaten him. That's why the exterminator appeared to the elder and his wife as a baby – helpless, chubby, and very tender to eat. Very tempting! The old cannibal could not help himself – he just had to grab that baby and extinguish its life – as if it were a piglet, or a lamb, or a small chicken. He wanted to roast the baby the same way he roasted an animal or bird – put it onto a roasting stick, put it in the open fire, and roast it as a delicacy – that was the fastest and easiest way to cook this gift! Naturally, they just killed the baby with no question, automatically grabbed the roasting stick, put the little baby onto it, and just leaned him over the open fire. Every once in a while they turned it over to brown evenly.

Once the baby was nicely cooked, and brown, and all that, the exterminator's power caused the old man to change his mind. Instead of eating the baby right away, he took it outside to hang over the scaffold and cool. That was where the pulsing hearts were stored. The old man put the baby on the scaffold and just forgot everything – just completely forgot! He walked into his wigwam and continued his daily existence.

Meanwhile, the apparent baby took himself off the roasting stick and became a man. He set out to find the secret place where the hearts were preserved – and then he opened the basket and saw the fluffy down feathers and those pulsing hearts sitting there. There were at least seven of them, and each one he touched very lightly with the roasting stick. He didn't hear anything and he knew that if he touched the one that belonged to the old man, he would hear him. Finally he touched the right one, and he heard the old man, just a little ways from the scaffold, scream, "Ah!!! Somebody...!" That was all he could say.

He got down from the scaffold and walked into the tipi, as a man, and the elders were so startled that they couldn't do anything but act naturally, as if they were being visited by a stranger. They offered him tea, made him sit in the best spot, the best area of the tipi, and treated him very cordially and respectfully. By this time they were totally beaten by the will power of the exterminator. The old man started to talk about where his sons were hunting and said they would be back later on that evening. From this, the exterminator knew that they would be home soon, so he left.

He went back up to the scaffold and started jabbing those pulsing hearts, one at a time – and as he stabbed each one, its owner just dropped dead on the spot. And that was that – the exterminator had done his job. There is no story about what he did to the females, whether he killed them after he killed the men, but once again there was peace amongst the area people.[5]

ICE HEARTS

This story happened just west of a lake called Washekami. There was a man who was trapping there in that area. He noticed in the fall that someone – some mitew – was bothering his family – and it was aimed at him. People begin to notice this unusual thing, they didn't know what it was, but they knew there was something around them which was evil. So they asked the man, and he told them there was a wihtigo that was sent by someone to bother them. So they says, "Well, get rid of it if you can, because we don't want nothing to do with this!" So he says, "Okay, whenever I can." He was a mitew.

One day he was walking away from the main camp when he felt

the thing following him. So he led it away to this particular muskeg area where there was tundra. He was walking through that, with this wihtigo coming behind him, when he suddenly turned around to see that the wihtigo was ready to grab him. So he just wrestle with that guy and, by the power of this mitewiwin, managed to trip his leg and smash him against the ice. This wihtigo just lay there, not moving. This man had known what he was doing – he had purposely led him onto the hard tundra hoping that, if he fell, the ice in its heart would crack. And that's exactly what happened. The wihtigo couldn't move because its heart was cracked.

The man just let him lay there and went to his trapping. And when he came back to make sure the wihtigo was still there, he saw that it had crawled away to another place to try and dig a hole to bury itself. It was just laying on its stomach in the moss, wounded. So he walked up to it and says, "If you bug me and my family any more, I won't help you and you will die here. But if you promise me that you won't bother us again, I will fix you up." So the wihtigo says, "Yes, please. I want to be healed." So the man just called in his helpers and they healed it. They put the ice back into form and the wihtigo got up and walk away. That's the story.

KETASTOTINEWAN

In Omishkego clanships there were usually about three families. And there was an old person who usually had the most powers to protect the family. And one time there was such a person – his name was Ketastotinewan – it means: hat off – as if you knock someone's hat off. And he was an expert killer of wihtigos.

So it happened that, even though he was so powerful, a wihtigo came into the group to kill them. It first had to find out who was the expert killer. To do that, he caught up with two young people in this family and asked them, "What's the name of the person who kills wihtigo?" So they say, "Oh, Ketastotinewan." So then the wihtigo just made the kids forget they ever saw him.

Later that night he went into the camp, right between the two tipis – and Ketastotinewan was in one of them. So the wihtigo calls from between the tipis, "Hey! You're invited!" So Ketastotinewan started going across to the other tipi and got grabbed by this wihtigo who took him into the bush and overpowered him. Yes, that.

So he was the leader for this family. But Ketastotinewan's wife knew this wihtigo would kill them all. So she put her life on the line – she followed the wihtigo into his camp, took his knife, and slashed him. The family was saved then – even though Ketastotinewan had died.[6]

Women and Men

WOMEN

So we will mention about women. There were some women who became shamans. There were good women who were bright and made very good homes because they were gifted to be medicine women – they were gifted to be healers. Women would train just like men, only, because they weren't strong enough to hunt large game, they did not have to develop those things.[1]

So women were not required to know the full-fledged mitewiwin, they had basic knowledge only. They were gifted to be seers, to develop intuition, and to be gifted healers. They could help people cure, and were also home-makers, small game hunters, and fishers. They knew how to use herbs, and plants, and animal parts to heal.

They also knew how to use the sweatlodge to help people who became dehydrated. For example, if a man walked and ran all day hunting big game, he strained himself very badly – he sweated a lot, lost a lot of water, and over-exercised his muscles. There would usually come a point where they had lost too much water, and became chilled right through the body. Then they could have a fit, like a convulsion (although when they get this far gone it is usually too late to heal them). The women always prepared the sweatlodge in the evening when her husband was due to come home, so it would be ready if he needed it. She prepared lots of water and Labrador tea, which could help avoid convulsions. Sometimes it only took two or three hours for him to recover. She didn't actually have to make a lodge – she only had to cover the man from his neck down and put stones and hot water inside, and a canvas on top so the guy would just sweat and sweat. He had to drink a lot too. So that was about all the sweatlodge was used for.[2]

OUR GRANDMOTHERS' POWERS

There are extraordinary stories about women in the past – our women, our ancestors, our great-great-grandmothers. They were gifted with women's intuition. This intuition was very accurate and they could use it to tell the future.

I know that my grandmother had this women's intuition because she could feel when her son was about fifteen miles away, coming towards home. How did she know that? And she would tell us, "Watch the dogs, they are going to know it too." And then we would go out and, sure enough, the dogs started to make little movements – then they would sit up and stretch and start to bark the way they did when they knew someone was going by. And then we would tell our grandmother, "Yes, they got up." And about two hours later he would arrive.

This was what women could do. They could feel things ahead of time – they could see and have visions. They didn't go out on dream quests as men did because they already had it gifted to them. They were very accurate when they described what was going to happen.

I know an old lady who was able to predict something four months ahead, and it happened exactly as it she described it. Three times in our camp where we were hunting, she predicted something, and it happened. For example, she was just sitting with her eyes closed, but she was fully awake, and she sat up and said, "Why do I have this vision?" And we asked, "What did you see?" And she said, "I saw people traveling towards the community, and they carried a small coffin, a small, white coffin. I don't know who they are, but they were carrying that little, small, white coffin." This was in November. In April, sure enough, a family living up the river brought down a child that was dead, I think about two years old – they carried this little white coffin to the village to be buried. That's how this lady was accurate, and that's the gift of some of the women who lived here.

That's not shamanism, that's different – but there are those ladies who developed shamanism and who were just as powerful as men. Mostly the women were gifted to be healers. When they were young, and as they got older, they had this dream.

One last story before I finish this. There was an old lady who died. Her son's face turned into a rash every April – his skin peeled off and he suffered. She had to just watch him suffer, because there were no hospitals in the bush. And one night, when she couldn't sleep, she sat by her son, trying to cool him off with a cold rag. She fell asleep and, towards dawn, all of sudden she heard a voice. The voice said, "Get up and go to the muskeg. In a little open space you will see some little tamaracks, they are about an inch in diameter. Cut two of those, bring them home, and cut them into blocks about an inch and half long. Take the inner skin, put it into a pan, and boil it. And then, with that water, wash the face of your son – wet every part of the skin that is broken." She did exactly as she was told by the mind, and the next day the boy's face healed – he never had that disease again. This is the truth – but this is not the mitewiwin, it was not a shaman thing – this is a gift that women had and there's many more stories about these things.[3]

WILDERNESS WOMAN

During their dream quests, some people encountered nature – like Thunderbirds, or hurricanes, and twisters – everything that is powerful and scary, they had to encounter in their minds. And one of these was the Wilderness Woman. She was fearsome and beautiful at the same time.

Physically the way they described her, they say she was the most beautiful woman there was – an indescribably beautiful woman. She could travel, she could take you wherever you wanted to go, and she could show you things that you had never seen. And she could bring very beautiful blissful joy – you could be so happy with her. It's like nothing in this world that you had ever experienced. They say it was more than sexual pleasure – it was an indescribable pleasure. Besides being beautiful, she also smelled good. So that's a little description about this woman.

Here is a short explanation from an old man. I asked him, "What is this Wilderness Woman? Did she actually exist?" And he says, "Actually she came to the mind of a person who was practising to have that vision – they could visualize her after awhile. In the wilderness during the summer time, before you saw her, you could smell the beautiful fragrance of flowers. And then she materialized there where there's beautiful flowers – that's where she appeared to you. And then she led you to enjoy that fantasy world where she lived. To the people who experienced her, it was something irresistible."

She could exist in a person's mind if he developed this during his dream quest. Only those who ventured into that dream quest could have her. When you prepared to be a mitew, many things were offered to you, as a young person. You could be invited to become a medicine man, or to be a powerful shaking tent operator, or to have general shaman power of everything. You could stop at any level you wanted, and you were able to understand the materials things on earth.

It was a risk to acquire the vision of her on your own – you had to have the guidance of an experienced elder who knew about this thing. If you did it on your own, or if you were too old – over twenty – it was not advisable for you to try to gain much of this thing. Aiming to get to the Wilderness Woman was very dangerous because it required a lot of fasting and many denials of this physical world. You even had to deny yourself your friends. Then you had to get out to the bush for a long time, go through the other regular procedures, and then go to the level where you could reach that point – where you could encounter the Wilderness Women.

If you were alone, you could get the wrong method of contacting this thing in your mind, and the Wilderness Woman became dangerous – over-possessive of you – and you began to lose your mind. You forgot the actual material world. She became the key person in your life, and you forgot about your friends, and your wife, and children – you just wanted to be in the bush all the time. And every time when you were in your home, when you were trying to provide for your family, she would come to you, she would be there. She would come and demand that you go to her. And that's where it was dangerous because if you refused, she threatened you, and you actually got scared.

My great uncle got hurt from the idea of the Wilderness Woman. He did that. He went against the rule. He was told not to follow the old traditional practices because he was already Christian – he was baptized in a Catholic Church. But when he was young there were many people who were involved in this traditional practice and he was fascinated by it.

So he went against the will of his grandfather and parents and tried to condition himself – he was aiming to reach the point where he could get the Wilderness Woman experience. He was not yet a married person. So he managed to get into that stage by himself, without the precautionary measures.

And then the time came when he got to be married and had children – that meant a lot of home activities to support his wife and family. But very often he was gone into the bush for long periods, without bringing food home, and he got in trouble with his wife. She says, "How come you're always in the bush and you don't bring us the food? You know your kids are now starving." He didn't want to say that there was a person out there, because she wouldn't believe that. And that's when his wife forced him to stay home with her and to look after his children.

Apparently the Wilderness Woman came for him – she went to his home and spoke to him from outside of his tipi. And he had to make an excuse to run outside so he could see her and try to hush her away. He would tell her, "Wait, wait – I first have to do this thing in my home, for my family." And then the Wilderness Women says, "If you want me, you deny them. You come with me to the wilderness and never mind this other stuff." And that's where the trouble began.

So he was trying to satisfy his real family and the Wilderness Woman – but he didn't know how to satisfy both. That's when he began to lose his mind – to go crazy. One time I saw him myself. We were sitting on the shore of the river with other children, my cousins and my sister, just on top of the riverbank. We were playing and the old people were coming in a canoe. Then all of a sudden the old man, who was in the front of the boat, began to paddle away from the shore. And he says, "Wilderness Woman, there she is, Wilderness Woman!" And then he really went crazy. And the old lady was mad. She says, "What do you mean? These are your grandchildren!" That's what I mean when I say it was dangerous.

He was really trying to get away from her then, and he had a big struggle to try to make her disappear from his mind. So what he did was, he turned to Christianity. He prayed more deeply, and all that, and he managed to get away from that, so he was all right. He died as a normal elder.[4]

MORNING STAR, A LOVE STORY, AND THE SPREAD OF THE CREE LANGUAGE

When the Omushkego people realized that their language spread way out to the west, as far as the prairies in Alberta, they asked themselves, how come? How come our dialects stretch out into that far distance? The question remains because nobody knows why.

So the story begins. Once upon a time there was a family in the Omushkego land who were in a very sad state. This married couple couldn't have no baby – every baby was still born, or lived only very briefly. Sure they were very frustrated and they wanted the children so much. The mother wanted to give up but the husband wanted to keep on trying because they wanted a child so much. So they prayed to the Great Spirit to give them a child that would live. They promised to the Creator to do their best to bring the child up into honesty and a good life.

In time the woman conceived again and she did everything not to have another miscarriage – and her prayers were answered. She delivered a baby who was alive and in good health. The mother called her Morning Star. She was happy, and so was her husband. They both loved their child.

Somehow, after she gave birth, the mother got sick – just a year after she had the baby. It was said that the delivery had caused her to become sick, but nobody quite understood why. In due time, she was very sick and a year later she died.

The girl became a beautiful, kind-hearted child. Other children loved to play with her. The mothers around her wished that they had a child so loveable. Her mother's mother, her grandmother, adopted her, which was the custom. Some years later, the grandmother also got sick and she died too. Now only the grandfather survived. The girl knew her mother had died when she was too young to remember, but she had known her grandmother and had gotten to think of her as her mother.

Now the grandma had died and she was broken-hearted. The only person she had left was her grandfather, and he did his best to love the young girl. She had only him to lean on and, when she was sad, she cried on his chest, to find warmth and comfort.

Some years later the girl became teenager. Like others her age, she turned out to be such a beautiful girl. All the boys who had once played with her now wanted her to be their girlfriend. Some parents who had eligible young men wanted to arrange marriage between their son and this upcoming young lady.

In summer the group migrated to the summer camp, which came alive again as people moved on to the open tundra. Two reasons. To get away from the mosquitoes, and because the open tundra provided an easy look-out for enemy attacks. This particular area was known to the Omushkegos as Mooshawow (Cape Henrietta Maria) – it means the barren land. Here are ridges that are actually sandbars, covered with lichen, white moss, and the tundra's wild flowers which give off a sweet fragrant scent, or a perfume. On these ridges you can see variety of colours of flowers, plants and local fruit plants in blossom. At the summer season, it's almost like heaven on earth because, in June and July and August, these plants produce flowers with colours and beautiful smells. The Omushkego men said the smell belonged to the beautiful Wilderness Woman – they seldom stayed home during this time, they went to the other ridge to see the beautiful colours and smell the flowers. When they came home, they would pin some of these nice smelling flowers on their wives' clothes or in their hair. It was in this season that this girl lived amongst the people. She blossomed like the wild flowers on the land, and for that reason all the young men wanted her to be theirs. Unfortunately she had a different priority – she wanted to look after her grandfather.

As it happened, the old man was now sick – he had a coughing disease, perhaps tuberculosis. That was the time the Omushkego would have developed tuberculosis which, when it was bad, could kill them in no time. He was going fast during the summer months and he knew that his time was near. He told his beloved granddaughter to be prepared in case he went.

One day a stranger arrived in the camp, a young man. As usual, as soon as the elders knew that he was not a danger, they accepted him as a visitor. In a matter of time the young women become aware of the young visitor. He was actually a mature man, fully capable of survival. He was from the west on the *mushkootew* – means the prairie land. The elders liked to ask him about his homeland and about the lands he had passed through – all this brought fascination to the Omushkegos because they had heard of the land to the far west, and of the rugged mountains.

Some young men, who were the same age, loved to hunt with this stranger and he gladly went along. Yes, he was a good hunter – his arrows flew straight and hit the target. Yes, the young Omushkegos admired his skills. The young boys liked to watch him play games with the other young men – he was good at sports. The girls they simply adored him. They wished he could be their husband in the near future and they all talked about this young visitor from the west.

In time, the Morning Star heard about that eligible young man, but, unfortunately, she was too preoccupied with taking care of her grandfather, the only loving person she knew. She had missed her grandmother terribly when she died, and now it seemed like she was going to lose her grandfather. She never wanted to waste her time doing anything but attending to his needs. She knew he would die in a matter of time. The story of the young man didn't affect her much, although she had become slightly aware of the opposite sex.

One day she was very busy – she had to carry drinking water to the camp from a stream that had fresh cold water, some distance away. That's where everybody got the drinking water. She walked there with her animal skin water bag and, as she turned to walk home, she saw a man she had never met before – tall, strong, and good-looking. He was standing by the stream, looking at the horizon. Quickly she walked home, carrying her water bag.

Soon the old man got sicker and he knew he would die soon. One day he talked to his granddaughter and said, "Child, I am going to die soon. Like your grandmother, I am old, I will not live forever. We are all going to die, but you are my grandchild. The only thing I regret about dying is leaving you here." The girl sat beside the grandfather's bed and held his hand. "No, you're not going to die. You're not going to leave me here alone!" she cried. The grandfather said, "No I will not leave you here alone. Someone will take care of you even better than I have done."

In past summer seasons the old man had been approached by some parents of the local boys who wanted to adopt his granddaughter if he died. He never told her about these things. They had brought up the subject of arranged marriages for his granddaughter and he had never said anything to agree or to disagree. He had only listened to the well-intentioned individuals speak on the subject. All he had said was, "I will know when the time comes."

Now was the time. That was why he talked to his only grandchild, who felt more like his own child than his grandchild. So he said to her, "My granddaughter, you have been the only reason I wanted to live this far. Now I am old – I cannot take care of you. You have been very nice to me – you always obeyed everything I told you to do. You have loved me and now I want to thank you and give you my blessing, before I get too sick to think straight."

He took her hand and put his hand on her head and said, "May the Creator bless you. May the Great Spirit bless you and protect you. May you find love and be loved as you have loved me. May the Great Spirit give you the kind of love every woman longs for. The love you have for me shall be repaid to you many times over because you have respected me as your own parent. There will be love for you, my child, love which you will enjoy on earth. There will be a man who will love as much I have tried to love you. But this man will be your husband, and you shall love him much more than you have loved me. Soon he will show himself to you – you will decide. That is my blessing." And here, they say, the old man died peacefully beside his granddaughter.

Relatives all came to the last respects for the old man. These people had known him as a kind and loving person and came to support the girl during her grief period. There was a farewell ceremony, singing, and a mourning period – and then the burial ceremony. All people attended.

When it was over and the people left the graveyard, the girl remained on the grave. She spoke to her grandfather as if he was still alive. With tears as in her eyes she said, "What am I going to do, grandfather? What will happen to me?"

As if he were actually speaking, she heard a voice. "Do not weep young girl, you shall be protected as I have promised. You will be happy. Take your head up, look around." At the same time she felt a hand touch her right shoulder – it was strong and felt kind. She turned around slowly to see who had come to her in time of her grief and sorrow, and she saw a man – a tall man with a kind voice. "Sit, let me help you."

At that moment she remembered the man she had seen at the spring, and she remembered the girls who had described him. Here, at her lowest moment, came the words of her grandfather. She dried her tears and said thank you to the man. With his kind smile he offered to walk her to her new home in her aunt's tipi, but she had to go to her grandfather's home to get her things out before the tipi was dismantled. And she says "yes" to this young man.

So they walked. Again the grief threatened to come back to her and she restrained from crying because the man was there. He offered to create a fire and make a drink for her, and she said "okay." While he was warming up the drink, a lady came in and asked the girl if she should dismantle the lodge now or later. The girl said, "Not now." The woman was her aunt who had taken it upon herself to become the foster parent of the girl. Morning Star was now sixteen – full grown in body, but inexperienced in nature – she had not yet been fully responsible for her own life.

She asked the young man who he actually was. Where did he come from? How long since he had left home? Why all this? So they stayed together awhile as he gathered her personal belongings and bundled them up. So they went to her aunt's tipi. He asked if he could see her again. And she said yes.

Next day the old man's tipi was taken down, with the help of the Morning Star. During that summer season she became friends with the young man from a distant land. One day he asked her if she would marry him. She said, "I don't know, I have to ask someone if it's okay." The young man said, "You are on your own now. You're the only one to say no or yes." She actually did not know what marriage was all about – she knew she would have to stay with the man and have children, but, besides that, she had no idea. She told her aunt and her aunt said, "It is up to you. Do you like the man?" And she said she did – so there it was.

She went to see her grandfather's grave again and speak to him. She said, "Grandfather, you have told me that someday I will marry and have children of my own. Shall I agree to marry this man?" She kneeled there a moment. Somehow the sweet smell from the flowers seemed to intensify, and the voice of her grandpa said, "Yes, you shall marry the man, you will be taken care of by him. You will find love in, and with, him." As she got up, a strong hand helped her – there was that man again. Without him saying a word, she said, "Yes, I will marry you."

The joy in his eyes and in her being seemed to wash away all the grief she had felt since her grandfather died. They married on the open tundra where the sweet smelling flowers seemed to give out their intensive smell to bless the marriage. One day her husband said, "Shall we return to my home?" By this time Morning Star loved her husband dearly, just as her grandfather had promised, so she said, "Wherever you go shall be my home. Wherever you go I always follow you. I am your wife."

A few days later, after preparation, they said farewell to the small clan she belonged to. The next day the Morning Star set out towards west.

The travel seemed to take only a few days, but in reality it took many moons before they reached his homeland. Finally, at the top of a hill, they looked down into a valley and saw many tipis. He pointed at them and said, "That is my home." And she says, "What is going to happen to me? How can I communicate? I speak my language and they'll not understand me." So her husband said, "Don't worry, I will speak for both of us." And then she was happy.

When she reached the camp, she was welcomed. And she was well loved because she was very kind woman, and beautiful. They lived happily and had many healthy children who eventually got married themselves.

By now, they were beginning to be an aged couple, but they were still healthy and having joy in life. And then one day when they were by themselves on the hill, walking, she looked towards east and said, "There is my home. Do you remember I told you that I wanted to walk to that place again?" And he says, "Oh no! Not at this time in our lives. We are not young anymore – it will be almost impossible to walk there." But he gave in, and he says, "Let me think, maybe we can go."

They traveled back east. She had been so happy when she was first married that she hadn't even felt all that travel. Now she was much older and she felt tired – but at the same time she was as happy as she had ever been. She still loved her husband as dearly as ever. And they traveled in the places they had walked through when they were just married and so in love with each other – and they caught that feeling again. And then finally, after many moons, they reached their destination.

They came to the forest region, and they came to the wilderness, and they reached the rivers that flow into the great salt-water Bay – and they finally reached the coastal region. They found the area where she'd lived – she eagerly approached the temporary village with her husband and found it just as it had been before she'd left.

They were greeted by the same people who had been young when they had married, but who were now as old as they were. And there were new members of the group. They welcomed them and they had a little feast. This was in the month of June. She wanted to stay there during the summer – so they stayed.

And she told the story about their journey towards his home in the west – how unforgettable it was. She talked about going from the tundra area into the deep forest – about how they had spent the winter in the forest area, and then finally reached the prairie land, the grass land.

And she described the prairie land, and the beasts that roamed in the prairie – beasts with shaggy hair on their shoulders and heads, and little horns, and very skinny behinds. And she described how many there were. "So, so many," she says. "sometimes they made the hills black." And she said how they had to move so slowly and carefully amongst them in order to go on with their journey. Some days they found other, much smaller, herds. One time, she said, the beasts were disturbed by a thunder storm which seemed to shake the ground, and she told how the lightning had actually set fire to the grass and had caused the whole herd of shaggy haired beasts to stampede. She described how the land thundered and rumbled when the beasts ran. And she described how she trembled and had to be held by her husband for protection. All this she described. She said that the prairie land is so vast that it took days to cross.

And then she described the tribes that moved along with the herds for their food – the men who hunted these shaggy beasts she calls them. She talked about how they used to hide from them because her husband knew that, if they saw them, there was a danger of her being snatched by the men – because she was beautiful. So he did his best to hide her and sometimes went out to lead them away from her.

All those stories were full of love, and joy, and adventure. And as they traveled, she had asked her husband if, some day in the future, she could travel the same land again to return to her home. She also asked him that she be allowed to speak her own language wherever they went, and to teach her children the language she grew up with. He had promised all these things because they were so much in love and nothing seemed to matter. The land seems to be all theirs to see.

Somewhere around July an unfortunate thing happened. A disease had emerged again, the year before, and was still with them. It was not spreading quickly but people who caught it usually just died very quickly – although some of them suffered for long time. Unfortunately, she got this disease and was very sick. Soon she was deteriorating within and she started to cough yellow pus and, sometimes, blood. She couldn't eat and she got weaker. One night she dreamed that she would die, and told her husband, "I will not be going home, I think this is it." So he said, "Well at least we did what we wanted to do. If this thing has to happen, then it will." She says, "We will take it as it is."

In the first week of August she died, at the same summer camp where her grandfather had died – almost the same month, when the wild flowers were in bloom and smelling beautiful, and the birds began to fly, and everything was so happy. She died. It was a sad time in the camp and in her husband was very broken-hearted. At the funeral service, it was just like it had been when her grandfather died – only this time it was her in the ground. And in that last service, in that small graveyard, her husband said farewell in sorrow and with tears in his eyes. He had lost his loving wife.

As he stood there, the flowers seemed to wave in the wind and bring out their perfume more intensely. He remembered his wife who was so beautiful, and his tears seemed to recede. For a moment he felt joy. And he was thinking, "Now what shall I do? Will I be able to get back, or should I stay here?" He heard the voice of his wife. "Yes, dear, you must go back. You should go back. You have to go back to be with our children, to give them support. For me, give them my love." So the man stood there and listened and visualized her beautiful face. And his heaviness lifted away. He took step towards west, saying, "Yes, I will go home."

And that is the story of the Morning Star. And it is a story about how the Cree language spread to the far west, past the prairie land. It was Morning Star who fulfilled this job. And the man went back and fulfilled his duty as a grandfather to her grandchildren who now speak the Cree language. And that is why the language spread way out west.[5]

This is the most general way of telling the story. But there is something else. The man himself was a shaman – he had the power to protect himself. There is that part in the story when they encountered the grass fire on the prairie – they had to find a small creek. They were able to bury themselves in grass and moss near the river until the fire went by. This was the time when they encountered the stampeding buffalos and had to jump into a small creek and stay in between rocks so they would not be tramped over. The little close calls like that she remembered vividly.

The man in the story is much admired by men. I think this story was expanded to teach men how to treat women. You had to be a total man to be able to have a beautiful woman.[6]

WIFE OF KETASTOTINEWAN

There were women that were beautiful, and very powerful, and dominant – just like men – they really didn't need men for anything except reproduction. They were very self-sufficient and they are in our legends. There was a woman who was a hero in a legend, and this has to do with the wihtigo story and cannibalism.

We talked before about the man named Ketastotinewan. He was an expert cannibal killer among this clanship, so he was feared by the cannibals. He was the protector for his clan because he was an expert.

A crazy cannibal man existed where Ketastotinewan was camping – he followed them secretly in the winter time, looking for a chance to get one of them. "Instead of that," the cannibal decided, "I'll get Ketastotinewan first!"

So this wihtigo, he went right into Ketastotinewan's camp, which had two tipis. He went right in between them and pretended to call Ketastotinewan from next door – he mimicked the voice from someone in another tent. Ketastotinewan was told, "Somebody's calling you," so he went out to walk across. He never reached there. After awhile people began to ask, "Where is Ketastotinewan?" He wasn't there, so they went to look for him. What they saw was blood dripping away into the bush. Somebody had killed him – and this somebody just went away and didn't even hide the trail.

And it was Ketastotinewan's wife who was fiercely angry. She was a very humble and very kind woman, and she had loved Ketastotinewan and respected him. And she says, "If he dies, I might as well be dead too. I've always supported him and always helped him in this dangerous job. If he gets killed, why should I still live? I'm going to die or I'm going to get this guy who killed him."

So she told the families, "I'm going after this guy who killed my husband." They said, "No you're not, you don't have the power – you don't have anything." "Try me," she says. So right away they say, "It's an impossible task – you would never do it. He will kill you." And she says, "I'll go."

And she went – she didn't even take anything, she just followed the trail into the bush. Not far from her camp she saw a huge bonfire, and she says, "There he is." She just walked up to him. There was human flesh cooking, and dripping, and everything. And she said, "You really have a delicious meal over here!" And he says, "Shhhhh. There is a camp with two tipis very close!" And his knife was hanging there in front of his braided hair – a very sharp knife.

And the lady says, "Is this the knife you used?" "Shhhh. There are two tipis over there!" So she says, "May I try your knife?" "Oh no, I have to sharpen it." He's whispering. She got hold of it. "Is this the way you kill a man?" as she slashed his throat open. She says, "Like this, eh?" She killed the cannibal and she saved the tribe. And that is the end of the story. This is the woman who saved the rest of the family – who risked her life to save the rest.[7]

A WOMAN, HER DREAM FATHER, AND A WIHTIGO DUEL

This story is not legend but it is considered to have been true a long time ago. It happened a long time before the European came. There was a woman one time who was gifted to be a prophet. And, like anybody else, she got married in an arranged marriage which was which was part of her culture in those days. Her husband was really a good provider, healthy, and loving, and fulfilling many of her other needs. But there was something that bothered this lady.

As long as she could remember way, way back when she was a just little, wee girl, she had a dream. This dream came back to her again and again – a dream that seemed so real, a dream that seemed to be so important. In the dream, she has been sent over to this land to accomplish something – she didn't know for sure what it was. As a young girl, she told her grandfather about it because he was her assigned teacher. He told her that she was a prophet and she was supposed to accomplish something that would benefit her people.

It was said that, before this young girl was born, strange things would happen every ten years or so – things that were very mysteriously controlled by some outside force the people didn't understand. In those days, there were many times when a cannibal would exist amongst the people and slowly kill them off. When they weren't eating human food, these cannibals would live like ordinary people, but the urge to carve and eat the human flesh was strong. Visit them, and they would be just the ordinary people – but they were cannibals. And this was the situation those days. So it was not very nice for the land. People didn't understand these forces because they didn't have no scientific explanation. There was no science in those days, and no people who break things apart to study them. There were not too many people who were comfortable sitting on their bums to look at the stars – to be astronomers. No, they didn't have that. But there were gifted people anyhow.

And this girl was one of them – she was gifted as a dreamer. And so she dreamed this dream while she was growing up. In her dream she was a lady, so she knew that she's going to get married. In her dream a person talked to her and says, "When you have seven children I will come and visit you. That's when you will be involved."

So it happened – she got married, and she had seven children. When the last one was born she knew in her being, that her dream would come true now. When her last child was about three years old, she told her husband everything. And all around them there were people who were terrified by cannibalistic people. They had been spared so far because they had lived somewhere else. She knew it would happen in that year's winter, so she told her husband, "One evening, when you are coming home, you will see tracks leading to our door. Do not worry, that will be my dream father – he's going to visit us for a while."

And one evening in March, this man was coming home and saw a track that led to his camp – a human foot, so heavy and big! And right away he knew this was a wihtigo – a big wihtigo too. Anyways, he remembered his wife's warning. As soon as he got to the door, his wife met him and says, "My father has arrived. I arranged the tipi and enlarged it a little bit so he can fit on one side and we can live on the other side." And he says, "What is this extraordinary size of man?" And the wife says, "He is my dream father. That's the one I told you I dreamed. It's a different kind of thing. He will be great – he will help the people." "Help?" said the man – because a wihtigo didn't help people. As soon as he walked in, he saw this being beside the wall – bigger than a man, maybe tall as tree.

So anyway, they live. The thing spoke to them and to the seven children. They became accustomed to it and they call "my grandpa." A month went by and the thing hadn't eaten anything, so the man began to worry. He told his wife, "All of a sudden this thing will turn against us and eat us!" She says, "No, no, no! He's going to leave soon. I'm sure he's going to leave soon." So she says, "Why don't you just bring some food to him?" That meant: go kill a man for him! But the lady so believed that it wouldn't eat them, because that was her dream.

After awhile this man just simply couldn't exist there – he even thought about leaving his wife and kids, and it was a terrible thing. He knew a few families not far from where he was camping. One day he went to visit them and there was a man there – a grown up man who was retarded. He was not a very good provider and just an extra burden to the family. So on his visit, he saw this particular guy and then talked to the elders about him. He says, "Well, I need some help at home. I need a person to help me and I was wondering if I could take this young man home to help me."

They were just glad that this person would be taken off their hands because he was he was in the way, so they said, "Sure! Just keep him as long as you want. It is no big deal." So he took the young man with him. Not far from his home, he could see the smoke from heir camp, he told the young man to walk ahead. He took his axe out and hit him behind his head and killed him instantly. He just picked up the body, threw it over his back, carried it close to the camp, and dropped it not far from the tipi. Then he went in, just like it was an ordinary day. He took his moccasins off. And his wife thanked him for the food he had brought, and everything. She didn't ask anything.

After dinner, when they were almost ready to go to bed, he said to his wife, "I brought some food for your father." So the mother said, "Okay, okay. He should be happy." So he told her father, "Father, I think there is a little caribou outside there for you."

The wihtigo began to stir a little bit and finally he says, "I am going outside. I'm going to make a fire out there in the bush and that's where I'm going to eat this." So he just sort of crawled out of the doorway – he was a big man.

After he went out, they could hear this sound as he broke the trees and put them into a big pile for a fire, and they could hear all this crackling, and everything. He made a temporary scaffold and hung the human flesh on it – and he made smoked meat out it. In our language we call it *kaakisikan*. It's just like exactly like barbecuing a hamburger outside – when the oil squeezes out and you can hear that sizzling sound. And that's exactly what he was doing. And it was a human body. And he began to eat and eat until there was nothing left.

Maybe a few days after that, late in the evening when the kids were already sleeping, this beast, the dream man, says, "I can't sleep. Something bugs me." So he says, "I think a stranger is going to come visit us. I'm sure. I mean a stranger who's like me. He's going to come. Much meaner than I am. He's going to clean off the land if he's not got rid of." He says, "I'm worried about my grandkids and you people. I guess I must do what you dreamed would come true," he said to his daughter. She said, "Yes, yes, father. I guess you have to do what you have to do." "Okay," he says, "tell your husband that we're going to have a visitor. Tell him to stay home so he can be here when the visitor arrives."

This was very close to the end of March. The next day was not very nice – it was one of those days when everything feels dull and people feel things aren't right. The old wihtigo was already preparing. And then says, "Towards midday we will have a visitor, I know for sure now." He says, "He knows I'm here and he wants to get rid of me so he can have all the people in this land. He is a wihtigo, way bigger than me – and he's going to stay here for a very long time if I don't try to get him away. He can kill me also." So he says, "I want your husband to cut a clearing around our home this morning – and be sure the trail is well packed because when this guy comes I will go meet him." He says, "But you guys and your seven children will stay in here. I want them to practise a song that they will sing." So he instructed, "Here comes the the wihtigo of wihtigos who is going to be taken out of this land so that the land will never experience another human wihtigo. Our grandfather has taken him away from this land so we will live in the land in peace."

This was the wording he gave his grandchildren. "When," he says, "this wihtigo arrives here, I will go meet him. And then I will challenge him to chase me. He will chase me seven times around your camp. And on the last time I will say, 'I am now leading him away from you.' These may be my last words! And then I will run to the east and he will follow me – and when I make my last farewell, my grandchildren shall come out and sing the song. They shall sing the song as long as they hear our foot sounds towards the east." So he was instructing. And the mother practised that song with the children that morning. Soon they had memorized all the words, and they waited.

At midday they could hear the usual sound that happens when a wihtigo was near – the sound of a heartbeat, only much louder – you could feel it through your body. But the wihtigo that stayed with the family said, "I shall absorb his shock so you will not feel fear – I will absorb it all, so you won't be hurt."

And that's what happened. The old wihtigo went outside and they didn't feel any fear. They heard the sound coming closer and closer, and then they heard them talking, those wihtigos, challenging each other. The home wihtigo was saying, "You cannot come and bother these beings, because they are my children. You can have them and all the land if you can kill me." He challenged him. So the other one says, "We shall do that." And then they began to tackle each other.

Instead of fighting in front, he began to chase the home wihtigo around the home: one time and two times and three times and a fourth time and a fifth time and a sixth time – and the kids began to get up, and they say, "Are we now ready?" And after the seventh time the old wihtigo said, "I am now leaving." So the children went outside and sang the song as they were told. And the wihtigos' foot sounds shook the ground for a long time, every time they stepped, the land shook.

When the shaking stopped, the children stopped the song. And that was the end of that wihtigo – the small one killed the big one, took it across from the island to the great waters of the salt sea, and dropped it there. And, in the land where they had fought, they had broken the ground up so much that, to this day, the land still shakes and there is a burst of flame every so often. And that's the last time a human wihtigo ever existed in the Omushkego land – the people have never experienced another giant wihtigo to threaten their existence. And that's the end of the story.

So this story is very important. The lady dreamed persistently when she was younger because she was being shown something that would happen in the future. This gift was not restricted to men; women could be gifted too. Women were usually given the gift in the form of a prophecy about future events to save their tribe. Sometimes women played that role. So it was one of these women who dreamed up this wihtigo to get rid of this giant wihtigo who was killing off her people. So she became a hero in this story, even though it took a bit of human flesh to feed this dreamed up father. So this is an important story about the women.⁸

WIHTIGO,
OR THE CONSEQUENCES OF NOT LISTENING

Amongst our people, the teaching was that similar to the Christian commandment which says: respect thy parents if you want to live long. It was very important amongst our people that the young people respect their parents, and their elders, if they want to live long. Even before Christianity, this commandment existed amongst us. It was said that if anyone did not listen to their elders, if they make fun of the elders, of the teaching they have told, they would have to experience punishment.

Now I'm going to tell a story about it. They told the young people, "No young person should shout outdoors between sunset and twilight – especially in the springtime." If the children were screaming or laughing or yelling outside after the elders have told them it was time to come in, or to be quiet, they would bring a wihtigo to the vicinity.

And one time this family was camping close by the river, after the spring thaw, when the rivers and creeks were starting to run. People usually moved closer to the creeks or rivers at those times. All the men were out hunting and trapping the otters and beavers. And this was long time ago – there is no mention of the existence of any white men.

The women were at the camp with their children. And there was one old lady among them who was the oldest – she was the elder. And one young boy was fifteen – he used to be a very juvenile-delinquent sort of person – he never listened to anything that the elders would say, and always challenged them. So one beautiful evening when it was quiet and very calm, the echoes carried sounds very easily. And so this young boy purposely climbed up a tree and yells down to his sisters and brothers from there. And it was after sunset.

He stayed up there in the tree, calling to the geese and whatever birds were flying around, and he liked to listen to the sound of his echo. So finally, before the twilight, his grandmother walked out and says, "Come on, my grandchild. It is time for you to come down and come inside. Your sisters and brothers must come in now. You must stop making noise – you might bring a wihtigo if you keep yelling at this time of the evening."

But the boy didn't stop – he didn't come down from that tree – he just stayed there and kept on calling. He even teased his grandmother – he kept on yelling, "Hey wihtigo, come on!" And finally his grandmother says, "You are going to see the results of your bad behaviour tonight. And you will be afraid." So the boy screams again, he says, "Come on, wihtigo! Come visit us!"

And then he finally came down. That's how he was, this young boy. There were such young people in times past – we did have some young people who did not listen to our elders – they even made fun of them and made them look ridiculous because they didn't believe the warnings.

Finally it got dark. Supper had already been served. Everybody had eaten for the last time, and the elders were only sitting around. And the young boy was still talking about the wihtigo that never showed up. But all of a sudden there was a terrible feeling of fear. The young boy, especially, was just gripped by fear. He started to tell his mother that he was scared, but his grandmother says, "Don't you say anything! You have asked for it!"

And sure enough, a wihtigo was near. And, as usually happened when a wihtigo was close by, they started to hear the sound of a heartbeat – that was the usual indication of the nearness of a wihtigo amongst our ancestors. The old lady recognized the sound and she says, "See what I say? See what I told you? It never fails."

And the boy was scared – he was shivering and gnashing his teeth – he couldn't cry, he just shook. The rest of the kids were scared too, but he was the worst one. His grandmother had fear too, but the old lady had experienced such a thing before, and she had learned to counterbalance the fear – she had developed some sort of a power within her to withstand it. The mother experienced fear too, but she managed to control herself.

Within a short time the sound came closer to their camp. The mother and the grandmother did not have the shaman power to counteract much of the thing, so they talked about what would be the best thing to do. They had recently moved to this camp from their winter camp, which was not very far away. Although winter camps were usually moss houses, their winter camp had been what they call a "spruce tree camp". By now there was no more snow – and all the willows and spruce limbs from that camp were dry. And the sound was coming from that winter camp.

The old lady had heard stories say that when a wihtigo came, it usually came in through an old campsite. Fear and discomfort was experienced by all the family, especially the young boy who had not listened. The old lady says, "I don't have any power to chase the thing. The next best thing I can do is what I used to hear in the stories – we have to create a huge fire – a bonfire – to keep it away, because it doesn't like to come to the light." She says, "I will go to it and create a fire within that spruce tree tipi where it's located."

With all the courage, she took all her belongings out of her birch-bark basket. This basket was usually carried by old ladies who kept all their sewings and their other possessions in it. The birch-bark basket was actually very thin material, like paper, so it could create a lot of fire. So she emptied her basket and put it into the open fire. And she says, "Open the door for me!" She lit the basket and ran towards the winter camp.

And she carried this fire basket on a long stick. She ran over there and put it inside the old camp and she started a fire there quickly – the fire caught in the dried branches and just puffed up in a big bonfire. And there was the sound of a heartbeat. As soon as it started to catch fire all around, she saw a being in there, a human form. It seemed to jump out from there and run away – and each step shook the ground. Finally the heartbeat faded in the distance. And that's the end of the story about the wihtigo. That is one of the stories that I used to hear as a young boy. And there are other similar stories.

These stories have never been written anywhere. They are very fearsome, and full of action and emotion – they are like horror stories. They were so vividly described and they seemed that you could experience fear when a person told you the story, especially the children. So these stories, I don't know if they were true, but I know they work. They are for disciplinary instruction.[9]

STORY OF A WOMAN HELPING A CAPTIVE MAN

Other tribes came to kill our people in various places between Moosonee and Fort Severn – even at York Factory. The group that we have many stories about were called Aatawewak.

One story is like this. One summer a group of people attacked an Omushkego village around the Cape Henrietta Maria. And it was so sudden. The men were out hunting, and the elders, and the young people, and the women were at home. One young man, who was sixteen years old, was taken captive, along with two or three young men, a young lady, and one elderly lady.

These attackers believed that, to survive, they needed to take captives to be sacrificed back at their home. This, they thought, would extend their lives.

They also liked to take an elderly woman to serve them, because she would be an expert at sewing things and all that stuff. Most of the time, they did not bring their own women on these raids, unless the woman was a warrior. On this particular time, they needed a woman to sew their moccasins – they had been travelling in muskeg, and sand, and stone, and it only takes one day to wear out moccasins in terrain like that.

After they had killed the women, and children, and elderly people, they took off towards their home. The captives were blindfolded but, because the Omuskego have a built-in compass, they instinctively knew where they went. They might as well not have been blindfolded. They knew they were heading south. Every day they could feel, and hear, and smell. They knew how many times they crossed over water, and where the prevailing winds blew from, and they could feel where the sun was. Finally, after many days, they reached birch-bark canoes. They travelled by these canoes and had many portages. Then finally they reached these peoples' home, on the shores of a great lake. The water was fresh and, where they come from, the Bay was salty.

They found that these people lived in a village and grew their food. It seems to describe the Mohawks or Iroquois. These people had warriors who went on raids to other communities for the same reason that these captives were taken.

One of the ladies in that camp happened to see the boy, and instantly was reminded of her son who had been lost in one of those war raids. Right away she walked up to the young man, and said, "My son! My son – you're back!" And she was told that this wasn't her son, that this was an Omuskego captive. So she begged the leaders and elders for this particular boy to be put in her custody until they came for him. Her request was so pitiful that they agreed, on the condition that there would be two sentries outside every day.

And this lady loved the boy so much because of the son she had lost. And through sympathy, and caring, and love, she taught the young man about mitewiwin. He picked it up very fast, and learned a lot from her.

One day there was a public meeting which they attended. One of the Omushkego captives was to be sacrificed. The boy watched carefully. By now he could speak the language of his adopted mother. She told him, "This is that prisoner's day to be sacrificed. He will be killed, and cooked in a pot, and everybody in the community will have a taste of the soup from his body." And the boy ask, "Why is it?" She says, "It's a holy sacrifice – a human sacrifice to extend our lives." So the boy ask, "When is my turn?" And the lady says, "It usually happens every three months. So if this boy is killed now in this fall, perhaps another one will be killed by February, and then another by early spring. I'm going to ask that you will be the last of your people to be sacrificed."

So the lady went to beg and at last it was agreed. Each day for the next six months she trained the young man to have the dream of escaping so that one day, when his time came, he would be able to escape and survive. Each day the boy learned many things from her – of course she was partially a shaman. And he had dream quest practice, with the encouragement of his foster mother.

Before six months was over he gathered enough knowledge and practice to have the dream vision that would save his life. The lady says, "I am glad that I was able to provide for you. I hope you will save your life and go back where you came from. I thank the Great Spirit that you came to rekindle my feelings towards the son I lost. Even though I will lose you too, I will always remember you that you are alive." This was a sad prediction for them both. The boy was by now truly attached to this lady, maybe even more than to his own mother.

And in the early part of the spring, it was time for him to be sacrificed. His foster mother had briefed him on everything that would happen, so he could try to fit his dream into the proceedings. And he knew that it would fit – that it would save him.

Then one day he was called in. He lifted up his head bravely and walked up to the council who were sitting in a circle. Whenever a person was to be sacrificed, they were given a last request. What would they want to have on their last day? The boy had dreamed a few things which would save him. Everything was ready inside the dwelling – it was one of those long houses – the pot was hanging there on an open fire, and people were sitting around, elders, and chiefs, and warriors, and all that.

So he said, "I want to dance – I want to have a last dance before I'm dead, with a tomahawk in my hand." The elders and council saw no harm in this, so they let him have his wish. The drums began to roll and the singers began to sing, and as the music picked up tempo, the boy began to dance. He danced so masterfully, because he had dreamed it. While he was dancing people sat around the open fire and he danced around them. They worshipped him as a living food. Some of them had their wooden spoons in their mouths and some of them had knives. Some of them actually wanted to kiss him as he danced by. And he happened to know this one elder who literally licked his wooden spoon because he could taste him already.

He had asked them to give him a tomahawk on the last round, and they did this. As he passed by the old man who so desperately wanted to eat him, he hit him over the head with the tomahawk, killing him instantly. And as soon as he did that, he jumped right through the hole at the top of the long house. Instantly he turned into a crow and flew away into the sky.

Everyone screamed and yelled and the warriors ran outside to shoot him with their bows and arrows, but they kept missing. The crow began to fly away and the best runner began to chase him, but he just remained flying, watching those people running after him. He disappeared into the sky and came around again. When he saw those elders walking back home and crying because they had lost the living food, he let go his droppings onto them, just to intimidate them. And finally everyone gave up the chase and went back home. And the crow flew away from them.

He went a little ways, landed on the ground, and then turned himself into a young man again. And this was what he had dreamed – this was what his dream quest had been. This dream vision had saved him, thanks to the guidance of the foster mother who loved him so much. So he went home to the Omushkego land and told the story.[10]

STORY OF A CAPTIVE WOMAN CONQUERING HER GUARD

This is another story about the different tribes who came to kill our Omushkego people on the southwest coast of Hudson Bay and the west coast of James Bay. One time a middle aged lady, who was a wife, was taken captive along with others when these warriors attacked. She was taken to serve the men – to sew their moccasins, and make new moccasins, and do the cooking.

She thought that her husband had been killed and so, once in a while, she couldn't help but cry for the loved ones that were slaughtered at her home. Usually the group would stop in the evenings and the warriors made a camp where they could scout around to see if there were any other people. She was left at the camp with another older man, who was the guard to make sure that she didn't run away.

One of those days, after the men left, her loneliness overcame her – she just let go of everything and really cried. And the guard, the old man that was there, didn't like the sound, so he says, "You stop this noise!" The woman didn't listen. She just went on crying, even though she was working. She cried until she couldn't cry any more. And the next day the same thing happened when they were stopped. The same old man was guarding her. He, too, was getting bored because he had to stay there.

And then one day when the lady cried, he really got mad, this old guard. Finally he says, "Why don't you stop crying, what do you want anyway? You're not starving, you eat good, and you sleep good, and nobody's done anything to you! Why don't you just try to stop crying all the time. I'm sick and tired of you! You make me so feel terrible when you do that!" So the lady tried to stop crying but she could not. And this old man was pretty mad. He didn't know what to do, so he walked up to the lady and says, "Here! Is this what you're crying for?" And he pulled out his sexual organ in front of her.

And the lady was so mad. She hated those men. What she did was, she says, "Yes! That's exactly what I want." The old man actually was startled and he just stood there. And the woman reached and began to fondle him and soon the old man was beginning to enjoy himself. Then she began to perform the oral sex on him, just to make him relax. As soon as he was really beginning to enjoy himself – she bit him! She just literally bit off his organ and ran away. And the old man just screamed and screamed – and he was still screaming when she could no longer hear him. And she's the one who told that story. She returned to her homeland and was lucky enough to never be caught again.[11]

Personages

THE DEFEAT OF THE GIANT SKUNK

Weasel was hunting by himself in the winter. He had travelled far during the day. Finally, towards evening, it was a time for him to turn towards home. It was one of those days when he was busy, but not very successful. He hadn't hunted very well, he was not lucky. He had enough for a light meal but he would rather have taken something more home. So he carried his catch on his back and, towards evening, he finally decided to head home by a short cut. The days were getting shorter. Finally, just after the sun set, he saw a trail ahead of him.

It was large. In his training he had been told always to be careful of which track he crossed – to always make certain first that it doesn't belong to the Giant Skunk. So this thought hit him right away. Because the law said that if anyone wanted to survive, he should never cross Giant Skunk's track.

He was already tired and had some distance to cover yet and, since it was already sunset, he decided to do the next best thing. Rather than go all the way around the skunk's track, which was a big distance, he decided to go under the track. He knew that the skunk wouldn't wander very far from his den and, because of his tired condition, he just didn't want to fool around. He hoped the

Giant Skunk would not find out that he had crossed his trail. Anyway, down he went under the snow – he crawled right down to the grassy bottom. He had to work very hard because the skunk's weight had really crushed the snow down under his track, and it was frozen hard right to the ground. But he went right under and dug through this hard crushed snow, hoping that the Giant Skunk was not going to find out. The weasel is very small and will only dig a hole of about one inch, so it was possible the Giant Skunk wouldn't be able to find it – at least that's what the weasel hoped! He crawled under the snow quite a ways, once he'd passed this crushed-hard snow, and came up to the surface far enough away for his trail not to be seen by the Giant Skunk. So off he went, forgetting all this.

He made it home after dusk. When he got there he was very tired and he gave his catch to his wife who prepared the food. The next day he didn't go very far. There were times when the male animals sat together and told stories about their hunting. And it was only the next day, not even in the evening, that he mentioned he crossed the trail of the Giant Skunk – he was just sort of asking people, "Do you think it's possible the skunk would detect my crossing his trail under the snow?"

So the news travelled fast in this small, connective society of animals – they carried the word across to each other and they say, "Well, the weasel has crossed the skunk's trail, and he is here with us. Surly the Giant Skunk is going to follow his trail, and he will find us as well. Surly we are going to be dead!" News of this mistake spread across the communities of other animals, so the wise animals came together to find an answer. They decided they had to move away and, hopefully, it would take awhile for the Giant Skunk to find out they were gone. They were certain that, by this time, he must be making an effort to locate whoever had crossed his trail. The animals had always made certain that they never cross his trail – they avoided the area where this Giant Skunk was living, in the winter especially. It wasn't too bad in the summer.

So the weasel was sort of put on the hot seat and he was told, "Why did you have to do that? You know it's easy for him to detect your trail in the winter! It would be all right if it was wet ground – he may have not found it. Nevertheless, it is too late now – we must move away!" So the elders and wise animals decided to leave the area to avoid being slaughtered.

The Defeat of the Giant Skunk

As the story goes, the Giant Skunk had very powerful shaman powers which surpassed all the animals, and he was the most feared animal there was because there was nothing they could do to him. There was no way they could avoid it, they knew for sure that he would find out eventually. He would track down the intruder.

The idea was that who ever crossed his trail would be his meal. We know that the skunk doesn't eat animals that often because he is more of an insect eater and vegetarian, but there are times, especially in the winter, when, if he could get a hold of animals, he would surely eat them. That's why it was dangerous to cross his trail in the wintertime. But anyway, after the decision was made by the animals, they say, "We might as well just take off, we will head west to the mountains somewhere."

They knew the Giant Skunk travelled very slow and preferred smooth ground to rough terrain, so they decided to head west where there were mountains and rocks and a lot of bad land. As they went, they were joined by all sorts of animals: squirrels, otters. The story doesn't mention the beaver, but it mentions all the four-legged animals who travel in the wintertime. The trail was packed – even the caribous joined in with wolverines, wolves, lynx, and all that stuff. And they all headed in the same direction. Among the animals, the wolverine was looked upon as being the wisest, and the caribous were looked upon as the most energetic – they could break the trail ahead. The herd of wild animals moved along, with the smaller ones behind – even the mouse family moved along with the weasels, squirrels and everything that travels in wintertime. They even had an eagle, and a raven, and any other animals that were in danger, so they said.

As they approached the mountains, they went across rugged ground. The only hope was that they would tire the Giant Skunk out, eventually he would be too weak to follow them.

Now leaving off the group of animals who were heading out – here was Giant Skunk in his home, the evening the weasel touched his trail. He was sitting comfortably with his wife, his family, when, all of a sudden, he could feel by his shaman power that he'd been touched. It was as if someone had touched his body. He says "Yum! Somebody is touching my trail!" And the wife, of course, was aware of what was happening. So he began to wonder who would be crossing his trail at that time of the day. It meant that he surely had a meal coming if he could catch the animal who had been trespassing. Somebody was asking to be killed, to be eaten! He says, "I will go look for it tomorrow," because it was too late already. The skunk went to bed but the animals and humans in those days were taught to leave before sunrise to go hunting.

So he left before sunrise to backtrack the trail where he travelled the day before. He went around but he didn't see no track – nothing whatsoever. The only thing he saw was a track of spruce grouse, and some owl marks, and things like that. And then he went home. He just couldn't understand how could he have made a mistake because he was very sensitive, his radar system was very keen – his shaman power never failed him. Whoever crossed his tracks usually touched him right way. And he told his wife, "Why, it is amazing! How could I be wrong?"

In those days the animals had a special ritual to reject their mistakes. What the Giant Skunk usually did was eat a certain kind of food cooked a certain way. If he ate this food and looked at his trail again, he hoped he would see the offender. So he tried first a small snake which was smoked – it used to work. So he asked his wife to prepare it for him and she went ahead and smoked the snake. He sat down to eat and began to backtrack in his mind.

He went out again to check all over – couldn't find a thing. So he returned in the afternoon and told his wife, "It's strange. I still couldn't find the track, what could it be?" He knew it wasn't a large animal, he knew it had to be underground, but he just couldn't find it. So he asked his wife, "Could you cook me a smoked bull frog like the one you cooked for me last fall?" So she says, "Sure." She went out and brought in a smoked frog. This kind of eating was a ritual for this purpose and he was the only one who would eat it. She offered the meal to him and he began to eat. As he ate, he sat as if he wasn't there – he was actually travelling on his track, looking back at it again. Finally he pinpointed the area in his mind and knew how to find it this time.

After he finished eating he went back out the same afternoon. Sure enough, he picked out the spot, and he had his axe that he used. He walked back and forth and found a small hole on the ground – just a small hole, made by a small animal. He followed it, and followed it, and finally came to the surface. This was the weasel! He says, "Ha! I know who it was!" So he says, "That was yesterday – they shouldn't be too far."

He didn't go that day. That evening he went home tell his wife that tomorrow he was going to follow. It was all just a ritual – he

The Defeat of the Giant Skunk

didn't really need to do all that but, because he was feared, and because he wanted to maintain his status, he had to do it. But he only expected to find the weasel family. Fortunately, it wasn't so.

The next day he found the trail again and followed it to the weasel campsite. And the family had left. And as he follows the family's trail, he saw where other animals had joined in. By the end of the day he knew there was a whole group of animals travelling in the westerly direction. They were found out! He would follow them.

He spent a night, and the next day the same thing happened. By this time the track was so wide and packed that he was just travelling very easily towards west. And days passed and he kept following. He was getting weaker, he was getting hungry because of all this travelling, but the animals seemed to just gain distance.

Finally, after many days, he could see the mountains – they seemed to be hanging in clouds. He knew they were going there. He followed and followed. Finally he reached the mountain region and began to climb up and down and up again, through the valleys. Sometimes he was too weak – he even had some cramps in his legs and had to rest. So he knew those other animals must have the same problem – especially the smaller ones, and the young. That skunk was not one to give up easy because he had to maintain his status as the most fearsome animal.

Now we come back to the animals. As soon as they reached the mountain region they began to feel safe because they knew the skunk would be having a difficult time and would be tired, just like them. Hopefully, by this time, he may have even given up and turned back! But those who were in charge of the expedition had a radar system also. The old animals scanned back along their track – and they could feel the skunk was not far. Actually it was gaining ground this time, because it wasn't as small as them.

So the wise animals, they say, "We have to make a stand! We can't just exhaust ourselves and let him pick us up one by one. We must stand together while we still have a strength, and we must choose the right place to make a stand." So it was agreed by all animals. There were caribous, there were moose, there were many others. There was only one extraordinary animal that was not around. This was the bobcat.

At that time, by freak of nature, he was more like a giant bobcat. In our language it's *mishipishew* – it describes a lion, the king of the cats. In our territory the bobcat was considered to be on the same level and status as a lion in Africa. So the animals decided to find it. Bobcats usually hang around in trees. They found a mountain valley where there were lots of trees. It had a large narrow lake, and at the end of it was a spring which had open water, because spring water doesn't freeze during the winter. So they stopped here, and surveyed the area. And those who were ahead of them said, "This will be all right!" So the wolverine and all the wise animals they say, "Yes this is the good place." They talked about what they would need, and how they would attack the Giant Skunk.

They decided the outlet of the lake, where there were tall pine trees, would be a good place to jump on the Giant Skunk. This was their attacking plan. Because the Giant Skunk was a gentleman – he would need coaxing before he would attack. They knew that someone would have to be nutty enough to make a wisecrack that would irritate the Giant Skunk and get him to attack. It was like when the gentlemen of England had their honour insulted – they would throw down their white gloves on the ground and make a date for a duel.

They had everything planned – all they had to do now was just wait for him. They knew he would come along their trail, so they went to the west end of the lake. They knew he would cross the lake on the ice and that somebody had to be on guard all the time, day and night. They placed some animals along the lake and made holes in the ice where they were looking out, so that, when the Giant Skunk walked across the ice, they would see the water moving up and down. This is one of the ways animals who live on top of the ice know when there are enemies nearby, so this was the system they used. Everybody was ready. And at the same time they hunted and maintained their life because life had to go on the same, even if there was a danger of them all being extinguished. It was a life and death stand they made.

Sure enough, the next day there was there was a yell says, "The Giant Skunk is on the ice!" Can't see him yet, because the length of the lake was so long – all they could see on both sides was mountains – in between they couldn't see anything. But they knew he was on the ice now, and so everybody prepared. They sent the females and the children away as far as they could, and the males made camp out there and waited.

Sure enough, time passed and in the middle of the lake appeared a speck, a dark object. And there he was – the Giant Skunk –

heading towards the end of the lake. It took time because, as we know, the skunk doesn't jump and hop but wiggles around. They knew it would take a long time before he got there, so they planned, and they planned, and they planned everything.

They had asked their brother bobcat to be ready when they called him to the scene. He had agreed but, true to his nature, he didn't want to come there for nothing – so he had said, "Call me when you need me."

Finally the Giant Skunk came too close, but it was a life and death decision they had made. The skunk had also decided that he wasn't going down without fighting. He had to keep his status – that was the most important thing, so he came, sure enough. As usual he greeted the animals respectfully. But one remark he made was, "I was just wondering, why in the heck did you have to make such a terrible travel trail?" He was now trying to create an argument to give himself an excuse to attack. But one of them already had an answer planned – it was the wolverine. The wolverine says, "Well we have seen the tracks of the pouch cheek – that's why the trail is so difficult!" So the skunk says, "Who is this pouch cheek? Who is this pouch cheek that you mention?" And then wolverine says, "It's a giant skunk! A giant skunk! That's what the pouch cheek is!"

That was all the Giant Skunk needed. He slowly turned around, ready to aim and let go of his killing. And, at the same time. all the animals just jumped into position. The wolverine had been instructed to jump at the skunk right in the rear end, where his spray would come from; that was his job because wolverines have very sharp and powerful teeth. Everybody knew that he was the only person who could hold off the stink and the spray. He had to do it, otherwise everybody would go blind and die.

It happened so quickly. The wolverine jumped and closed the opening. Once he was in the defence position, all the rest of the animals jumped on the Giant Skunk. Those who had teeth, or any other equipment, used them to attack the Giant Skunk – but without much damage. And, in the mean time, the wolverine had to hang on in all his might to hold off the Giant Skunk. And nobody could even do any damage to the Giant Skunk! Nobody had ever told them exactly how big that Giant Skunk was – he must have been bigger than a moose! Finally they said, "We can't do any damage!" The wolverine managed to say, from his position, "Come on! Do something! I can't hold this off for ever!"

So they finally decided, "We should call on our brother, the giant bobcat." They called this a giant bobcat to come and assist them but, true to this bobcat behaviour, he took a long time to come across the lake. Half way along he had to sit down because he had cramps in his legs. Finally he approached and he says, "Why in the heck do you have to bother me in my afternoon nap?"

So they said, "We have this Giant Skunk here, see, we can't do anything with it! And if the wolverine lets go, that's it – we've had it!" So finally he says, "I see." So the bob cat climbed on one of the big trees they had chosen and jumped on the Giant Skunk's neck. He began to work on him with his teeth and his claws – everything he had. It took a long time but finally there was an effect on the Giant Skunk. He began to sink on his front paws and rear end. Finally he fell limp and he died.

So the other animals won. They cheered, they screamed, they jumped. But the wolverine was still in there hanging on. Finally they said, "He's dead – you can let go." Due to the pressure that was there naturally, when the wolverine pulled away some of the spray went right into his face – through his garment and everything. And he turned blind. He couldn't see and he was suffering – just screaming and just twisting in the ground. So he begged, he says, "Take me into the water hole so I can wash my eyes!" The suffering had subsided a little bit, but he still couldn't see.

But the animals' wives, they say, "We can't allow you to wash in this lake because you will pollute the water, and the humans who will come to existence later may not be able to survive – same with the rest of us." So the wolverine says, "What am I going to do?" "Well," they said, "you should go and wash your body in the large body of water that was where we used to live, in the east." So he said, "Point me towards it." So they said, "Yes, we will point you towards it. Keep travelling until you hit the water and then wash." They pointed him east and instructed him, "Whenever you stumble, keep your faith up, don't give up. Ask the east where you are and it will tell you exactly where you are and how far the water is – and that will keep you going."[1]

Now we're going back to the scene of the slaughter. There lay the Giant Skunk, and wolverine had left. So the wise animals talked about it and said, "After we have eaten as much of him as we can, we must cut him in pieces." The usual thing was to burn whatever they could not eat, but they decided to cut the rest in pieces the size of the skunk today. So they cut it and scattered it all over the land. They carried it here and there, where a skunk usually makes a den. And then they said, "This is where he is going to inhabit the land and this is the size he is going to be when the humans emerge on the land." And then they went home, happy. So that is why today we have the size of the skunk we have – and this is why today the skunk wanders only in summertime. That's why the skunk hibernates – partially to be safe from the humans – and for all the rest of the animals that are required by human kind.

So the story ends. That is an example of a legend. It is related to the idea of evolution and is very old. There's nothing in there that tells us that there was any human existence. The Giant Skunk had shaman power – he was able to detect anyone that crossed his trail, whether he was at home, or in any other place. And he had to have a certain kind of a meal to refresh his memory or his detection power. Seems the way he ate helped him to increase his awareness, his keenness. And it tells us that all other animals are naturally afraid of skunks, its spray is painful to any animal. It tells us, most dramatically, that they prepared for the human to come later.[2]

THE LEGLESS MAN AND THE BOYS WHO DISOBEYED

There was a woman who was married. She had loved her husband and raised three sons. These brothers lost their father when they were very small, but their mother always took them out into the bush anyhow. She taught them how to hunt small animals and to fish, but she never taught them how to hunt the large animals, like moose. The youngest was only about thirteen and he was trained by his older brothers.

The lady had desires just like anybody else. She wanted a husband. So, in her dream quest, she dreamed that she would able to produce a new husband. When she lost the first one, she dream this. By that time her sons desperately needed an instructor for big game hunting, and the youngest boy, who was learning by his brothers' mistakes and disappointments, was not receiving the very best training. So, with all this in mind, this lady wanted her dream to come true. Now, let me begin the story again.

She told her sons one day when they were getting ready to leave, "My sons, I want to give you a small warning. Don't be afraid if you see something or hear something" – remember that it will be for me." The boys sort of wondered what she was talking about, so they asked her what she meant. She says, "One of these days, when you're out there hunting, you may hear or see someone – a man who will require my help. And you will have to come back and tell me." Of course, the boys didn't know what's going on. But they do know that every elder has the mitewiwin – mitewiwin means shamanism. So they know she must be a mitew conjuring up a man. So they were prepared, sort of.

They forgot all about this and just went hunting. That year there were hardly any moose and they were short of food – there's only the rabbits and fish – and they desperately needed the moose. So the mother prayed that her dream should come true now.

So one day those boys had been hunting and teaching their little young brother the best they could. They were on the way home late in the evening, almost sunset, walking across this small lake with very high banks and old trees. And, of course the two elder boys are walking ahead and the young boy was getting lazy – he was behind, playing with an imaginary foe, fighting trees, and hitting with the sticks and all that. And he was far behind. They started to run because their home was not far away. When the older boys were about three quarter across the lake and the youngest was half way across, he heard this voice. Distinctly he hears something. Now he got scared and ran as fast as he could. The other two boys had heard it too. So they all walked together. After awhile the voice says, "Kitoni niko nawanakamatawaskwe (do you have parents)?" And they looked. It came from the south section, more like, where there was a high bank and hanging moss. It says the same thing, "Kitoni niko nawanakamatawaskwe?" And then the elder boy says, "Do we say yes or no?" So they said, "No," they said, "no, we don't have both parents. Nikawiinan pwechimaatisiiw. Only our mother survived." And then the voice came again and the little boy was just terrified. It says, "Your mother will come and get me. Tell your mother to come and get me."

When they got home they greeted their mother in just the same way as ever. The food was ready and they had their moccasins off. The youngest boy was actually pampered and his mother was fussing over him. They were distracted by the food and the nice warmth, and the boys forgot all about anything. She kept on asking them, "So how did you make out today? What did you see?"

And then all of a sudden the youngest boy says, "You know, Mum, we heard someone on the lake." And she said, "Yes? So what was it the guy say? Did you see him?" He says, "No, we didn't see him. He just called us from the shore of the lake. And it's a man. And he says, "Do you have parents?" And then my brothers answered that we don't have both parents – only our mother is alive. And then he answered and says, 'Your mother must come and get me and drag me home.'"

She grabbed a toboggan and says, "Why didn't you tell me sooner?" And they were saying, "I forgot! Sorry Mum!" And she disappeared into the bush. The boys were sitting there wondering what's going to happen next. Will a man come? They waited.

They soon heard the very happy voice of their mother talking to someone and they just expected the man to come in behind her. But she came in pulling the toboggan and, to their surprise, in it was a man's head and his torso. No legs. The boys were just horrified for the time being. They sort of turned away because the mother says, "Don't look, turn your head that way, don't peek." So they hid their faces to the wall, and they could hear rustling and everything. By the time they turned around, there was a human body sitting there.

But it sat sideways, beside the mother. It was not a very nice thing for them because they're always used to seeing their mother fuss over them, and they always sat with her. But the boys didn't question. So, that's it. She went to bed with this man with no legs.

Soon they got used to this, this body of half a man. The main thing was that they were short of food, and the boys could not kill a moose. They needed an instructor. So, two blessings. He was a man to satisfy the hungry need of the woman, and he was an instructor for the boys. Maybe an angel. I don't know.

So one day the boys went out because they had seen a fresh moose track – but it got away. They were not good enough and they got home downhearted and sort of giving up. That night the man spoke to his wife, and the next morning she says, "Your stepfather says next time you find a fresh moose track do not follow it – just come home and tell us."

So they did that. The next time they found a moose track they returned home and said they had found a moose. So the mother says, "Well I have prepared the toboggan, and these are the man's snowshoes – extra pair. You take your stepfather to that thing."

And so the boys took the sleigh, put the body in there with the snowshoes, and dragged him over to where the moose track was. And he told them right there to turn their heads into the bush and not to watch until they knew he's gone. They wondered how this legless man was going to kill a moose for them, but they didn't question, they just did as they were told.

So they went to the bush and they could actually hear this man, as if he was standing up, and they could hear him putting the snowshoes on. Then off he went – they could hear the swish, swish, swish of the snow being shoved aside by the snowshoes. Powerful tracks – powerful legs! But he didn't have no legs!

So anyway, the man had said, "Follow me after awhile – give me time first." So they stay for a little while. Finally they hear a noise way in the distance – somebody's cutting a tree or something – so they knew he must have done something. They followed the trail and found the moose was dead. Already. And the man was not far – he had cut branches and now he's sitting in a little mat of the branches with the snowshoes standing beside. The boys had brought a little sleigh that they used to pull that legless man.

They began to hunt moose – they didn't hunt, but they'd always take this man and he would kill a moose. But they always had this strong urge to see what he looked like.

And then one time, when they took him into the hunting ground, they peeked as he put on the snowshoes, their curiosity was so strong – and they disobeyed the orders of their mother and that man. And then they look at him, yes. They didn't see anything – just a man getting up and putting his snowshoes on. And off he went. And then after that, when they went to follow, he had no legs, once again. He killed a moose and some caribous and then said, "Unfortunately this is the last time I'm going to be with you." They didn't say anything, the boys; they just took him home, same as usual.

The next morning their mother says, "You have not obeyed the rules. Your stepfather said you peeked at him and so he's not going to go any more. It's going to be your fault if you cannot kill and it will be your fault if you suffer." And he never went with them again. They almost starve to death, but they couldn't use him anymore because they destroyed everything with their disobedience. So that's the end of the story.

What does this teach us? You need an elder to pass on the knowledge for you to survive. And when you disobey, when you do not respect an elder or your parents, you will lose that benefit. So this is the way all stories are applied in our Omushkego culture. Even the legends teach us how to live. I have heard this story many times. Sometimes I heard it told in just a comical way, just to make us laugh. Sometimes it has been said very dramatically, so that we will respect our teachers, our parents who give us the benefit for our survival.[3]

JOHN SAKANEY AND BERNARD GULL

John Sakaney

Mitewiwin was part of our spirituality and our culture a long time ago before the European came. A mitew is a person who exercises such a thing. Mitewiwin is a noun.

There was a man between, say, 1900 and 1920. When the first fur traders began to operate in the James Bay lowland, they used to build the York boats in York Factory. Sometimes they have two masts and they were open decked; they don't have no floor or anything. And the Native people were required to sail them around the west coast of James Bay, because there were only two depots where they unloaded the stuff from overseas. One of them was in York Factory in Hudson Bay, and the other one was within James Bay, on an island called Akimiski (Charlon Island).

And at the beginning they didn't have no compass! Open decked. Open decked, and the rudder had no wheel – it's just a plain rudder that you had to fight with. Dangerous material! Dangerous stuff.

So this particular man, his name was Kakitewish, his Christian name was John Sakaney – he was not a big man, but he was a great man. And he was a mitew at the same time. We were told that he sailed these open decked York Boats, two masts, from York Factory right into the tip of James Bay. I don't think he ever lost one boat in a wreck.

He was very courageous, using the stars as his navigating aid, using the waves, able to understand the waves and where he was, and how far he was. It was very fascinating how he navigated, and what he used. Omushkegowak instinctively know their bearings, they have an inner compass. What was fascinating about this man was he didn't need the compass to go from one point to another. He knew exactly, he understood the salt water. When there were no stars at night, he knew how to use the waves to find out how far offshore he was, or whether there's any obstacle ahead—a few miles ahead. So he knows about these things. That's what was so fascinating about this John Sakaney – his Christian name. So that's the blending of his culture with the other culture – using the white man's boat and his own mitewiwin skill and knowledge to navigate storms in daytime or nighttimes, regardless. And he always found his way.

Bernard Gull

One small oral history that I want to recall is about a man who was important between 1890 and 1930, thereabouts. This was a man called Bernard Gull in his Christian name, or Kiyask in our language. In the Omushkego language we call him Penas Kiyask. He was one of the Hudson Bay key men – he was one of those guys who sailed the York boats on the southwest coast of Hudson Bay. Every summer he used to walk from Winisk into York Factory, which is about two hundred miles to the northwest from Winisk, to work for Hudson Bay Company – unload the steamship out in the Bay by York boat, put them into the York Factory warehouse, and then sail into a little community on the southeast coast for these goods to be sold to the Native people. And when he finished that, he was responsible, as a captain of this York boat, to beach the boat somewhere on dry land so it would be safe.

This man really did his best to get involved for the Hudson Bay Company, so he got good benefits – he had the materials that he wanted: process food, flour sugar, tea and all that stuff. And he has his own faults also.

So one story that's his: he had wrecked maybe three York boats and the last one he wrecked, or beached, he did it on purpose for his own benefit. He wanted to winter trap there around the coast, so he purposely beached the boat there without totally destroying the contents. And it happened! So he's an extraordinary man, he makes our recent oral history exciting. But I don't mean to be offensive – we do not tell the story about him because we want to offend him, we just want to show how Hudson Bay Company influenced people. It changed their style of thinking, increased the negativity in their character. We, all of us, have different inner faults. Some of us are so greedy. Some of us are wanting to be higher in the government and we'd do anything to get that.

Well this Bernard Gull was extreme about these things. He wanted to do what the white man do and he worshipped them almost. He wanted to be like them. And in that, he made a mistake – made himself so disgraceful – almost like a big laughing stock.

So two people: John Sakaney, who used his mitewiwin expertise to be able to accomplish something which was new to him, where he didn't even require the compass to find his way in nearly five hundred miles of open water, regardless of any storm. That could not be possible for an ordinary man, so we learn something about mitewiwin from him, an extraordinary person who was an accomplished shaman. He was gifted to navigate in the water. And the other – Bernard Gull – so extreme from one to the other! He was so greedy and took advantage of what he had. He made himself a shameful guy in the story, Bernard Gull. But we don't aim to degrade him or to make a laughing stock out of him. He did – he made himself a laughing stock at the time.[4]

AMOE AND SHEWEEPHAN

Amoe

This first story is about a person by the name of the Omushkego Man. He spoke the Ojibwa and Cree language, right in the middle – and he lived around what is called York Factory today. He was well loved because he was a kind person and, although he was a shaman, a mitew, he never misused his power or took advantage of people. So he was trusted and depended upon – if there was any need for leadership, he was asked to do that. He had four or five sons and, when they married, the families lived in his clan because he was a powerful family man.

It was said that he got his name from his dream vision. When he was trying to make himself a dream, as a young person, he heard about the bee: *amoe*. In the Omushkego land the bee is respected for his sting. He can stab you with this and you will puff up and really get sick. If it hits you close to the eye, you will almost go blind, and if it hits you near your ear, and then also you will be very sick. So the amoe is something that you don't take lightly, and the amoe fits the name of this man, because he could hit with his shaman power. Like a bee, he could sting, he could stab you!

Other shamans respected him, more like feared him, although he never showed any aggression or never was ever what they call impulsive. He was always humble, and for that reason people loved him. He was well-known and a good provider. He organized his people well, led them well, and he was well respected.

He traded for the Hudson Bay Company in York Factory, in Fort Severn, and in Kashechewan in James Bay, which is about six hundred or seven hundred miles distance in between York Factory and James Bay. To travel in there was something that not too many people could do. His home was right in the middle of the Omushkego land – all the land that he used was his, and he travelled extensively around the Bay and inland. We have stories about his deeds as a shaman protector.

There was a time when he was bothered by another shaman. One day he had enough and had to do away with this bothersome person. It didn't take him very long to do that and, for that reason, he established respect. So he was set. His friends loved him, and the people who considered him a foe respected him – even feared him.

When people came together in the spring, he was always invited to be something like a head man. These were times when the shamans were called upon to be the performers – to show their stuff. Of course Amoe was always reluctant, always modest, because he didn't want to offend anyone. He knew that if he could do something that the other shamans could not do, he would offend them. So he always respectfully declined. But this one time they somehow managed to coax him and he hoped that nobody's going to be offended at whatever he was doing.

Every other shaman there was so fantastic, doing things that are impossible for an ordinary person. One day they had this game. There was a little creek – this happened to be in James Bay where there are all those little creeks that run into the Bay. There are very nice grassy places and the creeks are usually very shallow – maybe you could walk across them when there's low tide. And this was where people were camping.

So, towards the evening, he was asked to come and see all this activity. He watched, and all those other shamans were performing things that are impossible – almost impossible. So everybody else did their thing in front of everybody. One guy they were so amazed with used a little bit of a canoe to go across without any paddle. And some people used some kind of a blanket to go across – they didn't sink, and it was very wonderful indeed. And one guy even used a pole. He put it in the water and stood on it, something like a one-legged water ski – but it's a tiny stick without any pull from the front. So he stepped on it and he went across and came back again! So everybody was fascinated and they really admired him. That was the end. He was the champion and they were going to give him the award.

And this Amoe lifted his hand and says, "Hold on! Wait a minute! Since you have invited me here, let me try!" So they asked him, "What would you need?" He walked to the edge of the little bank – and the tide was high. He says, "I'm just going to walk across!" They thought he was just going to wade across, with the water up to his chest, so they started to laugh. And then he just walked across the top of the water! Moccasin feet! He walked across the creek and back again. And that was it! Nobody else could do that, so he was the winner. Everybody was really mystified and they were cheering and all that stuff. Anyway, he insulted that other shaman.

The games and other activities went on. This always happened early in summer, just after the ice cleared from the river. The people used to have a temporary village with tipis all over the place. They visited each other and brought their food with them. It lasted maybe six days – it just depended on how much food they had brought in. And these were the real powwows.

And so everything went well. This was after the fur trade start because they had guns already. And one of those games they played was sharpshooters – and some of them were really experts, they could shoot a fly out of the air almost! Anyway they competed. At the same time, they used to have a hunting contest – they used to hunt loons. In that particular place there were usually a lot of red-throated loons. I guess that was before they get trimmed down because of the oil spills; now they don't have them any more. These loons are not easy to hit for anyone who isn't used to hunting loons. That's why they competed. They went out a little ways offshore, anchored the canoe with a stone, and sit in the canoe. When the loons took off and flew towards them, they would shoot them when they got close by. But only the expert shots could actually knock any down. So they used to do that.

So anyway, at the height of this game, again Amoe was invited to watch. Of course he didn't want to participate because he was afraid of hurting anyone's feelings. They were seeing who could reload their guns faster, and they were very fast. One was especially fast and it was fascinating to see him. He was the champion and was applauded and everything and they were going to give him the prize. Again, here is Amoe. He says, "Wait a minute! Wait a minute!" I guess he was carried away.

So they gave him a gun, like the rest of the others, and he began to shoot. But him, he didn't even have to load! He just kept pressing the trigger and the gun fired. And the other shamans were getting mad because he was using powers to do that. They used powers too, but he was much faster and more impressive and everything. And that was when he really insulted the other shamans. The guy who would have been the champion walked past him and said, "We will see who is fast!" That's a challenge – shaman against shaman. And so Amoe says, "We will see." That meant, 'okay'.

And then they went down south to Kashechewan (Albany River) to work with the Europeans. The summer went by and when the winter came Amoe went out in the bush by himself to hunt. He began to notice that he was not very lucky, that every time he hunted, he would miss! The things that he usually killed very easily with the gun he would miss, as if the gun was empty. And sometimes the gun wouldn't fire for no apparent reason. He began to suspect that this was another shaman's fault. After a long time he was getting hungry, so he finally decided he better find out about this thing.

So he set up the shaking tent and invited whoever was bugging him to come inside. He asked him, "Why do you have to bother me? I never meant to hurt or to insult anyone in the games. I ask you to stop. If you don't stop, I may have to take some action." So the answer was, "The action we must see." That was the answer. It meant the other person won't stop. Amoe was really getting annoyed because he couldn't hunt, he couldn't kill anything, and he was now depending on his friends, who were nearby, to feed him. They kept saying, "Why don't you do something? Why do you let this man bother you so much this way?" But him, because he was a modest man, he just hoped the other person would just simply get fed up if he could not provoke Amoe.

That was exactly what that other shaman wanted to do – push him over the edge so they could have a battle – because he thought he could beat the Amoe. Of course Amoe knew that but he didn't have to prove anything and so the challenge went on. Amoe ignored it for a long time. His friends said, "Let me fix him! Let me!" And other shamans say, "Let me put away that guy!" But he says, "No, no, no. He's going to get tired soon." But the other person wouldn't stop. These things happened so much. And so finally Amoe was convinced by his friend who said, "Why don't you just take action? Show him that you do not approve. Better still," he says, "get rid of him! Kill him!"

He actually didn't do much. He took his gun outside and he pushed a little plug inside it – just a little short moss – halfway up the barrel. And he says, "Well, let's see what he feels like if he fires his gun with a plug." So he just waits. The next day he brought this gun back and cleaned it up and everything. And then he says, "Actually, I think he's going to stop. I don't think he will need the gun anymore." They asked him what he did and he says, "I just plugged his gun so that, when he shot it, the plug would make it backfire and he would be blinded. And that's it."

So he didn't kill him but just blinded him temporarily. So Amoe began again to have luck hunting and trapping. He defended himself without actually killing a man.

Amoe traded furs honestly with the Hudson Bay Company when he was healthy and strong. But when he get older he was not as active, and just like anybody else, he began to lose his power. He remained a powerful shaman just the same, but by the time he died he didn't use it much because he wanted to be an ordinary person. It was said that he could almost do anything with his power.

Sheweephan

Amoe had a brother by the name of Sheweephan. It means: sweet lunged. He was younger than Amoe and not as honest. He was a bothersome kind of person. He was not properly mentally structured – he was a bit like a mentally retarded person.

Because of his character no one respected him and no women wanted to marry him. He was not well off and he was not well liked. He was a big man. When he realized that he was treated that way, he began to be resentful and was like an outlaw among his own people. He would steal, yes, he would steal if he saw a cache. What I mean to say is, when people left their stuff for later use, he would take it.

And then also he was aggressive – he took women by force for his pleasure. There were lots of arranged marriages, but if a man was not a good hunter or if he was not healthy, no person arranged marriage with him. This Sheweephan was not fit to be a married person and no family wanted to arrange for their daughter to marry him. That was his problem. So what he did was, whenever he could get hold of a woman by herself, he would just grab her and have his way – have his satisfaction. And he had that reputation and nobody trusted him. He was not a killer, never, until the end, until such time.

He frequented Kashechewan and James Bay. And at that time, in Kashechewan, there was a man who was a Hudson Bay manager. He had a Native wife. The years went by and they had children – two girls and some boys. The two girls became teenagers and eligible young women to be married.

But the woman was so proud of her daughters, she didn't want to give them to anyone but the very best – she was so protective. They were very beautiful women and many young men wanted to marry them. And, of course, our man Sheweephan also had looked at those women and he wanted them. He brought the fur into the Hudson Bay store many times for that reason. The Hudson Bay manager knew all the men and he knew about this guy, but he traded furs with him, just like the rest of them, and didn't treat him any different as long as he stayed away!

So Sheweephan was quite well known in Kashechewan area, and Fort Severn, but he lived by himself because people just sort of pushed him away, because of the way he was. When he began to bother women, sometimes even married women, he would be told to leave, and threatened sometimes. And he would leave, yes.

One time the Hudson Bay manager's wife, because she was an Indian, really wanted to go out in the springtime when the Canada geese are arriving, when the weather was changing and the spring was arriving. Omushkego women love to go spend time away from the winter camp, to wait for Canada geese to come. By that time the Omushkego people had guns so it was very easy to hunt – all they had to do was make a goose blind and a few decoys. But in those days there were not that many geese – at times there were very few Canada geese in the area, and at other times there were plenty. She begged her husband to let her go for a few weeks or even a month. She would go where people were camping not far from Kashechewan – there was a fort there. So the manager says, "Okay, but make sure that you look after yourself and the children."

So she left with her daughters. And it so happened Sheweephan was around – he had come to the community for the last time before the snow began to melt, to do some shopping. So he found out that the manager's wife was out camping with her two daughters and that gave him an idea. He thought, "Maybe if I go and approach them there, in the wilderness, maybe they will consent. Maybe the old lady will allow me." So he left the village and headed to the wife's camp.

He made it appear that he was just arriving and settling down there for the spring camp. The people knew better, they knew what he wanted, but it was too late to do anything. The spring was coming, and the ice would break soon, and why bother? So one day, Sheweephan came to the camp and asked the mother nicely, "I want to marry your daughter. I want you to give me one of your daughters." He even pointed out the one he wanted. But of course the mother just didn't want to hear at all. She even threatened him with an axe and chase him out of her home, and said, "Don't ever come near because, if you do, I am going to kill you!" And so, Sheweephan went back.

And then one day, he arrived again. They just barely saw him approaching the camp. He was carrying his gun – so what's wrong with that? Everybody carried a gun all the time. It was part of getting dressed – just put on your pants and jacket and moccasins and gun and axes – that was the way you dressed and there was nothing wrong with that, nobody thought about those things.

But the Hudson Bay manager's wife was so annoyed that she simply took out her gun and loaded it, and went to meet him. And she shot him. Sheweephan just stood there, stunned – his right arm was shot halfway between the shoulder and the elbow and was just barely hanging. So he just grabbed his gun with his left hand and loaded it very fast. The lady who shot him was so stunned that he was still standing that she forgot to reload! But him, Sheweephan, just simply expertly loaded his gun and took aim before she could reload. And he just aimed with his left hand.

He shot the lady right through the chest and she died instantly. Sheweephan just stood there, all open-mouthed. Everybody else was shocked also! So he just turned right back with his gun and his arm dripping with blood and hanging there loose, just like a rag, and he walked down to the bank where he come and disappeared back toward his camp. And those other people were just stunned and screaming. Everybody grabbed the lady but it was too late; there was nothing that could be done and that was a very sad situation.

The young girls were so stunned that they couldn't do anything. They were afraid this guy might come again so they asked a man, who was a sort of protector, to go and check whether the man was still around. So the next evening this guy went. And when he got to his camp, Sheweephan he was gone. He had disappeared. He had taken his camp away and everything. How did he manage? Nobody knew. And so he came back and told the girls and the others that Sheweephan is gone.

When the Hudson Bay Manager heard that his wife had died, he was so mad. He was looking for Sheweephan, and he was going to do the prosecuting because, in those days, the Hudson Bay manager was the judge, and the police, and everything.

And for that reason Sheweephan never went back to the community, he stayed in the bush. Nobody knows exactly what happened to him, whether he showed himself any place at all. But he never was found. So apparently he died somewhere by himself. But some people say he showed up some years later – somebody saw him in the bush. And he was simply hiding. He was not going to show himself anywhere. Especially, he was afraid of the white people. So that's the end of the story of the Sheweephan. And this story happens between that time, between 1775 and around 1845.[5]

Wisakaychak

Now I am going to pick this legend about a trickster. Some people call him Nanabush and we Omushkego people call him Wisakaychak. We don't know for sure how to translate this thing; what we can say is he was a pain in the neck, or any other part – that's the kind of person he was. He always tricked people to get his own way – not only people, tricked also animals. Most of the time he got his way, but sometimes he was beaten by his own making. So we are going to talk about this guy.[1]

WISAKAYCHAK THE ROCK MOVER

This guy plays many parts, fills in the answer where there is no explanation. In a way he plays a part that makes us laugh, and the mystery then can be just sort of eased away from your mind. That's what he does here in this story, and that's what he does in many stories. So there are mystery stories where Wisakaychak does things, this guy.

There is a place in the Omushkego land where there are some landmarks that are not understood, that mystify the Omushkego. One of them is in the area of this famous historical place for the Omushkego people – it's Cape Henrietta Maria. That's what it's called today by the white man ever since he came. But our ancestors call it Mooshawow. *Kinikimooshawow* – it means flatness of land. A place where there is no trees. But still, people lived there a long time ago. So that is where many things happen during the summer (nobody lives there in the wintertime).

So there is a shelter that could only have been made by an extraordinary man. There is a place not far from the Cape Henrietta Maria, maybe ten to fifteen miles from the exact peninsula where the James Bay and Hudson Bay is divided – on the south-west side of the Bay. And there is a landmark – a shelter – they say that is made of large boulders or flat limestone rocks (just about all we have around this area is limestone). So there is these pieces of large lime stones that have been placed to the northern section, and open at the south section. And they seems to be as if a human has put them there to make a shelter. But the thing is, these rocks, they're heavy. No one person can lift them. And how strong is the person who did this? So it must have been something.

The Omushkego people has been mystified by it. They have no explanation. Perhaps maybe someone once had the explanation – because in the past the Native people live there many years before the European came.

Some white people – the historians, the geologists, the anthropologists – have measured the time when the first men came to exist there. They didn't come from here – they came across the Siberian and the Alaska Strait. They came across from there, from Europe, that's what they say. They came here. Ten thousand years ago. So, for them, the people that live here understand only ten thousand years. That's the only period they cover. But our Omushkego people don't think that. They didn't measure years – they didn't measure time that way. They measure time by generations, one generation and then to the other one.

So anyway, to get back to this landmark, it has been done by some human figure. Human mind does that. No animal could do that. So, how old it is they never tell us, and they never know who did it. So it's just there. The mystery of these things people don't understand – where it comes from and why is there.

So, instead of just being stumped, instead of not having an answer at all, they make up a story around it. They say, "Well it was Wisakaychak, our hero! As he was traveling that way apparently he experienced a white-out storm and decided to shelter himself there for the night." That's a simple answer, very simple.

And not far away there is another landmark. They say it is still there. It's just a round rock in a football shape – but it's large – maybe five feet high or more. And it sits on these pre-arranged rocks. But these things weigh a ton. Who can lift the rock? So to make some explanation, our elders have said, "It is Wisakaychak, our hero, our giant." So, that's a second mystery in the same region – the first one is supposed to be Wisakaychak's shelter. If you look from the shelter towards the north-west, you could actually see that rock in the second place. So it could be somewhere around three to five miles away. So they say, "Why did he put that mark there?" "Well," they say, "he decided to have a crap in the morning. So after that you know, he just marked the place."

And the next one I am going to mention is the one that is shown in some lake. I don't know what they call it. Wunnumin Lake, I think they call it. Wunnumin is the name of the rock. And so they say that not far from the outlet of Wunnumin Lake that is shaped like a beaver house. And at the foot of that little hill is an outcropping that has grey rocks above red rocks. It appears as if the red rocks are cascading into the water. So people who look at this thing from the distance say you can actually see the hill that looks like a beaver house and, at the bottom of it, it looks like you can see blood. The red rock looks like blood. Not far from there, at the outlet of the lake, it looks like a dam is there – that's how the outlets look. So they say, "It is Wisakaychak, that's where he killed a beaver." After he kill the beaver, blood spill on the ground, and that's what we see.

They say that it's been so long ago that Wisakaychak existed that everything he did has turn into stone. The Native people understand that rocks age. The rock is first, it's very soft and that's a limestone, they know that. And then they have the certain other stage, the rock that is grey matter, and some of it that is red, and different color. They know it's in different parts, there's a different color of stone. So they have a basic understanding about the aging of stone.

And then there's a fourth, a mystery halfway along the Severn River. Severn River is one of the largest rivers that drains into the Hudson Bay basin, as the geologists would say. And it has very steep banks, many tributaries, and many lakes in the headwaters. It is very large, really, and very old. And halfway along there is fast water – rapids. It's big and dangerous and some people say that a person shouldn't shoot the rapid, they should be very careful. So they respect it. And it's located in the limestone place. The riverbanks have cliffs with the limestone. At an exact place there is a narrower spot and the water is white as moonlight.

And in that white water there is a rock that sticks out from this fast water. Again, it is a hard granite rock and it's black/greyish colour. And it has the shape of a little bag, like the one carry men carried around – they called it the medicine bag. It's a shape like that. It never moves, it's always there – it's been there for ages. How does it stay there? How come it never move? But in order to have an answer, they throw this guy Wisakaychak in there again. They say he jumped into the narrow spot of this river, and, while he was jumping, his medicine bag fell off. It dropped right into the middle of the river and he never bothered to pick it up. Across the river to the west side is a depression, right close to the river – they say this is where he landed. It looks like somebody stepped on the soft mud to make a depression. It has his footmark! And again, this thing happened so long ago that everything turned to stone.[2]

WISAKAYCHAK
AND THE WOMAN WHO PLAYED DEAD

Wisakaychak did some things that weren't supposed to be done. In stories, he sometimes plays a powerful person – he has all he making of a powerful man. But he also had human weaknesses – he has foolishness. He portrays foolishness at times and shows us the weakness of humans – men, especially. Sometimes he plays the part of a dumb person who really doesn't have knowledge – especially of the opposite sex. This is a simple one that I want to tell.

Once upon a time Wisakaychak traveled the distance between here and there. This was in summer, and the weather was fine. There was a woman who was picking berries on the ridges of the Hudson Bay, or maybe James Bay. She was by herself and she was told to always look out for bears and strange men – that she should always be ready to hide in order to save herself. Let us tell the story from the woman's side first.

A woman was picking berries in the afternoon and she was concentrating – there were so many berries that she forgot to lift her head every once in a while. She was too busy on her knees picking berries. Then all of a sudden she remembered that she should look, so she lifted her head and scanned the area. In a place where she was not expecting to see anything, a man's head appeared. She knew right away this was Wisakaychak and she knew how unpredictable he could be. He could be good one time and evil at another time – you never know what was going to happen or what he was going to do. For her safety's sake she just couldn't run away, so she just simply lay down on the ground and froze. That's the fastest she could think and it was the only thing she could think of. She pretended to be dead.

By this time, Wisakaychak noticed a human form laying on the ground. He had seen some signs of human and he was looking for their camp – he was not expecting to find anyone lying there! The person looked dead to him – you didn't usually find a person laying on the ground when you travelled in places. The first thing he thought was that this person couldn't be alive.

So he walked up to this lady and looked at her, and said, "What happened to her? What killed her? What happened?" He examined her the way that people examine a dead person or animal. He looked for what had killed this lady, a beautiful lady at that – and just recently! – the body was still warm! But there was no wound. So he turned her over and looked everywhere. Of course the woman had on a dress, so he lifted her skirt up and he says, "Oh! That's how she got hurt!" He thought that her sex organ has had a really deep cut. I don't know what convinced him to think that way – maybe it was her wrong time of the month – but he was so sure that the woman had been wounded between her legs. So that's the end of that story.

In this story Wisakaychak is showing how stupid you can get if you don't have elders, if you don't have parents, who teach you about the human body. So he played the role of an unfortunate person who was not well informed. This is how the legends worked. They gave you a feeling of excitement and then left you there hanging – and you would say, "But why, why does the story end?" And the storyteller, an old person, would tell you this guy was so stupid because he didn't know anything. So Wisakaychak was very stupid that time. At other times he's a very mighty, powerful man, and very tricky.[3]

WISAKAYCHAK PURSUES WOMEN

Wisakaychak was a wanderer, adventurer, and he was also a single man. He's not married. So they say he travelled – he appeared from the west part of this country, from this Hudson and James Bay. It was known he was expected to pass through the Omushkego country from the east, and moving towards west. But he didn't move right past – he stayed awhile with people and on the land. He knew all the rivers and all the lakes, the Bay areas – wherever the Native peoples enjoy most. He would participate in the seasonal activities – he would go into the Bay amongst the people wherever they have festivities, wherever they gather, and ask to know all the people. Then he moved to the next section. He came from the east doing the same thing towards west until he comes to the end of the land. That's the story. By doing this, the people around the Hudson and James Bay area knew that he would be passing through and that he would be staying amongst the people. Or sometimes he would join the animals. He was able to do that apparently around this area, when he was traveling through. He didn't stay with any one family at length – he probably stayed with a family for a season and then moved on to the next family, or other areas, for the next season.

So he's a loner type of person, but very adventurous, and very mystic. When he wanted something, he would play a trick on people or animals to get his way. I guess this is why people call him a trickster. He fits the description anyways. He was a shaman – he could do anything.

Now once upon a time Wisakaychak was traveling. It had been a long time since he seen a man and he's kind of lonely for a human being. So he decided to search for a family on the land – we don't know for certain where, but we think it's between James Bay and Hudson Bay area. There were lots of people then but no villages. The people lived wherever they could find life. So he wandered off to where he knew the people would be staying.

He had the same desires as a man. He needed a female companionship – he wanted sex, to be clear. There he has it in his mind because he hasn't seen humans for some time. Especially he wanted to see a woman. So he set off to find some people – he knew a family was not far away. He knew that there was an old lady, and her daughters, and some single people – anyways, he knew that there were some single women, and so he went. And that was exactly what he was interested in anyway.

And sure enough, a few days later he came upon the camp. He saw the tracks of the men hunting and could tell the direction of their camp, so he walked towards it. And this was close to the evening and the sunset would be very soon. The timing was right. He was really hoping to do something because he wanted sex right away.

So he decided to use a trick to help him get what he wanted. He thought about it while he was walking. How would he do it? How would he accomplish his wishes? By the time he reached the camp he had formed his plan and knew what he's going to do.

He knew the men would not be home yet because men always hunted in the daytime and didn't usually get home till sunset or even later – that's how he know for sure they would be away and all of the women would be home. And that's what he wanted. And so he had a plan. He was certain it would work – he would make it work, anyway. Sure enough, the closer he got, the more tracks and signs showed that the camp would be there. And now he was getting excited and trying to hurry. He re-ran his plan in his mind to be sure of the timing – it had to be done before the sunset. So he was alert and watching the roads and all that kind of stuff. This was the spring season – early or middle of April thereabouts – just when all the animals begin to stir and mate. He, too, began to feel that.

So finally he came upon this camp. It's a large camp with about three families. He knew that there would be single women – that's why he chose this camp. Anyway, he just hit a tree with his axe so they would know he's coming. Sure enough, a youngster came out and says, "There is a stranger." And a bit older children came, and then the teenagers, and finally the mother and grandmother.

So he took off his snowshoes, and put down his axe and personal possessions that he was carrying on his back. He hung it there outside. So, the women (it was a tradition to always invite a stranger) said, "We have some soup." (Soup is the only thing they had to offer because they had no tea then and soup was always available. We don't have to go through that, because we want to get to the story.) So they says, "Come in and have hot soup, you must be tired." And he says, "Yes, that will do. Sure, I'm hungry." And right away he said, "I can't stay. I want to make a distance." And that's all he says for the time being, just to let them know he's not going to stay. When a stranger arrived just before sunset, the usual thing was to offer him a place to sleep, and that's why he said right away he couldn't stay. This was – why would a person want to travel late in the evening when it's time to stop unless there's an urgency?

There was inside there an old lady, about sixty-years old. And there was her daughter, who was thirty-five or forty, and there were children. There was only a few girls. One was about twenty, and the other was a teenager. So he looked them over and desired to have them. He looked them over as they moved around and did things – when they prepared food and everything. So he wanted them. Really, sex was all he had in his mind – he didn't care about the food at all, but they were busy arranging to feed him, in keeping with tradition. Finally they offered him the food, they say, "Here's the food. You can have this soup for supper." And so he says, "Thank-you."

He tried to eat very fast, so he would seem to be in a hurry and the middle-age woman asks, "Why are you in such a hurry? What is so urgent?" And he says, "Why, I can't stay here. I should go on because I may not be good for you – I may have a disease!" "What kind of disease?" they says. Now the ladies were getting excited, and anxious, and all that stuff – and they really wanted to know what's wrong with him.

So this guy was Wisakaychak. They knew him – they knew who he was. So he kept calling them his sisters. He says, "My sisters, I'm sorry to have to say all this – I don't want to scare you, but there is a disease coming, an epidemic, and it's very bad. Kills people. So I was trying to move ahead of it." By this time the ladies were getting very curious, because the women were the medicine people – the nurses and doctors in the family – because they had all the knowledge about the herbs and plants to cure almost any disease. "How does this disease affect people?" And, "How do you cure the disease?" And Wisakaychak says, "Well I don't know, I really don't know. I never really asked, because I never really saw it – I just heard about it. I met some people on my travels and they told me there's a disease that kills and is very infectious. There's no cure for it, really. It's very quick – it arrives and it leaves." The ladies were really getting worked up now and they constantly ask, "Can you think of any cure at all for this disease?" And, "How did they describe it?" And, "How do they feel?" And, "What does...?" And he says, "I can't tell you! I really can't tell you, because it's a very strange kind of thing."

So by this time he was almost finished eating and it was sunset already, because it was getting dark inside. So he said, "Well I have to go. I don't want you to catch this thing. All I can do is to warn you – there is nothing else I can do." So they were very anxious, wringing their hands, and they didn't know what to do. Then, as he was going out, he suddenly says, "I didn't want to tell you this, because it's embarrassing. They told me that the only way you can prevent it is to stick your head into the ground and lift your rear end up."

So the women say, "Strange, really. Is it in the air we breathe?" "Yes, it sounds like that. That's maybe why you have to put your head down in the ground – so as not to inhale." "But how do you know when it's coming?" the women asked. "Well," he says, "it travels with the wind because this west wind seems to carry this disease. It usually comes with a gust of wind." So he says, "Good bye and good luck to you." And the women were just reluctant, they say, "If we were to leave, how far is it behind you?" "Oh," he says, "I don't know. It could be very close. It was only yesterday I met a man who said they had it, so I moved away from there. It could come any time, just prepare for it. So that's all you can do. Stick your bum in the air and hide your mouth in the ground. That's all you can do. That's all I can say."

So he went out. The menfolks were still out, but it was after sunset and soon they would be back, he knew that. So he took off towards the direction the wind was coming from and turned around, not far from the camp. He cut some willows and tied them together. Then he began to run toward the camp, dragging those willows so it would sound like gusts of wind. That was what he wanted the women to think. As soon as he reached the camp he heard a woman say, "There it is – there is the wind!" He ran around the tipi twice and then he took off his snowshoes and lifted the door flap. Here were the women putting their heads in the ground and sticking their bums up. So he just walked right in and he had his sex, as he had planned to do. Then he grabbed his snowshoes and travelled off again. Once again the trickster Wisakaychak had his way.

WISAKAYCHAK TRICKS THE BIRDS

So he went on. He had his way. He had tricked some people. The story picks up again later. And this time he was hungry. This was in the middle of August – somewhere there in August or September, just when the geese are beginning to find the coastal region of the Hudson and James Bay, and he was traveling by himself again, as usual. He decided that a goose dinner would be nice. He was very hungry, he hadn't eaten very well. All he had is a bow and arrow, tomahawk, probably a very rough knife – he also had a sling. Even if you are an expert, you only hit only one or two geese with the sling – you have one chance, one shot, unless the geese are moving. That's the time you can get as many as you want.

Because he was a wise man, besides being a trickster, he never killed more than he needed – he had to eat everything that he got. And on this day he wanted to have a feast. He wanted to satisfy himself with food, and he was thinking, "Why not have a feast all by myself?" Once in a while he would do that – kill an animal, usually a caribou or a moose, cook it the way he liked, and preserve the food. He wouldn't leave that area until he finished. So that's what he wanted to do now – only with geese.

He remembered this special small river, more like a creek. It used to be a place where the geese always ate – Canada geese and snow geese. So he went there. As he was walking on the shore, all of a sudden he heard a bunch of geese eating. He went up slowly, sneaking along the creek, and soon enough there was open water. It was quite a large pond – about three hundred feet long and two hundred feet wide and very shallow with lots of grass around – just the type of spot where geese and ducks like to eat. And sure enough, there were Canada geese, and swans – even some loons in there.

So he pulled himself back and began to plan. "What should I do to not only get one, but lots – so I could have feast?" Finally, he decided to trick them. "I wonder what would work?" he thought. He knew the Canada geese, and snow geese, and some other ducks, they're curious – especially the Canada geese – in the springtime. They're wise and they want to understand what they see to make sure that everything's safe and okay. Wisakaychak knew all these things about the birds and he used their curiosity to trick them. Instead of hiding from them, he came into the open – but before he exposed himself, he prepared his pack bag. He put lots of moss and stones in it to make it look like he was carrying something very heavy and bulky. The ordinary hunter wouldn't carry anything like that unless he'd had a successful hunt. Anyway, he walks.

The geese and ducks saw him, but he pretended not to look at them – he just walked on the shore. It was a nice, sandy shore on the north side. The north side is the favourable place for the people to camp because the sun can shine onto the shore in the middle of the summer. And the south side of the pond was wide open muskeg – all the birds were eating and washing there. The Canada geese were the closest ones to where he was walking. They wondered why he was not even looking at them, so they called him. "Hi Wisakaychak!" And he says, "Hi!" But he just kept on walking. So they say, "What's wrong with him? Something wrong?" So they say to each other, "What has he got in his bag? Let's ask him!" So they call him again, they say, "Hey Wisakaychak – tell us what you got in your bag!" But he didn't stop walking. And he says, "It's nothing that would interest you. My possessions." So they say, "What's in it?" They knew that humans didn't carry that big a bag – especially men. So they got more curious and lots of them came close by and they say, "Would you tell us what's in it?"

So he had their attention very closely now. "Well," he says, "if you want to know that bad, what I carry in my bag is my secret – my private possessions." They say, "What is it? Tell us!" So he says, "It's my songs." So all the ducks, and geese, and swans say to each other, "Songs? How a person can carry the songs in a bag? The ducks and geese, they do not carry the songs." So they say, "How do you carry the songs in a bag?" So he says, "I have my ways. You guys have your songs in your mind. Mine, I carry them." So that they found very strange. Finally they say, "So sing us a song." So he says, "No, this is a private thing. I don't sing any old time. There has to be a special arrangement. Got to be a stage." And they say, "Well, why don't you create it right now? We will wait for you. Daylight is still high and I'm sure you can do it." So he stopped and he says, "Are you serious that you want to hear my song?" And so they say, "Yes! We will wait, we will come!" So he says, "Okay, but you have to give me time."

And where he was standing there was a nice sandy beach with a few rocks, and over the banks there was a nice white mossy ground. And beyond it, away from the river, there were lots of trees – the kind people used for making a tipi. So he says, "I have to make a large tipi – there are quite a few of you I have to fit in. I do not perform to just anyone. You have to be invited." They say, "Okay!" And all excited. They hadn't heard him sing, but he must be very special to carry his songs in a bag! So they say, "Go ahead! We just will continue eating here. Call us when you are ready." So he said, "Okay."

So all the duck and geese went back to eating and feeding all the young. And you could hear in the bush a thrashing sound – this was Wisakaychak making a large tipi. At the back door, that's where he put his seat. He also created a drum which looked like it had been inside his bag. He planned to use this drum when he sang; it just made it more impressive to the ducks and geese and all of that.

So he calls them. He says, "Hey there brothers, I am ready! I'm ready to sing." So he finally got them to have a dance. In one song, he says, "This dance is for you to dance together, something like waltzing. So you listen to my instruction." He began to dance and drum – and half way through he says, "Now put your necks together." (You know how geese, and swans, and ducks have long necks.)

So by this time all the birds were just dancing very freely and totally enjoying themselves. And then once again Wisakaychak gave an instruction, and he says, "Now close your eyes!" And they closed their eyes, and danced, and wound their necks together. Then again he says, "Now move around! Move around!" And then they moved around together. By this time Wisakaychak was preparing as he sang, because the ducks and the geese were so busy dancing and enjoying themselves.

Wisakaychak picked up some roots that he had placed beside his seat and made a rope out of them. Then, as a bird passed, he would throw it over its neck and tie it quickly. And then he just choked it and threw it over the side as he sang. And everybody was busy – nobody knew what was happening because all they heard was the sound of their feathers rustling as they danced. They didn't know anything until the loon became aware that the dance place was not as packed as it used to be. And then some of the ducks also became aware that the room seemed more empty.

Then the loon, being sneaky as he is, opened one eye to see what's going on. Right away he saw Wisakaychak tying the geese together and throwing them aside. And he screamed and he says, "Wisakaychak is killing us!" And as soon as he say that every other remaining bird opened its eyes – and here was killing! They were being killed! And they screamed and rushed to the door. The loon that screamed, he wasn't very good at walking on the ground and he got trampled over by the door. By this time Wisakaychak had killed half of them anyway but, because the loon had given the warning, he just stepped on his back. That's why today the loon has a very ugly back, squashed-like, and that's why he cannot walk on the ground. And that's the end of that part.

Wisakaychak thanked his lucky stars that he was able to get so many birds, and he says to himself, "Now, I'm going to feast!" By this time all the remaining ducks and geese had taken off into the river and were really scared. Because there was no geese or anything around in the lake anymore, Wisakaychak was by himself. His trick had worked once again.

WISAKAYCHAK COOKS HIS GEESE AND LOSES THEM

He wondered, "Now what's the best way for me to cook these things?" Usually ducks and geese would be plucked and cooked, but he wanted to cook a special way. There's a way to cook geese when there are no pots or anything. He said to himself, "Well, I'm going to roast them in the sand."

Now first I'm going to explain how roasting in the sand was done. First of all, when they did it right, they would pluck the geese and sometimes leave the feet on – not always though. They would pluck them after taking the guts out and then wrap them in leaves – called lily pads – they have very wide leaves. Some people did it differently. They just made a large fire over the sand, a very large fire. Then after the sand was heated right down to maybe a foot or so, then they would just make a hole in it and bury the goose. After an hour or two the goose would be cooked very nicely.

But him, that Wisakaychak, he was so greedy and he was hungry. So he didn't bother to pluck the geese – he just put them right in. He made a large fire in the sand and, after he was satisfied there was enough heat, he put all the geese in, head first with the feet sticking out. So he buried them in the very hot sand and he left them there – there were lots. And he said it should take a long time to cook.

"And meanwhile," he says, "I might as well take a nap." He chose a place right on top of the riverbank – not a very high bank, really. He knew that there would be some animals traveling by and they might steal – foxes or even humans -so he decided to have a guard because somebody should keep an eye on his cooking. There was nobody around, so he talked to his rear end and says, "Well, you watch." So he lay down with his bum to the creek side and says, "You watch and let me know if anybody steals my food." And then he fell asleep. It's late in the afternoon. Usually it would take about an hour or so to cook the geese but, with the feathers in them, it would take a little bit longer.

And it so happen that there *was* some humans around. They, too, were looking for some food. They were hunting and this was famous place for them to hunt. That's why they were traveling this small creek. What the Native people did in those days was to drift along a river or creek – and if they see the ducks or geese they would stop. And then they would sneak to the shore and shoot the geese with the bow and arrow. And that is what they were doing – they were sort of drifting down the river and a guy was sitting in front of canoe, always looking ahead. If he saw a goose, they would back up to the shore and sneak up on the geese.

The leader in this boat kept his eyes open because this was a famous place for geese here. But there was nothing – the pond was empty. Then he saw somebody sleeping on the bank with their bum exposed. So he gave the sign to back onto the shore. "There's no geese," he says. "But I am sure there is somebody sleeping over there – see his bum sticking out!" "A bum sticking out?" they say, "But why?" And they begin to talk to each other. Who would do such thing? So they know that Wisakaychak was around and he always did something unexplainable – so it could be Wisakaychak. So they say, "Why would he do that?" And they talked about why he would do that and why there's no geese there now, and they say, "He must have killed the geese and that's why there's nothing left now." So they say, "Well let's take a closer look."

So this guy just went ahead by himself and looked at this person laying there. His bum was bare, and, when the bum saw him, the guy could see that it was going to fart. He ran back down to his group and he says, "You know this person is sleeping but when I exposed myself, you know, the bum wanted to fart!" So he says, "That's him alright! He must be using his rear end as a watch." So they say, "We will sneak behind him and you stay here. Just pretend that you are staying here and you are not going near him. You try that, and if we walk towards him and he's about to fart, you just give us a sign to stop."

So they tried it and, sure enough, as long as the leader made signs when the others should stop, the bum didn't fart. They knew this was Wisakaychak, so they moved very quickly. The guard kept watch and the rest took all the geese from the sand – they stole his geese. They cut the feet off and stuck them back into the sand. Then they rearranged the sand so it didn't show any tracks. And after they finished, this person who's taking care of the rear end walked away and they all went down the river. Then finally they take off. So they have stole his geese!

In the meantime Wisakaychak just slept. It was towards the evening by the time he woke up. He was all rested and everything and the first thing he thought about was his geese. So he says, "Oh my! I'm sure I overcooked my geese!" So he jumped up and grabbed his stick to dig out one. Nothing there! And he says, "Ah yes, I did overcook." Then he pulled up another set of feet. Same thing. Then he became aware that there was nothing attached to them – he began dig and there was nothing. All the feet had been cut from the bodies of the geese and buried again. So he began to realize that, while he was sleeping, some human must have stolen the geese. Only a human could do that – an animal would have just pulled the feet off and thrown them on the ground. He went to the shore but there were no footprints or anything. But at the water level there was a sign – footprints and canoe marks. So he was very certain that he had been robbed and he was very mad.

He didn't know where those people were now but he knew they would be far away and there was nothing he could do. He could only be mad at his rear end because it didn't give him any warning. So he talked to his rear end. So he says, "Asshole, why didn't you warn me?" And he took a switch and just whipped his bum. All he had to eat was those feet that were left over, and he still mad. Finally, he talked to his rear end again and he says, "I'll fix you!" The fire he had made was still burning so he rekindled it and put a stone in there. When it began to get hot he sat on it to punish his rear end. After he finished he decided that's enough punishment.

So it's said he went down to move on to other section of land. He was hungry because he lost all his food. His well planned feast hadn't turned out. It was his own fault. He was being repaid for his tricks to the animals that he killed; he realized that.

So he went down and traveled places. Then all of a sudden he noticed that, whenever he tried to hunt, he began to fart each time he moved even a little bit. Every time when he wanted to sneak up on an animal or anything, he would fart and scare it away. At first he thought it was very funny! When he walked with short steps he would make very short farts, quick ones. And when he took a long stride, there was a long sound coming out from his rear end. But soon enough he began to starve because he couldn't catch any food. Finally the day came that he was truly starving – the end just seemed to be just a few days away. And there was nothing to eat. And that's the end of the story about him starving.

WISAKAYCHAK TRICKS A BEAR AND LOSES HIS FEAST

The season went by and he survived. The problem with him was that he was too greedy – but he forgot his mistake, his greediness. He still carried on tricking anyone he could outsmart. And this time he was thinking about having a different diet. Again he was traveling on the creeks – people always used the creeks and rivers when they hunted because that is where all the animals and birds are always traveling.

Then one day he was following the river and, all of a sudden, he saw a bear on the riverbank. And it's late in September or thereabout, just when the berries are plentiful. He saw it eating berries – the bears like to eat berries, especially in the fall when they can eat ripe cranberries. When he saw this bear he realized that the bears, at this time, were nearly ready to go into their dens and would be very fat. And he thought about how nice it would be to have a bear steak. Again, he didn't go right up to the bear. He decided to trick him.

The bear looked up, a bit scared, and Wisakaychak says, "Hi brother!" And the bear says, "Hi!" So he walked up to the grizzly and he says, "May I join you?" The bear says, "Help yourself." So he says, "Sure, yeah, sure I will join you. Let's gather the berries." So the bear says, "Well, there's plenty." So they were like friends – they ate berries, and had a nap, and then they ate again – they kept on looking for the berries. By the end of the day Wisakaychak was getting hungry for a different kind of food. He looked at the bear. "That would be nice steak to have."

So he was forming his plan. How was he going to kill him? Can't just tackle him. Can't just kill him because he's more like a friend – trusting friend. But soon the bear's going to leave to go into his den. It's now or never. He knew that, whatever he wanted to do, the bear would just go along.

So then one day he began to play tricks on the bear. He says, "Do you see that thing there in the distance?" (Actually there was nothing there). And the bear says, "No, no I don't see anything." A little later, he pointed again and he say, "Do you see that crow sitting out there?" And the bear says, "No, I can't see that far." Wisakaychak knew there was nothing there, but this was just part of his trick. He kept on doing that to him, always pretending to see something that the bear could never see. Finally the bear says, "I guess I can't see very far. My eyes are not that good. Not like yours."

So Wisakaychak says, "I was like that a long time ago. I had very poor vision, especially at long distance. Then one day somebody told me how to cure my eyesight." And the bear says, "Yeah? How did that go? How did you cure your eyes?" Wisakaychak says, "I did get the cure and now I got very good sight. I can see far distance." "Yes," says the bear, "I would sure like to see far. I would like to have a good sight, like you." "Well it's no problem to do that. The cure is right there, you are eating it. The berries!" "These?" says the bear. "Yup! You have to squeeze their juice into your eyes. They will be sore, alright but right after that you will sleep, and then when you wake up you will see clearly." And the bear says, "That sounds easy enough. But these things, they hurt your eyes?" So Wisakaychak says, "Yes. They are very painful the first time, but you just have to close your eyes and go to sleep. After you sleep many hours you will be cured – and then you might have even better sight than me!" So the bear says, "Well, let me try these so I can see."

So Wisakaychak says, "Okay, let's go down the river right on the sunny side where we do our sun bathing. Nice afternoon for that." And so they picked a nice grassy place for the bear to lie down and Wisakaychak got lots of berries in his hand. He lay the bear's head on a pillow that was a stone. And the bear said, "This stone is hard!" But Wisakaychak says, "Well, that's the best way because that stone will reflect the heat in your head and comfort you." So the bear did what he says.

Wisakaychak began to squeeze the berries into the bear's eyes and the bear was just agonized. Finally Wisakaychak says, "That's enough, that's good enough. Now you lay your head here on the stone and go to sleep. And I'll sing for you." And then he began singing a song, sort of like a lullaby. He says, "I'll sing you to sleep." So finally the bear began to drift into a sleep and forgot all about the pain. The bear usually took afternoon naps after he ate berries and that's why Wisakaychak said that – because he knew the bear's going to sleep anyways.

So the bear went to sleep and Wisakaychak sat beside him and, by this time, he wasn't singing. When he thought the bear was fully asleep he looked around for a big rock. He walked up to the bear and lifted the big stone – but just before he before he dropped it, he slipped on a rock, Wisakaychak – so he dropped it just beside his head. This brought the bear awake. Wisakaychak says, "Oh, my brother! I was just exercising my muscles with this stone and I slipped and nearly killed you!" And the bear says, "I'm alright." He still couldn't open his eyes. Says, "How is your eyes?" "Still can't open them – they're very sore still!" He says, "Well go back to sleep and I will exercise a little distance away from you."

This time he made sure that the bear was sleeping – he was actually snoring this time. Then he picked up the rock again, balanced it in front of him, and dropped it right onto the bear's head. He killed him instantly. Once again he had his way and he congratulated himself.

Now he began remember the last time he lost his food. This time he's not going to lose it. So he took the bear up onto the bank and cut it into strips in the best way possible. He made a fire and roasted all the meat – the tenders and the fat. He was so eager to have a feast by himself! This time he didn't go to sleep. He just began to eat – but soon he was full. The bear was still hanging there and he was full – but it looked so delicious that he couldn't stop himself.

He decided he shouldn't sleep, even though he was sleepy, because he was greedy and he wanted to have his way as usual. So he decided, "I should squeeze myself between some trees so I can digest fast and eat more!" Not far away were tamarack trees standing close together – just the right size for his body. So he sat between them and talked to them and says, "Now squeeze, so I can digest the food in my stomach." So the trees started to squeeze, slowly. They squeezed and squeezed until he says, "No! No! Not too much, just a little bit – just gradually!" So they did. And later on they begin to squeeze hard again, and he says, "No, no, no! It's too hard! It's too hard! It hurts!" And then the trees twisted together on top of his stomach and held him there. And he says, "I can't move! Too much! Just stop!"

And now the trees say, "Okay you birds and animals – come and eat! There is some food here." And all of a sudden there were animals – foxes, and mink, and wolverines, and Canada jays, and all those flesh eating birds – ravens, crows and all that. They all came and began to eat this food. And Wisakaychak was held there by these two giant tamaracks. He said, "Let me go – let me go! They eat all my food!" And the trees didn't say a thing, they just held him there. Finally there were so many animals and birds eating that soon there was barely any of his food left there and he was getting mad. He fought but the trees wouldn't let go. Finally all the food was eaten and the trees let him go. And he was so mad at them that he twisted them – really worked them over. They say now that this is why the tamaracks are twisted out of shape – because Wisakaychak was mad at them. So once again he lost out.

So the moral of the story is that Wisakaychak, as powerful as he was, what got him most of time was his greediness. He was too greedy and so he lost out. He lost so many things and, for that matter, sometimes he lost very stupidly. So he teaches that you should live moderately and that you should not kill any animal that you can not put away or preserve for use. Most of all, you should not be too greedy because you will always lose out in the end.[4]

WISAKAYCHAK GOES WEST AND GRANTS TWO WISHES

When Wisakaychak passed through this Omushkego land he was very, very friendly. He loved everybody and actually never did any wrong to anyone. I don't think there is any story about him killing anyone at all. But there was a stupidity in him – sometimes he himself was almost killed because of his stupidity. But he was friendly to everyone, men, animals, even the environment, and he lived amongst the people for some time.

And then finally he decided to leave the Omushkegos. He says, "I am going to leave. I am going to leave you behind. I have been very nice to you. I am going to return at the end time. And the next time," he says, "I will not be very friendly." He's going to judge people – he's going to be very harsh.

They said he went west, to the land where the mountains touch the sky. That's where he sits now, facing west, taking care of this land. And he's been sitting there for long time – he's very old now – he has turned into stone. Moss grows on his head and forehead, and a huge pine tree grows on his forehead. And when the earth begins to end, he will get up again and walk on the land. So the story goes.

And there is a story about two people who didn't believe that. It happened long time before the European came, before the white man. One day two young men, hunters, were traveling together. One evening they were talking about this Wisakaychak. They knew that he went west and he sits there somewhere. So they were saying, "I wonder when he's going to come. I wonder what he's going to be like when he comes back." They had just finished their supper and were going to go lie down. They didn't have no tipi because it was summer – they just had a very small lean-to. And they were just looking at the fire, and sitting there, and the sun was getting set. All of a sudden they heard someone singing. At first each one thought it was only in his mind.

Finally they looked at each other and one guy says to the other, "You hear that?" And the other guy says, "Yeah! I thought you were humming." And the guy says, "Me? I thought you were singing!" And he says, "No I'm not." And they get up and they say, "Where does it come from?" The song came from the west and it was a mitew song. So they say, "Wonder who that guy is?" They thought it was just someone not far from their camp. So they said, "Well, tomorrow we'll go see." So they went to sleep. But the guy sang right past the sunset.

The next morning they never even thought about it. They just went back hunting and didn't care much about anything. And again, towards the sunset, they heard it again! They ask, "Did you hear it?" "Yeah, I did. Yes, I hear!" So they say, "What do we do?" "Well, it's too late now, there's not much we can do." So they made camp again and just listened to the song. So they begin to say, "I wonder how far that guy is?" And then they say, "Well, we should try to seek it in our dream." So they went to bed, tried to dream.

The next morning one guy says, "Yes I dreamt about this person who sings. He's just over here, not far away – we could see him if we travel that way." But the other guy says, "No, that's not the way I dream. The one we hear singing is far away – we would have to travel a long distance to get to him." So they finally agreed to go west.

So they traveled to the west and by evening they had traveled quite a distance. Just at sunset they heard the singing again – only it was a different song. For many days they travelled towards west. Same thing. Each evening they heard this song. Finally they came to this mushkootew – means the prairie. They travelled across that land for many days – and every evening they still heard this person.

And then one day when they were traveling, they suddenly noticed a cloud that seemed to be sticking up. It didn't seem to change at all. Towards evening that they began to wonder why it didn't moving and why it was so dark. And they began to realize that it wasn't a cloud – it was a snow-covered mountain. And again that evening they heard this person singing from the west. Finally one of them says, "Well, maybe we have been fooled. Maybe we shouldn't go any farther." But the other guy says, "We are already here. We might as well go just to the mountain and maybe we'll see him from there."

So they travelled and travelled and still the song came from the same direction. They now were so tired, there was no use turning back. And then they realized – this was Wisakaychak!

Finally they come to the mountain they had seen and they began to climb. When the evening came this voice was very clear and they say, "Oh yeah, that's him. That's Wisakaychak alright!" So they believe in him now. Says, "We don't have to see him. We know he's there."

The next day they finally saw him – from where they were at the bottom of the mountain, they could see this guy sitting up there on the mountain. Not on top of the mountain, on the slopes of the mountain – as if he's resting his back on the side of the mountain. This person was so huge that they worry whether they should go up or not – they didn't expect this thing.

Now they really believe and they know that this is a wise person, and he has a power to do almost anything. To them, it's just more like God. So one said, "What should we do? We've seen him. Don't we say anything at all to him?" And the other said, "Well, maybe we should. What can we ask anyway? What shall we do?" So they said, "Well, he's wise, he must know something. What about if we ask him our future because every wise person knows about the future, whatever it is." So they finally say, "Well, okay. Let's go up and ask him how long will we live. Let's go up and see. Let's go walk up to it."

So they climbed up the mound, right up to the bare rocks and everything, and there sat the giant. On its knees and shoulders there's white moss, and on its forehead stood a huge pine tree. And he just gazed to the west, not moving.

Finally he decided to speak to them. He just looked down and he says, "Hello there!" And his voice is so thundering that they were afraid and they wanted to run down. So he says: "Oh no! Wait." And he says, "What shall I do? What do you want of me?" So the two men couldn't think – they were just so startled, and stunned, and afraid, and fascinated. So finally one guy stammered, he say, "Well, I – I just wanted to know – I wanted to ask you if I could live forever. I want to live forever." So Wisakaychak said, "Want to live forever, eh? You sure that's what you want?" And the man was just so scared he doesn't know what to say except, "Yes, yes." Wisakaychak say this once again, he says, "Are you sure this is what you want?" And the man says, "Yes."

And then he bent down, this old Wisakaychak, and he says, "Come on, jump on my hand." So the man jumped on his hand and Wisakaychak lifted him up to his face and he says, "Are you sure this is what you want?" That's three times. And the man, by this time, was so scared – and he says, "Yes." Wisakaychak says, "Okay." He covered him with his other hand and rolled him in there, like a dice. Then he lowered his hand, as you do when your best wish is to get number seven, and threw him on the ground. And there he rolled – into the mountain – a sandstone. And Wisakaychak says, "There you are. Now you're going to live forever in this land."

The other young man saw this fantastic thing and he just didn't know what to say – he was just shook, standing there watching that his friend getting turned into a stone! And he thought, "I should not ask that request, but I cannot just go away – I have to ask him something." So Wisakaychak turned around and says, "What about you? What do you want me to do? Any request?" And the young man say. "Yes!" "And what is it?" say the Wisakaychak. And the young man says, "I don't want to live like him – not like that. I want to live long." So Wisakaychak says, "Are you sure?" And the man says, "Yes." And Wiisakaychak bent down again. "Okay, jump in my hand. You sure you want this? You sure you know what you want?" So the man says, "Yes, yes, yes, I know." And he picks him up into his level of sight and once again he says, "Are you sure this is what you want?" And the young man, by this time, was so scared – he just say, "Yes!" Finally, Wisakaychak put his hand over the other and covered him and shook him like a dice. Then he blew into his hands, opened them, and rolled the man onto the ground. And there stood a magnificent, fully grown, tamarack tree. "There you are! Now you're going to live long time, but not forever. Exactly what you ask. As you requested."[5]

Appendix

RECORDINGS BY LOUIS BIRD

Audiotapes and transcripts.

Centre for Rupert's Land Studies, University of Winnipeg. NOTE: The key CRLS reference numbers are at the left. Those with an asterisk may be found in audio and transcribed form on the website <http://www.our-voices.ca>. All recordings are copyright by Louis Bird.

*0002 Cannibalism. Date recorded unknown. Transcribed by Tamara Robinson.

*0007 Storytelling and Shamanism. Date recorded unknown. Transcribed by Doug Hamm.

*0009 OOHP Introduction. Recorded October 2, 1998. Transcribed by Doug Hamm.

*0011 Amoe and She-wee-phan. Recorded February 4, 1999. Transcribed by Doug Hamm.

*0012 Mitewiwin. Recorded April 12, 1999. Transcribed by Doug Hamm.

*0013 Cape Henrietta Maria (Mooshawow). Recorded March 3, 2003. Transcribed by Elona McGifford.

*0015 Spirituality. Date recorded unknown. Transcribed by Donna Sutherland.

*0016 Mystery Stories. Date recorded unknown. Transcribed by Dale Fontaine/Scott Stevens.

*0017 Competition and Pride. Recorded January 3, 1992. Transcribed by Brian Myhre.

*0023 Legend of Wiisaakechaahk. Recorded February 12,1993. Transcribed by Brian Myhre.

*0024 Ehep-Legend. Recorded December 26,2002. Transcribed by Brian Myhre.

*0025 Pakaaskokan. Date recorded unknown. Transcribed by Scott Stephens.

*0027 Original Cree Culture. Recorded January 8, 2002. Transcribed by Brian Myhre.

*0029 Mystery Stories. Recorded September 26,1986. Transcribed by Monique Olivier.

*0030 Traditional Education. Date recorded unlnown. Transcribed by Julian Johnson.

*0031 Shamanism. Recorded 2002. Transcribed by Julian Johnson.

*0032 Legends in Traditional Education. Date recorded unknown. Transcribed by Bobbi Fielding.

*0038 Legends and Oral History. Recorded February 27, 1997. Transcribed by Brian Myhre.

*0039 Prophecy and Dreaming. Recorded February 17, 1997. Transcribed by Brian Myhre.

*0041 Cree History. Recorded October 29,1991. Transcribed by Jennifer Orr.

*0046 Local History, Sweatlodge, Wiihtiko. Date recorded unknown. Transcribed by Jennifer Orr.

*0065 Cree Women's Stories. Recorded September 11, 1999. Transcribed by Alison Daily.

*0066 Skeleton Mystery. Recorded December 7, 1999. Transcribed by Monique Olivier.

*0067 Legless Man. Recorded December 9, 1999. Transcribed by Jennifer Orr/Bobbi Fielding.

*0068 Legends of Stones. Recorded January 11,1999. Transcribed by Kirsten Brooks.

*0075 Omushkego History. Recorded June 27, 1999. Transcribed by Jennifer Orr.

*0076 Omushkego History. Recorded June 30, 1999. Transcribed by Monique Olivier.

0080 Flying Skeleton. Recorded March 2003. Transcribed by Bobbi Fielding.

*0083 Stories. Recorded December 8, 1999. Transcribed by Amelia LaTouche.

0089 Wilderness Woman. Date recorded unknown. Transcribed by Kathy Mallett.

0092 Cree Woman Went West. Recorded February 6,1999. Transcribed by Tamara Robinson.

*0093 Oral History of Cree. Recorded June 30, 1999. Transcribed by Tamara Robinson.

*0095 Storytelling. Date recorded unknown. Transcribed by Jennifer Orr.

*0103 Residential Schools. Date recorded unknown. Transcribed by Monique Olivier.

*0104 Shamanism. Recorded February 8, 2001. Transcribed by Mark F. Ruml.

*0106 Mitewiwin. Date recorded unlnown. Transcribed by Kathy Mallet.

*0107 Shamanism (Cultural Story). Recorded December 8, 1999. Transcribed by Mark F. Ruml.

*0108 Shamanism. Date recorded unknown. Transcribed by Kathy Mallett.

*0114 Early Contact (Omens and Stories). Recorded February 27, 2002. Transcribed by Donna Sutherland.

*0117 Hunts Game. Recorded 2001. Transcribed by Roland Bohr.

*0126 Report for Canada Council #2 (Religion). Recorded May 31, 2002. Transcribed by George Fulford.

*0136 Legend of the Giant Skunk. Date recorded unknown. Transcribed by Kathy Mallett.

OTHER SOURCES

"Legend of Sinkepish." CRLS #2-Bird #401. Audiotape. Date recorded unknown. Transcribed by George Fulford.

"Legend of Wiisaheechak (Landmarks)." 2002. English 1 class visit, University of Winnipeg. Audiotape recorded February 28, 2002. Transcribed by Kelly Burns.

"Louis Bird on Cree Creation Stories." Audiotape recorded April 20, 2001. Transcribed by George Fulford.

"Questioning the Elders." Videotape recorded at the University of Winnipeg, February 8, 2001. Transcribed by Kelly Burns.

"Winter Territories." 1999. Audiotape recorded April 24, 1999.

HUDSON'S BAY COMPANY ARCHIVES, ARCHIVES OF MANITOBA (WINNIPEG)

Search Files: *Attawapiskat,* and *Weenusk/Winisk.*

Notes

PREFACE

1 0103 Residential Schools. Date recorded unknown.
2 Ibid.
3 Ibid.
4 Ibid.
5 Jennifer S.H. Brown, Paul W. DePasquale, and Mark F. Ruml, eds. 2005 *Telling Our Stories: Omushkego Legends and Histories from Hudson Bay* (Peterborough: Broadview Press).

WATER, EARTH AND SKIES

1 0041 Cree History. Recorded October 29, 1991.
2 0095 Storytelling. Date recorded unknown.
3 0031 Shamanism. Recorded 1992.
4 0039 Prophecy and Dreaming. Recorded February 17, 1997.
5 For a detailed discussion of Pakaaskokan see chapter 3.
6 For a detailed version of this story see chapter 2.
7 0013 Cape Henrietta Maria. Recorded March 3, 2003.
8 0068 Legends of Stones. Recorded on January 11, 1999.
9 0024 Ehep Legend. Recorded December 26, 2002. For another version of this story see *Telling Our Stories* chapter 2.

10 0095 Storytelling.
11 0068 Legends of Stones.
12 0106 Mitewiwin. Date recorded unknown.
13 0065 Cree Women's Stories. Recorded on September 11, 1999.
14 0114 First Contact. Recorded February 27, 2002.
15 Chakapesh. Recorded January 25, 2006.
16 0130 Mystery Stories 1. Recorded January 31, 2002.
17 0029 Mystery Stories. Recorded September 28, 1986.
18 0130 Mystery Stories 1.

INTRUDERS AND DEFENDERS

1 0076 Omushkego History. Recorded June 30, 1999.
2 0083 Stories. Recorded October 18, 1999.
3 0013 Cape Henrietta Maria.
4 0012 Mitewiwin. Recorded April 22, 1999.
5 0013 Cape Henrietta Maria. For another version of this story see Brown, DePasquale, and Ruml eds. *Telling Our Stories*, chapter 5.

PAKAASKOKAN

1 0130 Mystery Stories 1.
2 0066 Skeleton Mystery. Recorded December 7, 1999.
3 0029 Mystery Stories.
4 0080 Flying Skeleton. Recorded March 2003.

VALUES FOR LIFE AND SURVIVAL

1 0041 Cree History. Recorded October 29, 1991.
2 0017 Competition and Pride. Recorded January 3, 1992.
3 0131 Mystery Stories 2. Recorded March 10, 2003.
4 0027 Original Cree Culture. Recorded January 8, 2002.
5 0041 Cree History.
6 0030 Traditional Education. Date recorded unknown.
7 0027 Original Cree Culture.

RELATIONS WITH ANIMALS

1 0107 Shamanism (Cultural Story). Recorded December 8, 1999.

2 0117 Hunts Game. Recorded November 8, 2001.
3 0025 Pakaaskokan. Date recorded unknown.

MITEWIWIN HEROES AND VILLAINS

1 0027 Original Cree Culture.
2 0107 Shamanism (Cultural Story).
3 0012 Mitewiwin.
4 Ibid.
5 0126 Report for Canada Council #2 (Religion). Recorded May 31, 2002.
6 0106 Mitewiwin.
7 Ibid.
8 Ibid.
9 Ibid.
10 See the discussion about the Wilderness Woman in chapter 8.
11 0104 Shamanism. Recorded February 8, 2001.
12 0030 Traditional Education.
13 0039 Prophecy and Dreaming.
14 0030 Traditional Education.
15 0031 Shamanism.
16 0126 Report for Canada Council #2 (Religion).
17 0027 Original Cree Culture.
18 0046 Local History, Sweatlodge, Wiihtiko. Date recorded unknown.
19 0012 Mitewiwin.
20 0007 Storytelling and Shamanism. Date recorded unknown.
21 0076 Omushkego History.
22 0106 Mitewiwin.
23 0066 Skeleton Mystery.
24 Ibid.
25 0108 Shamanism. Date recorded unknown.
26 0015 Spirituality. Date recorded unknown.

WIHTIGOS AND CANNIBAL HEARTS

1 0130 Mystery Stories 1.
2 0095 Storytelling.
3 0002 Cannibalism. Date recorded unknown.
4 0032 Legends in Traditional Education. Date recorded unknown.

5   0016 Mystery Stories. Date recorded unknown.
6   0089 Wilderness Woman. Date recorded unknown.

WOMEN AND MEN

1   0108 Shamanism.
2   Ibid.
3   0106 Mitewiwin.
4   0089 Wilderness Woman. Date recorded unknown.
5   0065 Cree Women's Stories.
6   0072 Omushkego Woman Went West. Recorded February 6, 1999.
7   0089 Wilderness Woman.
8   0067 Legless Man. Recorded December 9, 1999.
9   0029 Mystery Stories.
10 0095 Storytelling. For another version of this story see Brown, DePasquale, and Ruml, eds. *Telling Our Stories*, chapter 5.
11 0104 Shamanism.

PERSONAGES

1   The animals were referring to Hudson Bay, which in Cree is called Winnipeg, "dirty water."
2   0136 Legend of the Giant Skunk. Date recorded unknown. For another version of this story see Brown, DePasquale, and Ruml, eds, *Telling Our Stories*, chapter 2.
3   0067 Legless Man.
4   0009 OOHP Introduction. Recorded October 2, 1998.
5   0011 Amoe and She-wee-phan. Recorded February 4, 1999. In his research in the Hudson's Bay Company Archives Doug Hamm identified the woman and family discussed in this story: Doug Hamm and Louis Bird, "Amoe: Legends of the Omushkegowak," *Papers of the Thirty-First Algonquian Conference*, John D. Nichols, ed. (Winnipeg: University of Manitoba Press, 2000), 144–60.

WISAKAYCHAK

1   0023 Legend of Wisakaychak. Recorded February 12, 1993.
2   0068 Legends of Stones.
3   0038 Legends and Oral History. Recorded February 27, 1997.
4   0023 Legend of Wisakaychak.
5   0068 Legends of Stones.

Suggested Readings

GENERAL BACKGROUND

Bauman, Richard. 1986. "Introduction." In *Story, Performance, and Event: Contextual Studies of Oral Narrative*, 1–10. Cambridge: Cambridge University Press.

Brown, Jennifer S.H., DePasquale, Paul W., and Ruml, Mark F. 2005. *Telling Our Stories: Omushkego Legends and Stories from Hudson Bay*. Peterborough: Broadview Press.

Cruikshank, Julie. 2003. "Discovery of Gold on the Klondike: Perspectives from Oral Tradition." In *Reading Beyond Words: Contexts for Native History*, 435–58. Eds Jennifer S.H. Brown and Elizabeth Vibert. Rev. ed. Peterborough: Broadview Press.

Mattina, Anthony. 1987 "Native American Indian Mythography: Editing Texts for the Printed Page." In *Recovering the Word: Essays on Native American Literature*, 129–48. Eds Brian Swann and Arnold Krupat. Los Angeles: University of California Press.

Murray, L., and K. Rice, eds. 1999. *Talking on the Page: Editing Aboriginal Oral Texts*. Toronto: University of Toronto Press.

Wickwire, Wendy. 2005. *Living By Stories: A Journey of Landscape and Memory*. Vancouver: Talon Books.

– 1992. *Nature Power: In the Spirit of an Okanagan Storyteller – Harry*

Robinson. Vancouver and Seattle: Douglas and McIntyre and University of Washington Press.
– 1989. *Write It on Your Heart: The Epic World of an Okanagan Storyteller*. Vancouver: Talon Books.

WATER, EARTH, SKIES

Cruikshank, Julie. 1990. "Getting the Words Right: Perspectives on Naming and Places in Athapaskan Oral History." *Arctic Anthropology* 27: 52–65.

Graham, Andrew. 1969. *Andrew Graham's Observations on Hudson's Bay, 1767-91*. Edited by Glyndwr Williams. London: Hudson's Bay Record Society.

Isham, James. 1949. *James Isham's Observations of Hudson's Bay, 1743 and Notes and Observations on a Book Entitled A Voyage to Hudsons Bay in the Dobbs Galley, 1749*. Edited by E.E. Rich. Toronto: Champlain Society.

Pike, Warburton. 1892. *The Barren Ground of Northern Canada*. New York: Macmillan.

Pilon, Jean-Luc. 1987. *Washahoe Inninou Dahtsuounoaou: Ecological and Cultural Adaptation along the Severn River in the Hudson Bay Lowlands of Ontario*. Report No. 10: Conservation Archaeology Report, Northwestern Region. Kenora: Ministry of Citizenship and Culture.

Robson, Joseph. 1752. *An Account of Six Years Residence in Hudson's Bay from 1733 to 1736 and 1744 to 1747*. London: J. Payne and J. Bouquet.

INTRUDERS AND DEFENDERS

Clayton, Daniel. 2003. "Captain Cook and the Spaces of Contact at 'Nootka Sound.'" In *Reading Beyond Words: Contexts for Native History*, 133–62. Eds. Jennifer S.H. Brown and Elizabeth Vibert. Rev. ed. Peterborough,: Broadview Press.

Lytwyn, Victor P. 2002. *Muskekowuck Athinuwick: Original People of the Great Swampy Land*. Winnipeg: University of Manitoba Press.

Malone, Patrick M. 1991. *The Skulking Way of War: Technology and Tactics among the New England Indians*. Baltimore: Johns Hopkins University Press.

Trigger, Bruce G. 1976. *The Children of Aataentsic: A History of the Huron People to 1660.* 2 vols. Montreal and Kingston: McGill-Queen's University Press.

PAKAASKOKAN

Ahenakew, Edward. 1973. *Voices of the Plains Cree.* Toronto: McClelland and Stewart.
Bloomfield, Leonard. 1934. "Plains Cree Texts." *Publications of the American Ethnological Society,* vol. 16. New York.
Brown, Jennifer S.H., and Robert Brightman. 1988. *The Orders of the Dreamed: George Nelson on Cree and Northern Ojibwa Religion and Myth, 1823.* Winnipeg: University of Manitoba Press: Part II.
Dion, Joseph F. 1979. *My Tribe the Crees.* Calgary: Glenbow Museum.
Parks Douglas R. (compiler). 1996. *Myths and Traditions of the Arikara Indians.* Lincoln: University of Nebraska Press.
Stevens, James R. 1971. *Sacred Legends of the Sandy Lake Cree.* Toronto: McClelland and Stewart.

VALUES FOR LIFE AND SURVIVAL

Brown, Jennifer S. H. 2005. "The Wasitay Religion: Prophecy, Oral Literacy, and Belief on Hudson Bay" In *Reassessing Revitalization Movements: Perspectives from North America and the Pacific Islands,* 104–23. Ed. Michael Harkin. Lincoln: University of Nebraska Press.
Doxtator, Deborah. 2001. "Inclusive and Exclusive Perceptions of Difference: Native and Euro-Based Concepts of Time, History, and Change." In *Decentring the Renaissance: Canada and Europe in Multidisciplinary Perspective, 1500–1700,* 33–47. Eds. Germaine Warkentin and Carolyn Podruchny. Toronto: University of Toronto Press.
Gray, Susan Elaine. 2006. *"I Will Fear No Evil": Ojibwa-Missionary Encounters Along the Berens River, 1875–1940.* Calgary: University of Calgary Press.
Hoffman, Walter J. 1885–86. "The Mide'wiwin or 'Grand Medicine Society' of the Ojibwa." *Seventh Annual Report.* 143–300. Washington, DC: Bureau of Ethnology.
Long, John S. 1986. "The Reverend George Barnley and the James Bay Cree." *Canadian Journal of Native Studies* 6(2): 313–31.
– 1986. "Shaganash": Early Protestant Missionaries and the Adoption of

Christianity by the Western James Bay Cree, 1840–1893. Ph.D. thesis. University of Toronto.

RELATIONS WITH ANIMALS

Adelson, Naomi. 2000. *Being Alive and Well*. Toronto: University of Toronto Press.

Brightman, Robert. 2006. "The Humanity of Animals and the Animality of Humans: A View from Biological Anthropology Inspired by J.M. Coetzee's Elizabeth Costello." *American Anthropologist* 108: 124–32.

– 1993. *Grateful Prey: Rock Cree Human-Animal Relationships*. Berkeley: University of California Press.

– 1990. "Primitivism in Missinippi Cree Historical Consciousness." *Man*, New Series 25(1): 108–28.

Carlson, Hans M. 2004. "A Watershed of Words: Litigating and Negotiating Nature in James Bay, 1971–75." *Canadian Historical Review* 85(1): 63–84.

Mullin, Molly, H. 1999. "Mirrors and Windows: Sociocultural Studies of Human-Animal Relationships." *Annual Review of Anthropology* 28: 201–24.

Preston, Richard. 2002. *Cree Narrative: Expressing the Personal Meaning of Events*. 2nd ed. Montreal and Kingston: McGill-Queen's University Press.

Ridington, Robin. 1988. "Knowledge, Power, and the Individual in Subarctic Hunting Societies." *American Anthropologist*, New Series 90(1): 98–110.

MITEWIWIN HEROES AND VILLAINS

Eliade, Mircea. 1987. "Shamanism: An Overview." In *The Encyclopedia of Religion*, Vol. 13, 202–8. Ed. Mircea Eliade. New York: Macmillan.

– 1964. *Shamanism: Archaic Techniques of Ecstasy*. New York: Bollingen Foundation.

Gill, Sam. 1987. "Native American Shamanism." In *The Encyclopedia of Religion*, Vol. 13, 216–19. Ed. Mircea Eliade. New York: Macmillan.

Hallowell, A. Irving. 1942. *The Role of Conjuring in Saulteaux Society*. Publications of the Philadelphia Anthropological Society. Vol 2. Philadelphia.

Kehoe, Alice B. 2000. *Shamans and Religion: An Anthropological Exploration in Critical Thinking*. Prospect Heights, IL: Waveland Press.

Marles, Robin J., Christina Clavelle, Leslie Monteleone, Natalie Tays, and Donna Burns. 2000. *Aboriginal Plant Use in Canada's Northwest Boreal Forest*. Vancouver: University of British Columbia Press.

WIHTIGOS AND CANNIBAL HEARTS

Brown, Jennifer S.H. 1971. "The Cure and Feeding of Windigos: A Critique." *American Anthropologist* 73: 20–2.
Brown, Jennifer S.H., and Robert Brightman. 1988. *The Orders of the Dreamed: George Nelson on Cree and Northern Ojibwa Religion and Myth, 1823*. Winnipeg: University of Manitoba Press, Part II.
Brightman, Robert. 1988. "The Windigo in the Material World." *Ethnohistory* 35(4): 337–9.
Brightman, Robert, David Meyer, Lou Marano. 1983. "On Windigo Psychosis." *Current Anthropology* 24(1): 120–5.
Hamm, Doug, and Louis Bird. 2000. "Amoe: Legends of the Omushkegowak." *Papers of the Thirty-First Algonquian Conference*. Ed. John D. Nichols, 144–60. Winnipeg: University of Manitoba Press.
Howard, Norman. 1982. *Where the Chill Came From: Cree Windigo Tales and Journeys*. San Francisco: North Point Press.
Morasty, Marie. 1974. *The World of Wetiko: Tales from the Woodland Cree*. Ed. C. Savage. Saskatoon: Saskatchewan Indian Cultural College.

WOMEN AND MEN

Bear, Glecia. 1992. *Kôhkominawak Otâcimowiniwâwa: Our Grandmothers' Lives as Told in Their Own Words*. Eds Freda Ahenakew and H. Christoph Wolfart. Saskatoon: Fifth House.
Beardy, Flora, and Bob Coutts, eds. 1996. *Voices from Hudson Bay: Cree Stories from York Factory*. Montreal and Kingston: McGill-Queens University Press.
Cruikshank, Julie. 1990. *Life Lived Like a Story: Life Stories of Three Yukon Elders*. Lincoln: University of Nebraska Press.
Flannery, Regina. 1995. *Ellen Smallboy: Glimpses of a Cree Woman's Life*. Montreal and Kingston: McGill-Queen's University Press.
Landes, Ruth. 1938. *The Ojibwa Woman*. New York: Norton.
White, Bruce M. 1999. "The Woman Who Married a Beaver: Trade Patterns and Gender Roles in the Ojibwa Fur Trade." *Ethnohistory* 46(1): 109–47.

PERSONAGES

Brown, Jennifer S.H., and Robert Brightman. 1988. *The Orders of the Dreamed: George Nelson on Cree and Northern Ojibwa Religion and Myth, 1823*. Winnipeg: University of Manitoba Press.

Hultzkrantz, Ake. 1983. "Water Sprites: The Elders of the Fish in Aboriginal North America." *American Indian Quarterly* 7(3): 1–22.

Thompson, Stith. 1929. *Tales of the American Indians*. Cambridge: Harvard University Press.

WISKAYCHAK

Ahenakew, Edward. 1929. "Cree Trickster Tales." *Journal of American Folklore* 42: 309–53.

Carroll, Michael P. 1984. "The Trickster as Selfish Buffoon and Culture Hero." *Ethnos* 12(2): 105–31.

DePasquale, Paul W., and Louis Bird. 2005. "Omushkego ('Swampy Cree') Traditional Literatures: 'Wissaakechaahk and the Foolish Women' and 'The Cannibal Exterminators.'" *Algonquian Spirit: Contemporary Translations of the Algonquian Literatures of North America*, 247–91. Ed. Brian Swann. Lincoln: University of Nebraska Press.

Scott, Simeon. 1995. "The Legend of Weesakechahk and the Flood." *Cree Legends and Narratives from the West Coast of James Bay*, 34–9. Ed. and trans. C. Douglas Ellis. Winnipeg: University of Manitoba Press.

FURTHER READINGS

Brown, Jennifer S.H., and Roger Roulette. 2005. "Waabitigweyaa, the One Who Found the Anishinaabeg First." In *Algonquian Spirit: Contemporary Translations of the Algonquian Literatures of North America*, 156–69. Ed. Brian Swann. Lincoln: University of Nebraska Press.

Christy, Miller, ed. 1894. *The Voyages of Captain Luke Foxe of Hull, and Captain Thomas James of Bristol, in Search of a North-West Passage in 1631–32*. Vols. 88, 89. London: Hakluyt Society.

Cooper, John M. 1938. *Snares, Deadfalls and Other Traps of the Northern Algonquians and Athapaskans*. Washington DC: Catholic University of America.

Cruikshank, Julie. 1984. "Tagish and Tlingit Place Names in the Southern Lakes Region, Yukon Territory." *Canoma* 10: 30–5.

Davies, Wayne K.D. 2003. *Writing Geographical Exploration: James and the Northwest Passage 1631–33*. Calgary: University of Calgary Press.

Decker, Jody. 1988. "Tracing Historical Diffusion Patterns: The Case of the 1780–82 Smallpox Epidemic among the Indians of Western Canada." *Native Studies Review* 4: 1–24.

DePasquale, Paul. 2005. "Natives and Settlers Then and Now." Introduction. *Canadian Review of Comparative Literature/Revue Canadienne de Littérature Comparée*.

Dickason, Olive P. 2002. *Canada's First Nations: A History of Founding Peoples from Earliest Times*. Toronto: Oxford University Press.

– 2006. *A Concise History of Canada's First Nations*. Toronto: Oxford University Press.

Ettinger, Kreg. 2002. "Cree Place Names and Myths as Evidence of Past Use and Occupancy: The Offshore Islands of Eastern James Bay." Paper presented at the Annual Meeting of the American Society for Ethnohistory, Quebec City, QC.

Fogelson, Raymond D. 1989. "The Ethnohistory of Events and Non-events." *Ethnohistory* 36(2): 133–74.

Francis, Daniel, and Toby Morantz. 1983. *Partners in Furs: A History of the Fur Trade in Eastern James Bay 1600–1870*. Montreal and Kingston: McGill-Queen's University Press.

Fulford, George, and Louis Bird. 2003. "'Who Is Breaking the First Commandment?': Oblate Teachings and Cree Responses in the Hudson Bay Lowlands." In *Reading Beyond Words*, 293–321. Eds. J.S.H. Brown and Elizabeth Vibert. Rev. ed. Peterborough: Broadview Press.

Goddard, Ives. 1978. "Synonymy [for Iroquois]." *Handbook of North American Indians*. Vol. 15: *Northeast*, 319–21. Ed. William Sturtevant. Washington, DC: Smithsonian Institution.

Goetzmann, William H., and Glyndwr Williams. 1998 [1992]. *The Atlas of North American Exploration from the Norse Voyages to the Race for the Pole*. Norman: University of Oklahoma Press.

Granzberg, Gary, and Nathanial Queskekapow. 1999. *Nathanial Queskekapow: Cree Shaman and Storyteller*. Winnipeg: University of Winnipeg.

Hamilton, Virginia. 1988. *In the Beginning: Creation Stories from Around the World*. New York: Harcourt Brace and Company.

Honigmann, John J. 1978. "West Main Cree." *Handbook of North American Indians*. Vol. 6: *Subarctic*, 217-30. Ed. William C. Sturtevant. Washington, DC: Smithsonian Institution.

Long, John S. 1985. "Treaty No. 9 and Fur Trade Company Families: Northeastern Ontario's Halfbreeds, Indians, Petitioners and Metis." In *The New Peoples: Being and Becoming Metis in North America*, 137-62. Eds. Jacqueline Peterson and Jennifer S.H. Brown. Winnipeg: University of Manitoba Press.

– 1995. "Historical Context." In Regina Flannery, *Ellen Smallboy: Glimpses of a Cree Woman's Life*, 65–75. Montreal and Kingston: McGill-Queen's University Press.

Lytwyn, Victor Petro. 1999. "'God Was Angry with Their Country:' The Smallpox Epidemic of 1782–83 among the Hudson Bay Lowland Cree." Papers of the 30th Algonquian Conference, 142–164. Ed. David H. Pentland. Winnipeg: University of Manitoba Press.

Macoun, John. 1881. "Ornithological Notes." *Annual Report of the Department of the Interior for the year ending December 31, 1880*. Ottawa: Queen's Printer.

Matthews, Maureen. 1995. "Thunderbirds." *Ideas*. Toronto: CBC Radio, 15 and 16 May.

Moore, Christopher. 2000. *Adventurers; Hudson's Bay Company – The Epic Story*. Toronto: Madison Press Books for the Quantum Book Group.

Morantz, Toby. 1984. "Oral and Recorded History in James Bay." *Papers of the Fifteenth Algonquian Conference*, 171–92. Ed. William Cowan. Ottawa: Carleton University.

– 1992. "Old Texts, Old Questions: Another Look at the Issue of Continuity and the Early Fur Trade Period." *Canadian Historical Review* 73(2): 166–8.

– 2001. "Plunder or Harmony? On Merging European and Native Views of Early Contact." *Decentring the Renaissance: Canada and Europe in Multidisciplinary Perspective 1500–1700*, 48–67. Eds. Germaine Warkentin and Carolyn Podruchny. Toronto: University of Toronto Press.

Neatby, L.H. 1976. "Henry Hudson." *Dictionary of Canadian Biography*. Vol. 1: 374–9. Toronto: University of Toronto Press.

Norman, Howard Allan. 1977. "The Cree Personal Name," Master's thesis. Indiana University.

Payne, Michael. 1984. *A Social History of York Factory, 1788–1870*. Ottawa: Parks Canada.

Powers, William. 1982. *Yuwipi: Vision and Experience in Lakota Ritual*. Lincoln: University of Nebraska Press.

Powys, Llewelyn. 1927. *Henry Hudson*. London: John Lane, the Bodley Head.

Preston, Richard. 2000. "James Bay Cree Culture, Malnutrition, Infectious and Degenerative Diseases." *Actes du Trente-deuxième Congrès des Algonquinistes*, 374–84. Ed. John D. Nichols. Winnipeg: University of Manitoba Press.

Purchas, Samuel. 1906. *Hakluytus Posthumus or Purchas His Pilgrimes Contayning a History of the World in Sea Voyages and Lande Travells by Englishmen and Others*. Vol. 13. Glasgow: James MacLehose and Sons.

Rordam, Vita. 1972. "The Old Blind Squaw." *Oakville Journal Record* (April).

– 1998. *Winisk: A Cree Indian Settlement on Hudson Bay*. Nepean, ON: Borealis Press.

Schorcht, Blanca. 2003. *Storied Voices in Native American Texts: Harry Robinson, Thomas King, James Welch and Leslie Marmon Silko*. New York: Routledge.

Seed, Patricia. 1995. *Ceremonies of Possession: Europe's Conquest of the New World 1492–1640*. Cambridge: Cambridge University Press.

Shandel, Tom. 1975. *Potlatch: A Strict Law Bids Us Dance*. Vancouver: PacificCinematique.

Sutherland, Donna G. 2004. "Kokum's Story; Wiihtiko or Victim of Circumstance?" In *Aboriginal Cultural Landscapes*, 337–47. Ed. J. Oakes, R. Riewe, Y. Belanger, S. Blady, K. Legge, and P. Wiebe. Winnipeg: University of Manitoba, Aboriginal Issues Press.

Thwaites, Reuben. 1901. *The Jesuit Relations and Allied Documents: Travels and Explorations of the Jesuit Missionaries in New France, 1610–1790: The Original French, Latin, and Italian texts, with English Translations and Notes*. Vol. 72: CIHM: 07606. Cleveland: Burrows, 1901.

Treat, James, ed. 1996. *Native and Christian: Indigenous Voices on Religious Identity in the United States and Canada*. New York: Routledge.

Tyrrell, Joseph Burr. 1931. *Documents Relating to the Early History of Hudson Bay*. Toronto: Champlain Society.

Young-Ing, Greg. 2001. "Talking Terminology: What's In a Word and What's Not." In "First Voices, First Words," ed. Thomas King. *Prairie Fire* (special issue) 22.3 (2001): 130–40.

Index

Aatawewak, 39–40, 148
Adam and Eve. *See* creation stories
Amoe, 167–9; challenge by other shaman, 170; honesty, 171; humility, 168; self defence without killing, 171
animal helpers *(pawaachikan)*, 92. *See also* dream helpers
animals, 71–80, 84; dangers of, 92, 102; disease among, 114; giant, xix, 24, 114, 157–8, 160; giving up lives, 72, 77, 88, 107; instinctive powers, 71, 73; knowledge of Creator, 88; learning from, 78, 89; messages to humans, 73–4; Mitew ability to become or create, 53, 87, 105–6; respect for, xx, 72, 75, 77, 193; shamanistic powers, 72–4, 102; sinning against, 72, 76–80, 193; in snaring the sun story, 33–5; spiritual relationship with hunter, 78. *See also* specific animals
Anway, 118, 120–2; exterminator of cannibals, 116–17
assini (stone), 14
astral projection, 90
astronomy, xviii, 17, 19, 22; night sky, 21–2. *See also* moshegiishik (the universe)
attacks or intrusions by other tribes, xviii, 9, 39–50, 148, 151; captives, 39–40, 43–4, 47, 148–9; fights over land, 40; killing to extend life, 43, 149; Omushkego responses to, 42–4, 46, 103

Bag of Bones. *See* human skeleton (Pakaaskokan)
balloons (mysteries in the sky), 37–8
balls of fire (mysteries in the sky), 37
bears, 71, 92, 102; in Wisakaychak story, 190–2
beaver, 88; destruction of land, 89; respect for, 89
becoming a mitew, 90–2, 97; 90; animal helpers, 92; dream quests, 92; early start, 90, 99; getting over fears, 91; instruction and guidance, 90–1; obtaining dreams, 91; for survival, 93
bee *(amoe)*, 167
belief, 78; in dreams, 99; non-belief, 106–7; power of, xx. *See also* faith
bestiality, 79
Bible, xvi, 55, 60; fasting in, xx
Big Foot, 113
Bird, Louis, *xxv, xxvi, xxvii*; demonstrating gun, *xxix*; early life, xi, xii; on importance of oral history, xiii; prizes, xv; residential school, xii, xiii; *Telling Our Stories*, xv, xx

Bird, Thelma, *xxvi, xxvii, xxviii*
birds, xx, 75, 86, 105, 108, 118, 139, 146; balloons and, 38; migrating, 22; powers, 71; Wisakaychak and, 184–7, 193. *See also* thunderbird
black bears, 92; powers, 71; similarity to Native behaviour, 102
blasphemy, 79–80
blood-suckers, 9, 41
breasts (in White Milk Lake), 9, 41
burning of wihtigos, 113–14, 116, 122

Cain and Abel, 55
cannibal hearts, 114, 122–4. *See also* ice hearts
cannibals and cannibalism, 24, 113, 115–22, 141–3; cannibal exterminators, 116–17, 123, 125, 140; prolonging life, 39–40, 42. *See also* human sacrifice; wihtigos
Cape Henrietta Maria, 10, 12, 40, 44, 175; first European contact, 49–50; as Garden of Eden, 42; ship stories, 49; summer place, 41–2, 45
captives, 40, 43–4, 47, 148–9; for human sacrifice, 39–40, 149–50; women, 39–40, 43–4, 149, 151
caribou, 20, 41, 77; instinct for danger, 73; messages to humans, 73–4; shamanistic powers, 72, 74, 102
celestial bodies. *See* astronomy
Chakapesh (legend), 24; dream quests, 30; mental telepathy, 28; and the moon, 36; need to learn lesson, 29; power of mind over matter, 25–6; snaring the Sun, 29–36; swallowed by fish, 27–8; travel with mind power, 23
Chookomolin, 46; dream of thunderbird, 47; special method of scanning, 46
Christianity, xix, 64, 131; appeal to Omushkego people, xx; cause of competition among ancestors, 62; condemnation of shamanism, xviii, 61–2, 70, 87, 111; destruction of native cultural and spiritual beliefs, xx, 61, 63, 83; for group or universal use, 69 (*See also* churches; communities); as protection from bad medicine, xx; and respect for animals and nature, 77; sacrament, 39; similarities to Omushkego spiritual beliefs, 39, 60–1, 146; women and, xx, 62

Christian missionaries: intolerance and ignorance, 7, 62–3; trickery, 62; use of human skeleton legend, 55
churches, 7–8, 59, 64, 69; one belief held by group, 63
code of ethics, xx, 78; blasphemy, 79–80; cruelty or misuse of animals, 72, 76–9, 89, 193; *maahchihew* (taboo), 76. *See also* consequences; moral laws
communities, xix, 42, 63–4; "living together" or civilization, 69
confessions, 76
consciousness, 59
consequences, xviii, 25; animals no longer available, 76, 78, 88; death by nature, 79; in giant spider story, 15; of not listening, 28–9, 36, 146, 164
conservation, 77, 115
creation stories, 15–17, 55
Creator, 4, 8, 17, 60; animals provided by, 77–8; ensuring survival of all species, xx. *See also* God; Great Spirit
Cree language, 45; story of its spread to the west, 139

dignity, 70; alienation from, 69. *See also* pride and shame
disobedience, 25, 28, 164; in giant spider story, 15. *See also* consequences
Distant Early Warning radar station. *See* radar station
dream helpers, 86–90
dream quests, xviii, 30, 75, 86–7, 89, 92–3, 97; to escape captors, 150–1; sharpening senses, 94; for Wilderness Woman, 129–30
dreams, 20, 26, 142, 151; about stars and universe, 18–19; control through, 85; dream visions, 87, 89, 97, 167; the elements (wind, etc.), 92–3; establishing spiritual nature, 75; healing, 60; mind power through, 94; obtaining, 91; overcoming fears through, xviii, 59, 91; places to dream, 96 (*See also* sacred land or places); seasons for, 95; special powers through, 74; thunder and thunderbird, 47, 84–5; for understanding, 74–5, 88–9; women's use of, 129, 142–4, 161–4
ducks, 40, 184–6

eagles, 9, 71, 85–6. *See also* thunderbird

Index

Ehep (giant spider), 15–16
Ekwan River, 103
elders, xii, xiii, xiv, xv; guardians and teachers, 91; guidance of, 90, 130; instruction from (for spiritualism or shamanism), 59–60; interpreting life, 16; needed to pass on knowledge, 98, 164, 179; respect for, xx, 98, 106, 146, 165
European missionaries. See Christian missionaries
Europeans: arrival, 47; first contact, 49–50; lack of understanding, 7, 89
European style of living, 69, 114; destruction of land and, 61, 68, 89
evil spirit, 20, 52
evolution, 161
extermination process: burning of wihtigos, 113–14, 116, 122; cannibals, 116; hiring of person to kill wihtigos, 114. See also killing
extra-sensory perception *(pimootahgosiwin)*, 94–5
eye for an eye, xx, 82, 107

faith, xx; in dreams, 99; healing and, 66, 68, 81–2; in yourself, 69
fasting, xx, 59, 83, 97; Jesus, 61; for spiritual power, 24
fear, xviii, 58, 60–1; Amoe, 167, 169; of bad mitewak (shamans), 20, 116; of cannibals, 24, 117, 122; eagle, 85; Giant Skunk, 157; human skeleton, 53–8; of mitew, 82, 108; overcoming through dreams, 59, 91–2, 94; thunder, 84; wihtigos, 114, 145, 147–8
fire sticks. See guns
first love and intimacy, 36
First Nations descendants: dignity, 69–70; pride and shame, 61–2
fish, xxvii, xxxi, 26–8, 38, 92; beavers and, 89; dream quests and, 86, 93; fighting for, 40; mind power and, 105; women as fishers, 127
foxes, 41, 79, 86
fur trade, 165, 168; Native competition, 62

gatherings, 103; of mitew to entertain or show power, 82, 103; thanksgiving, 82
geese, 9, 19, 40–1, 184–9; arriving, 172; Wisbaychak and, 184–9

giant animals, xix; bears, 24; Narwhal whisker, 10–11
giant bobcat *(mishipishew)*, 157; in Giant Skunk legend, 157–8, 160
giants, 5, 23–5, 29
Giant Skunk (legend), 153–60; evolution idea, 161; shaman power, 161
giant spider (Ehep), 15–16
giant wihtigos, 145
giant wolves: killing people, 114
God, 7–8, 55; Jewish, 69; same as Great Spirit, 68
good spirit, 19, 52
grandparents, 59, 79, 115, 147; guardians and teachers, 90–1. See also elders
great shaman *(kitchi mitew)*, 105
Great Spirit, xx, 52, 89, 95; animals' knowledge of, 88; as Creator, 16–17, 60, 68, 95; elders and, 90; mind power and, 95; Moshegiishik and, 19; predetermination, 97; same as God, 68; survival and, 5, 75, 77–8; thanks to, 78; ways of maintaining population, 114–15
greed, 166–7, 187, 190, 192; losing out in the end, 193
Gull, Bernard, 166–7
Gull, Joseph, xii
guns, xxix, 64, 72, 108, 169–70; lightning gun, 47; in mitew contests, 171; Sheweephan, 172–3

hawks, 9, 86, 92
healers and healing, 48, 60, 99; exposure to extreme cold, 99–101; Jesus, 66; medicine men, xv, 60, 66–8, 81–2, 90, 98–101; menstrual problems, 101; women as healers, 127, 129
high ground. See sacred land or places
historical events. See Omushkego history
Holy Spirit, 60
horror stories, 148
Hudson Bay Company, 168; influence on character, 166
human flesh. See cannibals and cannibalism
human giants. See giants
human sacrifice, 39–40, 42, 149–50
human skeleton (Pakaaskokan), 9; predictions, 51, 54; sound of human voice, 51, 53–7; stuck on treetop, 54–5

humility, xix, 48, 61, 168
hunters: training for, 21, 161; up before sunlight, 20
hunting, 40, 73, 171; importance in First Nation culture, 20; learning from wolves' behaviour, 78; mitew contests, 169; overhunting, 113; small groups, xix; three men and the white foxes story, 79; using mitewiwin for, 75, 77, 108. See also animals; nature
hunting ground or territory, 7–8

ice hearts, 113, 116, 124
immortality idea, 64, 66, 107–8, 149; human sacrifice to extend life, 40, 42–3; medicine, 40
Inuit people: attacks on Omushkegos, 40, 45
Iroquois, 149

Jesus, xx, 60–1, 63; healing, 66
Jewish God, 55
Jewish scriptures: creation story, 55; holy sacred calves, 39; ten commandments, 4

Kakitewish, 165–7
Keewatin ("Mister North"), 85
Ketastotinewan, 125, 140
killing: medicine as power to kill, 90; mitew right to kill, 82; for nothing, 77 (See also sinning against animals); Omushkego beliefs, 78, 107, 115, 193; using animals for, 105–6. See also eye for an eye; nature's law
killing to extend life, 43, 107–8, 149. See also cannibals and cannibalism; immortality idea
Kinosheo Rivers, 46
Kinosheowisip River, 45
kitchi mitew, 105
Kiyask, 166–7

Labrador Tea, 100, 128
land, 83; destruction of, 61, 68, 89; fights over, 40; lack of understanding (European), 89; mysterious landmarks, 175, 177; Native need for so much, 7; respect for, xx; spiritual connection to, 4, 6
language development: Cree language, 45, 139; mind knowledge and, 18; not important for life in wilderness, 69
leeches, 9, 41
legends (or stories): created from history of the people, 52; geographical differences, 6–7; importance of, 6; moral lessons, 4; multiple layers or levels, xii, xvi; similarities across Canada, 7; teaching system, xiii, xiv, 4, 54, 61, 75, 165
life after death. See immortality idea
lightning, 18
lightning gun, 47
"living together" or civilization: alienation from First Nation culture, 69; destruction of land, 61, 68, 89. See also communities
loons, 9, 186
love and intimacy, 36. See also sexual satisfaction
love stories: helping captive, 149–51; Morning Star, 132–9

maahchihew, 76
medicine: to extend life (immortality idea), 40
medicine man, xv, 60, 66–8, 99; gifted to help others, 81; gifts from people they helped, 81–2; medicine as power to kill (turned to evil), 90; respect for, 98; symbols and rituals, 100–1
menstrual period, 27, 76–7, 93, 101
mental power. See mind power
mental telepathy, 28, 36
mice, 41
midgets, 23, 25
migratory life. See nomadism
"Milk White Water Lake," 41
Milky Way, 22
mind power, 46, 87, 105; development of, xiv, xv; limitations, 95; mind over matter, 25–6, 84; third mind (extrasensory perception), 95; through dreams, 94; travel by, 23, 46, 89
miracles, 66, 68, 95
mitew, xv, 10, 12, 21, 75, 90; ability to create or become animals, 53, 87, 105; ability to leave body, 23, 46, 87, 89, 105, 113; challenges between (See mitew duels and insults); control of other people, 87; control of thunder-

birds, 46–8, 85; control of wind, 85; humility, xix, 48, 61, 168; knowledge of astronomy, 17–18; magical travel, 46, 89, 105, 109–11; naturally gifted people, 98; power to extend life, 66; power to fight off wihtigos, 113; proper use of power, 10, 48, 60, 98, 117; right to kill, 82; scanning power, 7, 103; training and development, xviii, 21, 69, 82, 89–93, 97, 99; use of animals to kill, 105–6; Wiskaychak as, 180; as worst kind of wihtigos, 113–14

mitew competitions or performances, 82, 103, 168–70

mitew duels and insults, xviii, 104–6, 170

mitewiwin, 4, 24, 165; achieved through life practice, 59; acquired individually, 59, 82, 99; in animals, 73; comparisons with European spiritual beliefs, 70; condemned by Christianity, 70; connected to whole environment, 51; European lack of understanding, 7; everything having a spirit, 69; incompatibility with Christianity, 87, 111; levels or degrees of, 48, 61, 83, 85, 89–90; limitations, 104, 106–7; mind over matter, 25–6, 84; necessary for people to survive on the land, 60, 75, 93, 116; need to grow up with, 21, 69, 87, 90, 99; non-belief and, 106–7; performing miracles, 95; places to practice, 7–8; rituals for, 59–60; submerged after Christianity (practiced in secret), 107–8; through dreaming, 74–5; tricks and, 10–11; useless against white man, 104, 107. *See also* mind power

mitewiwin gone bad, 60, 108, 116; killing for immortality, 107–8

Mohawks, 40, 149

molting season (ducks and geese), 41, 45

moon, 19, 23, 36; full moon, 27; as round rock, 14

moose, *xxxi*, 20, 71, 92; shamanistic powers, 74

Mooshawow (Cape Henrietta Maria), 8–10, 12, 40, 44, 133, 175–6; first European contact, 49–50; impassable during early summers, 45; where everything happens in summer, 41–2, 45

moral laws, xviii, 4, 78, 80. *See also* code of ethics

morning star, 18, 21

Morning Star (love story), 132–9

Moshegiishik (man called), 20, 23; interest in stars, 21; predictions, 22; respect for, 22

moshegiishik (the universe), 19, 21. *See also* astronomy

mouse, 34, 86

Mr. Bones. *See* Pakaaskokan (human skeleton)

muskrats, 86

mysteries, xiv, 22, 115; about stones and rocks, 12, 14; coldness of north, 18; Ehep, 16; explanations for, 56; Pakaaskokan (human skeleton), xviii, 9, 53–8; of universe (line), 19

mysteries in the sky, 37–8; predictions of death, 37–8

mystery stories, xviii, 51–2, 55. *See also* legends (or stories)

Nanabush. *See* Wisakaychak

narwhal, 12

narwhal whisker, 10–11

Native spiritual values: individual nature of, 63, 68–9; predating European arrival, 63. *See also* mitewiwin

Natowaywak, 39–40

nature, 88; death by, 79; harmony with, 63; respect for, xx, 75, 77–8; retraction of benefit from, 76–8, 88 (*See also* code of ethics)

nature's law, 83

navigation: inner compass, 165; using stars, 17, 22

night sky, 21–2

nomadism, xix, 68; following the seasons, 42, 102; preservation of land, 61

non-belief, 106–7

north: dreams of, 18; power of, 85

Northern Lights, 22–3

North Star, 18, 21, 85

O*chakatak* (the Great Bear), 21

O*chakwish* (Little Bear), 21

Omushkego cosmology, xviii, xix

Omushkego culture, 82–3; based on knowledge of wilderness, 83; loss of, xx, 80, 82; spiritual connection of the people to the land, 4

Omushkego history, xxi, 52; mitewiwin or shamanism, 82–3; in story telling, 5, 166

Omushkego individualism, 59, 63, 68–9, 82, 99

Omushkego people, 3; attacks or intrusions by other tribes, xviii, 9, 39–50, 103, 148–9, 151; belief in immortality, 64, 66; connection to land, 4; inner compass, 165; nature's law or wilderness rules, 83; nomadic lifestyle, xix, 42, 68, 102; power of the mind (importance), xix; teaching system, xiii, xiv, 4, 54, 61, 75, 165; useful ways in pre-European time, 69; westernization, 69

Omushkego spiritual beliefs. *See* mitewiwin; Omushkego world view

Omushkego world view, xvi, xvii, xviii, xix, xx; comparisons with Christianity, xx, 60; outsider views of, xxi

opposites, 20, 90

orphans: as cannibal exterminators, 123; Chakapesh story, 24–5; power of, 64–5; shaman power, 99; as wihtigos, 113

Ostigwan Nowakow (skull beach), 43–4

other-than-humans, xix, 112–13. *See also* wihtigos

other tribes. *See* attacks or intrusions by other tribes

over-population and overhunting, 113

owls, 41, 71

paastaho, 77
paganism, xviii, 9, 61–2, 70
Pakaaskokan (human skeleton), 51, 53; fear of, 56–8; mystery of, 54; predictions, 51, 54; secrecy or silence about, 53; sound of human voice, 51–7; stuck on tree top, 54–5
pastahowin (sin against nature), 115
Patrick, Michael, xiii
pawaachikan (animal helper), 92
Peawanuck, 14
personages, xix, 153–74
pimootahgosiwin (extra-sensory perception), 94

"*pisk*," 14
places in the skies. *See* creation stories
polar bears, 92, 102
prayer, xx, 98; public *vs.* private, 63
predetermination, 97
predictions, 51, 54, 57, 128; of death, 37–8; weather, 17, 21–2
pride and shame, 61–2. *See also* dignity
prophecy, xviii
punishment, 59, 146, 189; death by nature, 79; retraction of benefit from nature, 76 (*See also* consequences)
Pwaatak (Sioux), 39–40

rabies, 114
radar station, xii, 9
ravens, 71
residential schools, xii; effect on Omushkego culture, xii, xiii
respect, xx; for animals and all nature, xx, 75, 77–8; for elders and parents, xx, 146, 165
respect for total environment: highest form of belief and worship, 78
resurrection stories, 64–5; restoration of life, 48; shaking tents, 90
revenge, 25, 106; eye for an eye, xx, 82, 107
rituals: medicine men, 100–1; for mitewiwin, 59–60; denial of luxury, 59; fasting, 59
rocks. *See* stones and rocks
rules of morality. *See* moral laws

sacred land or places, xviii, xxi, 7; high ground, 8, 96
Sakaney, John, 165; blending of cultures, 166; mitewiwin expertise, 166–7
Sasquatch, 113
scientific explanations, 18, 22, 84, 142
seals, 40, 45
seasons: bears and, 102; for dream quests, 95; following the seasons, 42, 102
secret places, 96
self-discipline, 98; fasting, xx, 24, 59, 83, 97
self-inflicted punishment: as ritual for shamanism, 59
sexual satisfaction, 180; denial of, 59, 98; forced, 171–2; by trickery, 183
shaking tents, 12, 60, 75–7; Amoe's use

of, 170; for entertainment, 82; to fight other shamans, 105; levels or degrees, 88; resurrection from dead, 90; used to find help, 117
shaman. *See* mitew
shaman illusions, 48, 53
shamanism. *See* mitewiwin
Sheweephan: disappearance, 174; as killer, 173; outlaw among his people, 171; taking women by force, 171–2
ship stories, 49
shooting stars, 21
shrew, 35, 86
sin against nature *(pastahowin)*, 115
sinning against animals, 76–9; killing for nothing, 77
skull beach. *See* Ostigwan Nowakow (skull beach)
Sky trail (Milky Way), 22
spiritual beliefs and practices. *See* mitewiwin
spiritual world: blending with material world, 53; existing at same time as material world, 52
squirrel, 34
stars, 18, 21; navigation using, 17, 22, 165; weather prediction, 17, 21–2
starvation, 112–13, 115
stones and rocks: mystery, 12, 14; stories about, 12–14; water, 12
story telling, xiv, xv. *See also* legends (or stories); mystery stories
strands (of hair) for snare, 31–2, 35–6; first love and intimacy, 36
string image: in giant spider story, 15–17
subconscious, 89
sun, 23, 29–30
supernatural beings, 52. *See also* other-than-humans
superstition, 77
survival, 77, 88–9, 93, 116, 164; of all species, xx; animal powers for, 71, 74; outsider views of, xxi; using mitewin for, 60, 75, 93, 116
swans, 184–5
sweatlodge, 101, 127–8

taboo, 76
teaching system, xiii, xiv, 4, 54, 61, 75, 165; disciplinary instruction, 148
Telling Our Stories (Bird), xv, xx
thanksgiving gatherings, 82

third mind (extra-sensory perception), 95
thunder, 8, 93; fear of, 84
thunderbird, 8, 46–8, 85, 93; common to all First Nations people in Canada, 48
thunder sticks. *See* guns
tobacco, 81–2
trading, 40
travel: with mind power, 23, 46, 89; mitew magical travel, 46, 89, 105, 109–11
trickery and tricksters, 10–11, 175, 181–3, 190–1; Anway's tricking of the cannibals, 118–19; in Christian conversion, 62

UFOs, 37–8
universe (moshegiishik), xviii, 17, 19. *See also* astronomy

verbal skills: unnecessary for life in wilderness, 69. *See also* language development
violations and consequences. *See* consequences
visions, 25, 53, 128

Wabagamushusagagan Lake (White Milk Lake), 9, 40–1
walrus, 45
weasel, 33–4, 86; in Giant Skunk legend, 153–4
weather, 8; mystery of, 84. *See also* north
weather prediction, 17; stars, 21–2
westernization, 69
whales, 45; dreams about, 89
White Milk Lake. *See* Wabagamushusagagan Lake
wihtigos, xix, 113, 124–5, 142–3, 146–7; burning of, 113, 116, 122; created by starvation, 112–13; duels, 145; extermination process, 113–14; giant, 145; half human, 113; mitews as, 113–14; orphans as, 113; from over abuse, 112–13, 115; from sin against nature, 115. *See also* cannibals and cannibalism
wihtigo stories: disciplinary instruction, 148
wilderness, 6, 8, 63, 69, 97–8; nature's law, 83; need for higher level of understanding, 69
Wilderness Woman, xix, 129–31, 133; dangers of, 130–1

wind, 85, 92–3
Winisk, Ont., xi, xii, *xxvi,* 166
Winisk River, *xxviii*
Wisakaychak, xix; granting of two wishes, 196–7; greed, 187, 190, 192–3; mystery stories, 175–8; portrayed as powerful and tricky, 179; portrayed as stupid, 178, 193; repaid for tricks to animals, 187, 189; the rock mover, 175–7; as shaman, 180; showing need for elders, 179; tricking birds, 184–7; tricking of bear, 190–2; tricking women, 181–3; turned to stone, 193; as wanderer and adventurer, 180
wolverine: in Giant Skunk legend, 155, 158–60
wolves, 71, 92, 102; killing only for eating, 78; shamanistic powers, 102
women, 101, 127–51, 171; appeal of Christianity, xx, 62; breasts, 9, 41; captives, 39–40, 43–4, 149, 151; conquest of guard, 152; gifted as dreamers, 129, 142, 145; gifted without dream quests, 94; grandmothers, 19, 79, 115, 137, 148; as healers, 127, 129; helping captives, 149–51; intuition, 25, 128; killing of wihtigos, 125, 140, 148; men mystified by, 93; menstrual period, 27, 76–7, 93, 101; mother representing Great Spirit, 16; predictions and prophecies, 128, 141, 145; preparation of sweatlodges, 127–8; rule against stepping over animal meat, 76–7; shamanism, 88, 117, 127, 129, 150; training, 127; visions, 128; wise women (Chapkapesh's sister), 23–5, 36
written records, 17, 52
Wunnumin Lake, 177

York boats, 165–6
York Factory, 13, 51, 165–7